D-DAY TO ARNHEM

SECOND ARMY

30 CORPS

50 (N) INF DIV

8 ARMD BDE

79 ARMD DIV

3 CDN INF DIV

43 (W) INF DIV

49 (WR) INF DIV

7 ARMD DIV

11 ARMD DIV

GDS ARMD DIV

Contents

Preface

I have written this book for a number of reasons. Firstly, I believe it is a good story. Secondly, there are many books about D-Day and the 1944 War in Europe, but not many of them have been written, as this is, by those who took part in the day-to-day fighting. Most of the literature comes from the generals who disposed us, or from war correspondents, and later from historians and authors using the documentation and second-hand accounts of others. Much is US oriented, nearly all the films and documentaries being American produced and financed, or designed to catch the American market. The D-Day landing was primarily a British success, and most of the fighting in Normandy against the German Armour was done by the British and Canadians and later the Poles. Thirdly, the role of the artillery in Normandy was one of the decisive factors in the success of the Allied armies.

Finally, the Hertfordshire Yeomanry, with whom I served, were an outstanding regiment. Their contribution to the preparation and organization of the Normandy landing, and their performance on D-Day itself, have been little recognized and I think their story is one which should be told.

I have deliberately not made this a military history. It is the story of my own short war told from my own memories, from my diary written at the time, and from original diaries, notes and memories of others in the regiment, notably Lieutenant-Colonel George Fanshawe, who commanded the 86th Field Regiment on D-Day, Captain Stephen Perry, who commanded 'B' Troop of the 341st St Albans Battery, Captain Garton Ash, who commanded 'D' Troop of the 342nd Hertford Battery and Lieutenant Sidney Beck, the Gun Position Officer of 'B' Troop, who has provided a War Diary compiled from the contemporary day-to-day Battery Command Post log of the 341st Battery supplemented by extracts from letters to his wife. This has been invaluable both in itself as an *aide-mémoire* and as a date fixer.

The book, therefore, is a combined effort, and the accounts given are first-hand and often eyewitness accounts. The opinions are my own and I have tried to make it clear whether the opinions were expressed in 1944 or whether they are my later opinions subject to hindsight.

In order not to interrupt the flow of the narrative, I have included as an Appendix information about weapons, gunnery and our regimental organization which I advise the reader to digest before chapter 3. The Glossary and short Bibliography will also be found helpful.

Apart from my co-authors above mentioned, I would also like to express my thanks to the following. Margaret Archer for endlessly typing, retyping, editing and correcting so efficiently and patiently. Clive Partridge for drawing all the original maps from my scribbles and for his comments on the text. My wife Letty, Alison Stanko (my daughter) and Sophie Nunn (my step-daughter) for reading, correcting and for many suggestions to improve it. Colonel John Sainsbury for reading it, for many improvements and for his great help with photographs and facts. Mrs Fanshawe for her help and delightful contribution about George Loveday in chapter 11. Chick Bullen for his account of the Lingevres battle extracted from *Panzers in Normandy – Then and Now* published in 1983 by After the Battle, and Mr Ramsey, editor and After the Battle for permission to use these extracts and for information on German Panzers. Reg Munt also for reading it and for his D-Day contribution. My publishers, their referee and their editor Michael Coultas for their refining and improvements and helpful suggestions. A number of others in my family and outside who read it and encouraged me.

Acknowledgements for illustrations are also made to the Trustees of the Imperial War Museum (Crown copyright Imperial War Museum) for Plates 7, 9–24, 27–42, 45 and 47, to Triumph Processing of Putney for reprinting Plate 8, to the Illustrated London News Picture Library for permission to use Plate 46, and to Colonel Sainsbury for Plate 48.

Foreword

SUMMER 1938 CORNWALL

Roseland Cornwall in a hot summer haze, St Mawes and its estuary, fluorescent at night and placid with the sun's heat at midday. Two eighteen-year-old lads with a lug and missen boat and beauty all round. The last summer of peace with threats of war developing, but ignored.

The delights of Pimms No. 1 at a shilling a half pint in the Ship and Castle. The two of them sailing with two young ladies off Zoze Point and landing on an empty sandy cove to while away the afternoon playing strip poker on the sand.

Nights when they threw bricks into St Mawes harbour to see the phosphorescence and ended up swimming with their arms dripping light.

SUMMER 1944 NORMANDY

The red and yellow dawn, blotched with mushrooms of smoke, breaks over the coastline from Arromanches to Courselles. A windswept and angry sea.

0530 Peace is shattered. A cruiser, HMS *Belfast*, opens the party by firing star shells at the Ver-sur-Mer battery of German guns. Allied bombers also start pounding the coastline.

0630 The destroyers have opened fire.

0650 The SP guns open up with their 'run in' shoot. Weather terrible.

0725 'H' hour. The AVRE tanks land. A German gun hits one on the beach. It goes up and the landing craft with it and then two more are brewed up. All the way along the beach the 5th East Yorks and the 6th Green Howards are ashore. Something big has blown up at Courselles on the Canadian front to our left.

Strong resistance in La Rivière on our left front. The rising tide is littered with blazing or drifting craft and the beach with blackened tanks and vehicles.

PLATE 1. *The author, Captain Kiln, in 1943. In officer's service uniform, RA badges on lapels, Hart badges on shoulders.*

1
Preparation: 1939–1943

The author's story from 1939 and the outbreak of World War II through to the spring of 1944. His service as a Gunner in the Honourable Artillery Company. His becoming an officer in the Hertfordshire Yeomanry 86th Field Regiment RA in June 1940, and his service and training in the United Kingdom in preparation for D-Day in June 1944.

1939

'Consequently this Country is at war with Germany.' At 1100 hours on 3 September 1939 at City Road, London, Neville Chamberlain's speech on the wireless announcing the outbreak of war with Nazi Germany comes over loud and clear to the assembled troops of the Honourable Artillery Company (HAC).

That morning the various regiments of the HAC's voluntary soldiers are being embodied into the regular army. Each member in turn takes the Oath of Allegiance and receives five pounds, five shillings and fivepence. I am one of those waiting in the queue as the National Anthem follows Chamberlain's speech. While the notes of the music die away, the wail of air raid sirens takes over and shatters the peace of that lovely late summer morning, and we see the barrage balloons all around the city gradually rising into the sunlit sky.

That was how the war started for me. Like many of my fellow soldiers that day, I had been a teenager through most of the 1930s and had grown up with the menace of Soviet Russia and Nazi Germany. After the Munich crisis in September 1938 it was obvious to most of us that war must come, although some felt that it would be between Germany and Russia.

At the beginning of 1938 I had left school and started a career in Lloyd's in the City of London and my spare time was taken up playing rugby. In late August 1938 I was invited to go on holiday with the family of a school friend near St Mawes in Cornwall. There we had a fortnight of glorious summer weather and I learned to sail. In fact, we sailed the Carrick roads and across to the Helford river and out round Zoze Point in all sorts of wind and tide, and by the end of my holiday I had cured myself of being seasick. The next time I sailed the English Channel, six years later, I was to be grateful for that holiday.

I remember so well returning home in September 1938 during the Munich crisis. It coincided with the start of training for the new rugby season, which I took seriously, and on our training evenings the discussions were all about volunteering for the Territorial Army. Many went off and joined. I waited, as I had to spend two evenings a week working for insurance exams and two evenings training. Then Chamberlain returned from Munich waving his piece of paper on his arrival in London. My immediate reaction was of a profound relief, which lasted a month or so. However, I joined the Honourable Artillery Company as a gunner in 'A' Battery early in 1939, along with hundreds of others. In March 1939 I was moved into 'C' Battery. We trained on two evenings a week and on several weekends. We learned basic gun drill, that is, how to lay and fire our field guns, to drive our vehicles, to use wireless sets and to shoot our rifles.

The Honourable Artillery Company was the oldest part of the British Army, tracing its decent from the City of London's trained bands of the Middle Ages, which had been brought under control by the Tudor monarchs. They were entirely, and always had been, a volunteer force. In 1939 the Company contained Infantry, Anti-Aircraft Artillery, and Field Artillery.

At the start of 1939 the field gunners consisted of 'A' and 'B' Batteries. In the early months of 1939, two additional Batteries, 'C' and 'D', were formed. 'A' and 'B' Batteries formed the 11th Royal Horse Artillery (RHA) and 'C' and 'D' became the 12th RHA. The Royal Horse Artillery was a proud title, as opposed to the more ordinary regiments of Royal Artillery, but the distinction in World War II was purely one of tradition. Nevertheless, the HAC were the elite of the Territorial Army.

My realization that war had become inevitable came at Easter 1939 when I was on the Old Merchant Taylors Easter rugby tour and staying in Teignmouth, Devon. The news of Mussolini's invasion of Albania came through on Easter Saturday morning as we were climbing into our coach and just about to set off to play Plymouth that afternoon. Any residual doubts that Britain could avoid the forthcoming War were dispelled in the summer by the Nazi–Soviet non-aggression pact.

In mid August 1939 one in ten of the HAC volunteers was called up for a 'Key' party to prepare for mobilization and to dig air raid shelters across the HAC playing fields in City Road just north of Moorgate (Plate 2). This was my first introduction to archaeology. As we dug our trenches through Moorfields we unearthed layer upon layer of London's rubbish, including relics such as arrowheads and stone aiming posts from the medieval archery training grounds. These were carefree days of summer weather, digging all day and driving up to the West End most evenings in an army signal truck.

PLATE 2. *HAC Key Party digging air raid shelters at Armoury House, Finsbury in late August 1939.*

On 1 September the rest of the regiment were called up, and thus we were all assembled to be embodied on that Sunday morning of 3 September. The dramatic sound of the sirens taking up from the National Anthem was no surprise to us as we expected an instant German air raid on London. Together with other members of the Key party, I guided our comrades into the air raid trenches we had dug for them (Plate 3). We were then issued with crowbars, shovels and pickaxes, formed into one of London's auxiliary ARP (Air Raid Precautions) Rescue Squads and marched off to take shelter in the basement of the HAC squash courts with the barrage balloons still gently rising.

In our shelter we huddled together, listening to what we imagined in our emotional state to be bombs dropping. Imagination is a strange thing, and I know that morning we all heard the crump of bombs. We surfaced three-quarters of an hour later to the same peaceful sunlight outside. No bombs had fallen; in fact no German aircraft had even crossed the English coast, and London had to wait a full year before its bombing started in earnest.

Having been enrolled as soldiers, some eight of us decided that we should celebrate, and around two o'clock, with our embodiment monies in our pockets, we made our way to the Great Eastern Hotel at Liverpool Street Station, where we had a splendid lunch of porterhouse steaks – an unheard

PLATE 3. *Completed shelters being inspected 3 September 1939.*

of expensive luxury to us. Some three hours later we repaired by taxi to Piccadilly for tea and a conference. There on the pavement outside the Regent Palace Hotel we listened to the broadcast by the King, and afterwards had a long argument as to the next move. We were all really expecting London to be bombed that night. The braver souls among us made off to Soho to die with their boots on, or off; we the more timid, slunk homewards out of London to protect our loved ones.

Those first few days of the war were curious; a perpetual twilight with no lights on in the underground trains, all car headlights papered over with pin-point lights only, and of course, windows blacked out. We reported for duty as soldiers every day and did almost nothing. Then one day we were told to report with full kit, as the regiment had been posted and would move off by train the next morning. We paraded and marched all of 400 yards to Moorgate Station where our families and friends waved a fond farewell.

None of us lowly gunners knew our destination, but France was the usual guess. I had a lovely girlfriend called Anne who had enrolled herself in the HAC to be with me, and there she was in her army uniform waving a tearstained handkerchief. She too was moving that afternoon, and no doubt we would be reunited in Calais. In the event we moved twenty-five miles to Borehamwood in Hertfordshire! This was about ten miles from my home, so I borrowed a car and drove home the next day to visit my family. Anne moved to Bulford Camp in Wiltshire, and this alas was the end of our romance.

We were billeted all round Borehamwood in private houses, and while learning to become a soldier, I helped organize the regimental rugger side and led the scrum. This pleased the Colonel as it showed initiative, so in order to facilitate rugby training, he appointed the rugby side Regimental Policeman (RP). This was a plum job as it relieved us of all sentry duty, cookhouse fatigues and other unpleasant duties. We also had a comfortable police room with a roaring fire and armchairs. One of our duties was to watch the morals of the troops, and wearing our red armbands we had to move the local girls out of regimental property. The regiment had taken over two film studios and, I suspect, a few starlets as well!

A second duty of the RPs was to check the food stores against theft or pilfering. Inspection of the cookhouse stores and collection of the police rations was a pleasant task. This meant that our police headquarters always had plenty of rations; hot buttered toast was served to off-duty policemen and off-duty starlets most evenings, and of course, with our red armbands, we cleared the pubs at night and had the freedom of Borehamwood.

The autumn of 1939 and the cold winter of 1939/40 were part of the twilight war. Hitler's invasion of Poland was over, and Russia and Germany were allies. Russia had invaded Finland and, with little help from anyone, the Finns were fighting a heroic struggle. British volunteers, including two friends of mine, fought in Finland, but for those of us in England war was still remote. There were no German air raids on Britain, and the British Army in France was dug in on defensive positions along the French border.

At Borehamwood we drilled, learned to fire rifles and small arms, and longed for the day when we had real guns, as all the 25-pounder field guns with which we were to be equipped were quite properly earmarked for France. The regiment's time was spent guarding vulnerable points (VPs) such as Battersea Power Station and various bridges. However, as a Regimental Policeman, I was excused these duties.

We learned something about army life in the ranks, the value of comradeship, the ability to make yourself as comfortable as you could, and the gradual assumption of discipline and pride in your battery. The lesson I learned above all was the ignorance of the ordinary soldier, and how vital it was for officers to communicate with their troops all down the line.

In World War I the British Expeditionary Force (BEF) sent to France in 1914 had contained some of our best Territorial or Volunteer Regiments.

PLATE 4. *A Section of 'C' Battery 12th RHA (HAC) on parade in Borehamwood, November 1939.*

The Honourable Artillery Company in 1939 were of that calibre. However, they were not sent overseas, but deliberately kept at home to be trained as officers. In September 1939 some of the more senior members of the regiment were sent to Officer Cadet Training Units (OCTUs). In December 1939 selection of another thirty from our regiment started. Those on the shortlist were interviewed. At that stage my reputation as a soldier was pretty low; my Battery Commander had publicly announced that I was 'a sloppy sort of soldier', and he was quite right – my battledress always had butter stains down the front! However, the week before the interview I had sprained my ankle playing rugby for the regiment; I entered the interview on crutches and of course, was one of the chosen few. One lesson which I have learned is 'If you want a job be different!' Somehow you have to make a mark so that you are remembered. Crutches, provided your wound is an honourable one, are a very good way of making your mark on a selection board.

1940

On New Year's Day 1940 the thirty chosen officer cadets assembled at King's Cross Station en route for our OCTU at Filey on the Yorkshire Coast – bracing in January! 'Assembled' is perhaps overstating it, as three of the party had to be wheeled onto the platform on luggage trolleys and put in the guard's van to sleep off their New Year's Eve in London.

We spent six months at Filey drilling, learning gunnery, motor maintenance, men management and signalling, interspersed with PT on the beach, route marches, and digging beach defences, passing from winter into summer of 1940 and Dunkirk. Having started as an ignorant gunner of 19, I was commissioned a Second Lieutenant in the Royal Regiment of Artillery in June 1940, and much to my surprise, came fourth in our group of thirty on passing out, failing only on smartness, and thus not being posted to a regular Royal Horse Artillery Regiment (RHA), who took the cream. I was posted in June 1940 to the 86th Field Regiment (Hertfordshire Yeomanry) who were then guarding the coast of Northumberland against a German invasion from Norway. I could not have wanted a better home, and while the war lasted or I lasted, I stayed with them, being very careful never to volunteer for any dangerous jobs like parachuting, gliders or commandos. I liked gunnery and was good at it, and the Yeomanry did not mind sloppy soldiers, they were somewhat relaxed themselves.

When I joined my regiment, their Regimental Headquarters was at Linden Hall, Longhorsley, just north of Morpeth and some twenty miles north of Newcastle. The regiment's role was to provide the artillery support for the defence of the beaches from Blyth northwards to just south of Berwick on Tweed. When I arrived in June there were very few guns, but gradually they arrived, collected and scavenged from all over the place. They were French 75mm guns from World War I or from the USA, medium guns recovered from parks in Edinburgh and howitzers from somewhere else. Ammunition varied too, but by July we could fire effectively on the beaches. Some guns were mounted just behind the beaches to cover them by firing over open sights. Others were placed 2000 or 3000 yards to the rear, dug in near farms or in hedges with observation posts on the beaches themselves. The first time I found myself in the sand dunes with two guns was at Druridge Bay, to the north of Blyth. We took our role seriously, as no doubt did the rest of the British Army playing the same role on beaches all round Britain.

Of course, East Anglia and the Channel were the expected areas of invasion. Nevertheless we were expecting a German invasion across the North Sea from Denmark, north Germany and southern Norway, either as a diversion or as a supplement to a cross-Channel invasion: the Germans had plenty of ports and ships in that area. The North Sea crossing is some 300 or more miles, but German air cover was good, and the beaches were easy to land upon and less prone to storms than the West Coast.

It was part of our thinking to work out the German plan and it is interesting to see their problem in comparison with the Allied problem four years later. In 1944, as we shall relate, the direct cross-Channel invasion to the Pas de Calais would be used by the Allies as a bluff, and the actual invasion in Normandy would be in a more remote area away from the Germans' main defences and separated from them by major rivers, notably the Seine and the Loire. This sector could be isolated by air power to prevent easy reinforcement and was in a lightly populated region. There would have been very similar advantages to the Germans if they had invaded Britain using, for instance, an airborne division and one or two divisions from the sea between the Tyne and the Tweed. Strong natural defences on the Tyne or Tees to the south and the Tweed or the Cheviots to the north, with an advance along Hadrian's Wall to the Solway Firth, would have cut England off from Scotland and would have been very difficult to dislodge.

This was our appreciation and certainly we took it very seriously. Whether the Germans ever even considered it, I know not. In July I moved inland and we took delivery of two medium guns, 60-pounders which had been sitting in an Edinburgh park since 1918 and hastily pressed into service. We had prepared large sandbagged gun positions dug into a hedgerow backed by a small farm track and carefully camouflaged. The gun position was about 4000 yards from the sea so that the guns could fire indirectly over a wide area of the beaches. They arrived on their own iron wheels and were carefully manhandled into the prepared gun pits. The No. 1, that is, the sergeant in charge of each gun and his crew spent several days seeing how they worked and oiling all the parts carefully. Then the shells arrived, separately from the propellant charges. These charges consisted of canvas bags of loose explosive, and we were to use one or more bags according to the distance we wished the shell to travel.

The great day dawned when we were to fire the first practice rounds. No one knew how much explosive to use or how far the shell might travel, so the area between us and the sea was hastily evacuated by the police. It was deemed advisable by all concerned, and especially by me as the Gun Position Officer (GPO), that we should pull the trigger by remote control. A long length of cord was attached to the firing lever and this led to a safe position behind the lane. The guns being loaded, we all retreated and the No. 1 pulled the string. The first time nothing happened so I, as the guinea pig, had to investigate. The problem was simply that we had not removed a safety block that we had placed behind the firing lever. Once the block had been removed all was well: the guns actually behaved beautifully. We calibrated them and ranged them in on our various beaches and there is no doubt at all that they would have been a formidable anti-invasion weapon.

The summer passed peacefully for us. The Battle of Britain hardly affected us. Only the occasional appearance of German aircraft kept us alert. One gunner regiment to the south of us claimed to have shot down a German aircraft over the sea with a field gun, but this news was received with scepticism by us.

In September I was sent on an engineering course at Darlington to be trained in demolition techniques, that is, how to blow up bridges, and to fell trees across a road with an explosive charge to delay enemy tanks and vehicles. I always enjoyed these courses; they were like a holiday away from the discipline of school and away from responsibility, along with ten or twenty young officers. I learned something new, and was free to enjoy the evenings. Darlington was great. I had a fortnight there and fell in love with a local girl. We danced and walked up Teesdale and I spent many nights with her and her mother, who was deaf, when I should have been safe in barracks. We spent our last Saturday evening at a dance in the George Hotel at Piercebridge. Dancing in such lovely riverside surroundings was most romantic. When I finally arrived back at our billets in the centre of Darlington, I heard that the German invasion had started. Concentrations of German troops and craft around Boulogne and Calais had led our Intelligence to think that the invasion was about to begin, and the code word 'Cromwell' signifying this had been passed that evening. At two in the morning I donned full kit, with steel helmet and gas mask, and proceeded through deserted streets to our rendezvous position, only to find that the alert was over and everyone else had long since gone to bed. I retired to bed with a hangover, and reported back to my regiment the next day.

The invasion season was drawing to its close. The Battle of Britain had been won in September, and the autumn and winter blitz of 1940/1 was starting.

Our regiment was withdrawn from the beaches and billeted for the winter on Coquetdale. Regimental Headquarters were at Rothbury. This was a part of England which we all came to know well and to love during that winter. There is something special in the light of Northumberland, a blue sheen on the hills, which is like nowhere else.

Our various batteries were billeted at Cragside, Lord and Lady Armstrong's fantastic nineteenth-century castle, Thropton and Harbottle; Harbottle was my resting place that winter, tucked up under the Cheviot Hills and remote from the real war being waged in the Atlantic and in North Africa and from the blitz on London (Plate 5). That winter was a very cold one, and when the snows came we were out clearing the roads. We also trained on the Northumberland hills in all weathers. My only experience of the blitz was

PLATE 5. *Officers of 462nd Battery at the Star Inn, Harbottle, December 1940. Left to right: Lt. Shepherd, Capt. Humphries, Mr Brady (Landlord), Lt. Cleminson, Capt. Tuke, Capt. Woodbridge, Lt. Morgan.*

arriving at King's Cross on leave early one morning, in January 1941 to the sight of fires and the acrid smell of smoke lying like a pall over London.

1941 AND 1942

These years passed for us with no fighting and little exposure to bombing. In early 1941 we left Northumberland for Tewkesbury in Gloucestershire where, on 14 May, I celebrated my 21st birthday. I had obtained forty-eight hours leave, and returned home to Northwood, twenty-five miles north-west of London. My father had arranged a party for me at the Café de Paris in London. However, at the last moment he changed the venue to the Spider's Web roadhouse near Watford. The party went well, and as we returned home the sky to the south of us was ablaze with the fires of that night's raid on London – including the Café de Paris.

During these years we felt mere spectators of the events of war, and became increasingly guilty as our friends and families were bombed, or were fighting in Africa, the Far East, in the air over Europe or the seas of the Arctic and the Mediterranean. Many volunteered for the commandos, for Africa or for the paratroops, but few were taken and those that were not became restless and disillusioned. War is, I suppose, like life itself, long periods of inactivity punctuated by blasts of action, but it was difficult to accept that we were being usefully employed sitting around Britain while so many others were fighting or working hard producing weapons or food. It was therefore vital to keep morale high, and in this we were lucky in two ways.

Firstly, in 1942, George Fanshawe became our Commanding Officer and remained so through D-Day and Normandy. He had been the Regimental Adjutant in the 1930s, and in 1939 he was promoted Brigade Major of 54th Division. George Fanshawe was a regular officer in charge of a bunch of amateurs. He both terrified and inspired us. He bristled, and spoke in a distinctive nasal voice. He had piercing blue eyes and a decisive mind. He was a driving, dynamic force, and there is no doubt that his personality and his long association with the 86th made them into one of the most innovative and successful field regiments of the war.

Secondly, from 1942 onwards the Hertfordshire Yeomanry became increasingly involved in combined operations. We gradually became, in Britain anyway, the leading specialists in the role of a field regiment during an opposed landing, i.e. to provide artillery support from the sea during the actual assault and then to land quickly and to continue that support from the beach as the advance moved inland.

In the meantime we trained as gunners. We drilled ourselves and our troops in how to fire our guns in all sorts of conditions and weather, how to deploy them quickly, how to camouflage and how to move at night. We took part in exercises at troop level, at battery level, at regimental level and joined in with other regiments in Army exercises.

These major exercises were conducted all over Britain, and had code names we will always remember, like 'Spartan' and 'Bumper'. I remember one during which we always moved at night, when every night for a week I led a battery of guns through English lanes, following a route on a map by torchlight. Every wrong turning meant a monumental pile-up, and George Fanshawe's nasal castigation over the wireless at about 3 am and worse, in person as dawn broke. It taught me the skill of reading a map and a sense of location which I have never lost.

Long before we knew that Normandy was to be our objective, we took part in an exercise in the Devonshire countryside around Dartmoor, in tiny lanes with high banks, where if you missed a turning, there was no way you could turn a tank or back it out. Lessons about the vulnerability of vehicles, including tanks, in such country were imprinted on our minds before we saw the same 'bocage' again across the Channel.

We also gained the ability to do without sleep. One exercise meant four consecutive nights with no sleep for me and I slept whenever I sat down, whether it was day or night. I often found that, having overcome fatigue on the first night, I did not feel the need to sleep on the subsequent nights.

Training too was designed to create a team, and this team training went on continuously, at all levels from the gun team of six men upwards to the regiment. Discipline and routine were part of this process, to ensure that our actions were automatic and instinctive. However, the most important thing was the development of trust in our comrades, and respect and love for them. Discipline in battle arose not from fear of punishment, but much more from the fear of failing one's comrades. Training was always competitive; each gun team was determined to be the best gun in the troop, and each troop to be the best in the regiment. I will relate one example.

In 1941, at West Down ranges near Larkhill in Wiltshire, each of the six troops in the regiment competed against each other. The competition was simple. The Troop Commander (TC) proceeded along a road leading to the firing range, with a signal truck 100 yards or so to his rear. About two miles behind them came the Gun Position Officer (GPO) leading his troop of four guns at a steady pace. Somewhere along the route one was never quite sure where the Troop Commander would be stopped by an Instructor of Gunnery (IG), who would point out a target on the range ahead. Once the target was known and identified, the IG put us under starter's orders, and only then was the TC permitted to start issuing his commands. The winner was to be the first troop to deploy their guns, fire, range and hit the target, and to lay a telephone line between the Troop Commander's Observation Post (OP) and the Gun Position.

We had been told the day before of the route we were to take, and given the night to prepare our plans. I was GPO of E Troop of 462nd Battery and my Troop Commander, Peter Woodbridge, was a real competitive hunting type. The rivalry between troops was intense. Our appreciation of the situation was firstly that somehow we had to speed up the laying of a telephone line, so at midnight our signal truck laid out wire, well hidden along the morrow's route. Secondly, we had to delay the IG's starting order for as long as possible, and in the meantime forewarn the guns to get in action as fast as possible. When the IG stopped Peter Woodbridge, his signaller sent a short morse signal to my signaller, and I, as GPO, started to deploy the guns into action. This meant I had to find a suitable field off the road, and a suitable exit.

Peter Woodbridge was now 'acting stupid' with the IG, so that by the time he had 'identified' the target and called the guns into action, we were already in action and nearly ready to fire. At the same time the signals truck at the OP end taped into the pre-laid wire and ran that to the OP. The signallers at the gun end likewise tied in to the pre-laid cable. We won that competition by a record two minutes.

Complaints were registered, but the IG overruled them and said we had shown great initiative. It all sounds petty now, but Peter Woodbridge's troop would have followed him anywhere and done anything for him.

Other activities organized for us were courses. The Army were always running them in some skill or other, mainly for officers. We left the regiment for one or two weeks or a month to do an intensive training in a particular skill and then returned to teach others. Responsibilities were left behind, and usually the evenings were passed in good company. I used to volunteer for as many training courses as I could. The most popular one was vehicle maintenance at Rhyl which I never made as my senior officers always snapped up the vacancies on that one. They presumably had visions of running garages after the war. Apart from my training in bridge demolition at Darlington, which I have already described, I learned cooking and catering at Scarborough. This was not a popular course, but was actually much underrated, as we were billeted in a first-class hotel on the front and instruction was in the hotel's kitchens. The food was superb and we were allowed to have guests twice a week, which meant that invitations to sample Army rations were highly sought after. Scarborough was full of Wrens billeted around the North Cliff area. I nearly did this course twice! A survey course for a month at Larkhill was more like hard work, but we had every weekend off and free transport to Salisbury every evening. I also went on gunnery firing courses at Okehampton and in North Wales.

Best of all was a naval liaison course at Poole Harbour where we lived in a Naval Mess. Even in the middle of the war, dinner was served by delicious Wrens in white gloves, and we had unlimited brown sugar in our coffee; this in wartime Britain where a tiny ration of white sugar was everyone else's lot! If we wanted to spend an evening in Bournemouth the Navy would lend us a car, complete with a Wren driver to take us there and back. I have had a healthy respect for the senior service's organization ever since, a respect confirmed by its D-Day performance.

During these years we were constantly moving round Britain from Tewkesbury to Wiltshire, then to High Wycombe, to Suffolk, to Yorkshire and then in the spring of 1943, to Codford in Wiltshire.

I must digress a little, because my memory of our various travels round England always conjures up visions of Wrens, although my regular girlfriend of those years was a WRAF officer (she married an RAF officer later). My recollections of English girls at war will always be tied up with erotic visions of Wrens and Wrens' uniforms and Wren officers' three-cornered hats. Wrens at Scarborough, Southwold, Poole, Southampton and Bletchley. I have fond memories of fierce mixed hockey matches on Boxing Days, and of climbing home at night from Southwold to our billets in Walberswick by going hand over hand across the broken-down bridge between the two.

When we returned from a course we were expected to practice our new skill. Having been to Scarborough, I became Regimental Catering Officer. This again was a much despised job, taken on in one's spare time from regimental duties. I revelled in it. Once or twice a week I said goodbye to my troop for most of the day, took the Regimental Quartermaster Sergeant and a cook, and proceeded to the nearest Naafi depot, where I ordered and received the regiment's rations for the week. We ate lunch in the local mess and returned gently to Army life that afternoon.

Thus it came about that I was Regimental Catering Officer when the regiment was stationed in Suffolk at Christmas 1941, and the Colonel decided that we ought to give the troops a proper Christmas dinner. I was detailed off to provide it. This, in the middle of food and beer rationing, was no easy task. One of our officers was a director of Benskins Brewery at Watford, and he persuaded them to provide the beer. I tried turkey farms in Suffolk and Norfolk with no success. My father worked in London next to Leadenhall Market and knew some of the poulterers there. He somehow procured me enough turkeys, and a week before Christmas I took a quartermaster and a driver with me in a three-ton truck and set off for Hertfordshire and London. We spent forty-eight hours at home, then collected the beer and the turkeys, and headed back in glory for Suffolk. The dinner was a resounding success, and my stock with the Colonel went up several notches. By such deeds are reputations made. My promotion to Captain came the following spring.

While all these activities continued, officers and other ranks were being posted and gradually the rest of us attained seniority. By summer 1941 I was troop GPO, and that autumn became the Senior Battery Subaltern of 462nd Battery or Command Post Officer (CPO) under Battery Commander Robin Higgens, who with his Northumbrian wife looked after me and to whom I owe a great deal. In the spring of 1942, I was promoted to Captain, as Troop Commander of 'A' Troop of the 341st St Albans Battery at Westleton in Suffolk. Then later in 1942, I was again promoted, this time to Battery Captain of 341st Battery, and second in command to my Battery Commander, Major George Loveday.

For two years, from 1942 to 1944, I served under two Georges, George Loveday as my Battery Commander and George Fanshawe as my Regimental Commander. There is no doubt that I was fortunate in both. Their quality was evident even then, and it was no surprise to me after the war that George

Loveday became Chairman of the Stock Exchange and George Fanshawe a Major-General.

Battery Captain (BK) was the best job in the Army; I had no direct responsibility for a troop or a battery and I was excused parades every morning. My work was to organize the smooth running of the battery's administration, including supplies, food, transport, petrol and billets. While the regiment was moving frequently around England, the second in command and the three Battery Captains always formed the advance party to reconnoitre and pick billets. The same procedure took place on campaigns with this reconnaissance preceding a move in battle. Billeting was a matter of supreme rivalry between the Battery Captains, and the choice or the allocation of the best area for one's battery was a point of honour and importance. We might be sent to a village or part of a town and given a list of vacant houses or barns. We would then allocate these as troop quarters, headquarters, stores or officers' mess. Often the local vicar or local publican would find other empty houses which we could requisition or rent. All this and reconnaissance of all the possibilities could take a week or so, and was a superb way of seeing and getting to know Britain and all manner of local people.

During these years I grew up and educated myself. Having left school at seventeen and joined up at eighteen, my experience of life really had been very narrow, but by 1943, at the age of twenty-three, I had become used to taking decisions, thinking quickly and assuming responsibilities. I think many young officers of my generation did the same. The ability to command the respect of one's men does not come naturally, especially in a volunteer unit where many of one's troops are older, more experienced and as intelligent and educated as oneself. It takes time and hard work. These years enabled me to grow up so that by 1944 I had few doubts as to my ability.

Part of this growing up was educational. I read a lot and studied geology, history and church architecture. Moving around England and Scotland gave me many, many opportunities to put my knowledge into practice.

I shall never forget my first real introduction to Norman church architecture at Durham in 1940. My wonder at the interior of the cathedral and the position of the city itself has never left me. The geology of the countryside, too, was before my eyes, from the scarps of the Chilterns or Cotswolds to the volcanic rocks of the Cheviots and the U-shaped valleys of North Wales. I also read history and military history of all ages. I knew Hannibal's and Marlborough's campaigns and many others well. I think a soldier should study the great soldiers of history, and an early favourite of mine was Jenghis Khan, the greatest of all military organizers.

1943

By early 1943 we were training in earnest for the invasion of Europe. At the beginning of that summer we were stationed at Codford in the Wylye valley between Salisbury and Warminster, and in furtherance of our projected role in an assault landing we received our first self-propelled (SP) guns. The essential difference of this gun was that instead of being mounted on wheels and towed behind a gun tower, the 25-pounder gun was mounted on a tank chassis. The gun thus became part of the tank and could travel as a tank. More importantly, the tank chassis with tracks could negotiate the wet sand of beaches, and once the tank engine and exhaust had been proofed against water, could drive through several feet of water.

George Fanshawe described their reception by the regiment as follows:

> One day I had a message from the Station Master that 24 tanks had arrived by train addressed to the Regiment, and would I please send someone to take them over. Not unnaturally we thought a mistake had been made as no previous warning or notification had been received by anyone. However, it was found that they were for us and were self-propelled guns. Fortunately we had recently had a Subaltern posted to us who had been in a Tank Regiment, so he went down to the station, only a few hundred yards away, and drove all 24 SP guns to the camp, and so the Hertfordshire Yeomanry were the first or almost the first Field Regiment to become self-propelled. In retrospect I presume the ex-Tank Corps Officer had been posted to us by design.

From then on our training proceeded apace. We all had to learn to drive a tank. The transition from steering a wheeled vehicle to steering one with tracks is difficult to make. With a tank, a wide turning circle can be made by slowing one track or speeding up the other, but a tighter turn means a controlled skid on at least one track. On tarmac roads, particularly during a hot Wiltshire summer, there is soon little soft tarmac left and what remains is a mangled mess. On concrete or cobbles the ‘skid’ is hard to control.

One incident will always stick in my memory. One Sunday morning a troop of our guns was proceeding through a peaceful Wiltshire village to the ranges. Corners were generally carefully negotiated, but one driver misjudged one of his turns and the 25-ton SP caught the corner of a house, causing the wall to collapse. The first-floor bedroom was laid open to view, with the bed protruding and suspended in the open air. From the bed erupted a massive male figure in a torrent of words. We had unearthed a Regimental Sergeant Major home on leave from the 8th Army in North Africa and enjoying his first Sunday lie in!

The gun crews soon got used to manning their guns mounted on tank platforms and we became intensely proud of our new monsters.

We spent some time now liaising with the Navy, and moved down to Blandford Forum where we practised and worked out how to load ourselves into a Landing Craft Tank (LCT), a flat-bottomed craft with a wide door and ramp at the front and bridge to the rear which could carry about six tanks.

LCTs were in very short supply and none were available for practice at this stage. However, we found out the dimensions of the craft and laid out our own mock LCTs on the turf at Blandford. We could then load and reload until we were sure we had packed them in as full as we could, with the guns able to fire from the craft and over the top of vehicles in front of them.

The idea was to provide support to the infantry as they landed and we were given the task of perfecting the technique of firing from moving ships, the 'run in shoot'. The first experiments were carried out at Poole, on Studland Bay, in July 1943 using 25-pounder guns on a Valentine tank chassis shackled in the hold of LCTs. Later a demonstration was given to the Master Gunner of St James, Field Marshal Lord Milne, who travelled in the LCT carrying the four guns of 'B' Troop of 341st Battery. He watched the regiment's fire concentrated on the beaches, while the LCTs steamed at 6 knots towards the target area. The LCTs were kept on their correct line of approach by wireless signals from an accompanying motor launch fitted with radar.

It only remained to perfect the technique. Further demonstrations and experiments were carried out at Kilmarnock and Tignabruich in August 1943. After experiments with American equipment (the Priest 105mm SP Gun), the regiment was finally equipped with Sextons (25-pounder guns mounted on a Ram tank chassis).

By autumn 1943 we had fully mastered all the techniques, and we had written the military manuals on how to load field guns on landing craft, to debouch into six feet of water, to go into action on a beach, and to fire the guns accurately at targets on shore from a landing craft as it approached the beach. The whole concept of the field artillery's 'run in shoot' was our speciality.

We had developed a technique to hit an unseen target on shore from a field gun lashed into an LCT and unable to transverse, where the gun platform was pitching up and down and back and forward with every wave, and each gun was scheduled to fire 200 rounds before it landed. The position of the LCT was 'fixed' or known in the sea at the start. The LCT proceeded towards the shore, pointing to the target bearing, and was kept on course by a launch fitted with radar. The officer in charge of the guns, the Gun Position Officer (GPO) started a clock which synchronized with the speed of the craft. An LCT travelling at a steady 6 knots moved approximately 200 yards in a minute. Therefore, about every minute the range was dropped by 200 yards; this was done for us by the clock. The gun layers altered the range, and on the order to fire, had one minute to fire with the gun level. They had to wait until both spirit bubbles for pitch and roll were level and then fire up to four rounds in the minute before the range was dropped. If the bubbles did not level up within one minute, those rounds were missed, and the gun layers had to wait for the next time.

The technique was simple and effective. Hitches could occur and George Fanshawe described one as follows:

> The firing technique was to use a naval clock which showed yards and moved at the same rate as the LCT so the GPO could order the range to decrease at the speed the LCT was moving at; the shelling therefore remained stationary. Trouble occurred during one 'Run In' shoot when I had a Posse of VIPs, including one Lt Ryder RN VC, just above the target area, the clock apparently stopped and the shells instead of staying on the beach climbed up the hill towards us. The first into the slit trench was Ryder VC, you do not earn a VC without learning a thing or two. However, all was well and we stopped the firing.

Lastly, the Observation Posts (OPs) were in motor launches cruising a few hundred yards off the beach, with the target in view, and could therefore observe the fire and correct it by wireless to the LCTs which were initially some 12,000 yards out at sea.

The guns fired until the LCTs were about 2000 yards from the beach, then firing ceased and decks were cleared. The SP guns were unshackled, spare ammunition loaded up and everything prepared for landing. Directly the LCT touched ground, the ramp went down and the guns and command vehicles drove off into the water and up the beach to take up their first firing position, either on the beach itself or just behind it. Landing was difficult. The LCT had to be kept facing the beach while disembarkation went on, and of course one never really knew the depth of water, the softness of the sand, or whether there were pot holes on the beach, let alone whether there were German obstacles and mines. On D-Day, Royal Engineers laid down mats ('roly polys') to allow vehicles to cross the soft mud and sand.

In addition, careful planning was vital, not just to organize the loading of the guns and operational vehicles on their landing craft, but also to work out the priorities for all our supporting vehicles and stores which would come ashore days or even weeks later so that we kept in action with enough ammunition, petrol, food and the workshops and transport to keep the guns firing and mobile in the field. We had expected to land in Sicily, then to capture Rhodes, then to invade Europe in 1943. However, we realized that we were booked for the invasion of Europe itself in 1944. Where and when we did not know. We became teachers to the Essex Yeomanry, and then in the winter of 1943/4 to the 90th Field Regiment of 50th Division who had returned from Italy.

George Fanshawe remembers his reaction when told that we would be part of 50th Division for D-Day:

> In late 1943 we were told that we were to join 50th (Tyne and Tees) Division just back from Africa. So we met these terrific war heroes, the more cowardly of whom only had one MC – most of them had three! I don't think we had a medal between us all, so we all felt about 1 inch high. They were terrific and, as I subsequently found on D-Day, worth every medal they had or could ever earn. They said 'We know all about Desert Warfare but nothing about invasions, you teach us.' Well, we didn't either, but after that to work with them was the greatest period of the Herts Yeo's war life so far.
>
> Their CRA was Cyril Norton, and we were to replace one of their Field Regiments and help retrain two others to aquatic work and SPs. After the landing their third Field Regiment would come out and replace us.

We moved to Walberswick in Suffolk that autumn, and then spent the winter months at Norwich, which was US Air Force country. Their bomber and figher crews dominated the city at that time, and the centre of Norwich was so full of Americans and US dollars, US cigarettes and nylons, that impecunious British soldiers stood no chance with most of the locals. In fact, the overwhelming US presence gave rise to so many incidents that we and all our troops were banned from the centre of Norwich and did our drinking in the pubs on the outskirts. Most of our time that winter was concerned with learning the techniques of waterproofing our vehicles so that they could dive into six feet of water and still proceed ashore.

1944

As the spring of 1944 approached we knew that invasion was near. We thought it would take place in May at the latest, and guesses as to where it would be ranged from Norway to Calais and even to the south of France. We, like the rest of the invasion force, moved into embarkation camps. Ours was C.14 just outside Romsey in the New Forest. Here the regiment moved in with our tanks, guns and vehicles well hidden under trees. The whole area was full of the 50th Division and other British invasion forces. In the West Country the US forces were similarly behind Weymouth and Plymouth. We carried out final exercises in Studland Bay, co-operating with the infantry and tanks, using live ammunition under the watchful eye of General Montgomery.

May was an idyllic English summer month. We waterproofed our vehicles, which consisted of sealing all holes and cracks with metal, tape and 'Bostik', a dark and sticky substance, and providing extended exhaust pipes for engines. This sounds simple, but the practical work had to be very carefully

PLATE 6. *86th (Herts Yeo) Field Regiment RA officers in camp outside Romsey late May 1944 before embarking at Southampton. Middle row seated left to right: Capt. Perry, Capt. Kiln, Capt. Hankins, Major Swan, Major Morgan-Smith, Lt.-Col. Fanshawe, Major Scammell, Major Loveday, Capt. Pamphilon, Capt. Turnbull, Capt. Felsted. Standing behind (Left half only): Lt. Mackie, Lt. Beck, Lt. Craston, Capt. Street, Capt. Hall (behind), unknown, Capt. Ash (between Capt. Swan and Major Morgan-Smith).*

planned and meticulously carried out. One stalled vehicle could block the exit from a landing craft for all those behind it. Our Royal Electrical and Mechanical Engineers (REME) squad under Lt. Revie worked it all out and supervised it, and as far as I know our regiment, in contrast to some others, did not have a single failure of waterproofing on D-Day.

Part of our pre-invasion briefing was a visit by General Bernard Montgomery ('Monty'). Much has been written about General Montgomery and his conduct of D-Day and the Normandy campaign, and I will add my own comments as this book progresses. There is no doubt, however, that Monty had charisma and no doubt that he inspired confidence in himself from those he commanded. At this time he was already a legendary figure to 8th Army veterans, but to us he was almost unknown as a commander and I vividly recall his visit.

We were up on parade early that morning and the whole regiment marched for several miles in the rain to the rendezvous with Monty. When we arrived at the clearing in the forest, where we were to meet him, the weather was sultry and insects biting. We were all extremely cross, sweaty and fed up.

I remember my own feelings of resentment and scepticism at the whole proceedings.

Montgomery arrived in a jeep. He was wearing a ridiculously large black beret. From that moment on he electrified all of us. He spoke from the back of the jeep. None of us afterwards remembered what he actually said – it probably did not matter anyway – but his personality and magnetism came over like a shaft of light. Within a minute he was holding everyone's attention. He then dismounted and walked among us, stopping to talk individually to most officers and quite a number of other ranks. He was a small man, which surprised me. He had bushy eyebrows and light blue, piercing eyes which dominated his face. He passed a few words with me, but afterwards none of us could recall exactly what he said to them. I certainly could not, and cannot to this day, but we were all inspired by his performance, of that there was no doubt whatever. My resentment and scepticism vanished. George Fanshawe years later described his reaction as follows:

The next memorable event was Monty's visit to his troops. I had heard how he harangued the soldiers and then waved them up to his jeep. In fact he did his review in Brigade groups. Each Regiment was drawn up in two lots of four lines facing inwards with a gap between the two groups, the CO meeting the Great Man at the beginning of his Regiment. So I met him for the first time and fortunately I remembered my own name and the Regiment I was commanding; because he did not pretend to know my name he said 'What is your name and what is your Regiment' and we started walking slowly down the lines: while we did this he waved to the soldiers and said to me, 'I am doing this so all the officers and men know their Commander by sight.' After his visit, if Monty had said 'JUMP', I would have cleared the moon.

His performance was, of course, carefully rehearsed and repeated many, many times that spring, but like all good performances, it was inspiring. I can only say that Lawrence Olivier as Henry V had nothing on Monty. I saw both.

Montgomery was a great general, but whether he was an outstanding one history still has not yet decided. He certainly convinced his troops that he was, and that is half the battle a general has to conduct.

C.14 was an idyllic camping site. The sun shone every day and we disported ourselves in the shade, waiting and waterproofing. Then the final briefings began. We were shown aerial photographs of the landing beaches and the first maps and sand models. At first these were all nameless. We were, of course, locked in or confined to the camp, being allowed no leave or outside visits. Then briefing became selective. At our level our Colonel was the first to know where we were going. Afterwards there were briefing sessions with the three Battery Commanders and the tanks and infantry they were to support. At the end of May no one below the rank of Major knew where we were to land.

I remember one briefing very clearly because George Loveday was unable to attend and I, as his deputy, was detailed in his place. Our beaches were talked about as La Riviera and Creully and Arromanches and they meant nothing to me except that they sounded French. I had no idea exactly where they were. Then 'Cannes' and I thought, we're off to the Riviera. But the pronunciation was not quite right, and when someone discussed our D-Day objective as including Bayeux, the scales fell from my eyes and I knew from the Bayeux Tapestry and the invasion of 1066 that we were off to Caen and Normandy.

2
The Waiting and the Sailing

The embarkation of the 86th Field Regiment from the camps near Romsey in the New Forest to board their various ships and craft at Southampton. The waiting, as D-Day was postponed, the tension created, then the sailing on 5 June and the crossing of the Channel.

As June arrived in the New Forest, the regiment completed its briefings and waterproofing and had its photographs taken (Plate 6). It was then split up into task forces for specific jobs on D-Day. The various different boat or shiploads were gathered together to move early in June to load at Southampton's Royal Docks.

From this point onwards I will tell the story as it was witnessed in the personal diaries of observers on the spot: by myself, BK of 341st Battery, sailing with the Naval Commander King Red Beach in his Landing Craft Headquarters (LCH), by Captain Stephen Perry, Troop Commander of 'B' Troop, on his LSI with the 7th Green Howards, and by Lieutenant Sidney Beck, GPO of 'B' Troop with his four guns on their LCT.

ROBERT KILN

For my LCH, destined to lead the way to King Red Beach, we are six from the Army: Major Humphrey Dixon, the second in command of the 5th East Yorks, his assistant and signaller, Captain Richards, of the 4th/7th Dragoon Guards, his assistant and myself with my assistant, Bdr Child. We are due to drive down on the morning of Saturday June 3rd from Romsey to Southampton docks, but it is not as humdrum as that. Richards has other ideas, and he takes me under his wing. He says he is going to leave England in style in his own car. So we see the others safely loaded into their lorry and proceed to drive ourselves, or rather he to drive me, down in a Chevrolet car which he had 'liberated' from the Canadian Army. We even stop for a drink en route, carried in the Chev! It is a fine sunny morning and as we drive through Southampton, no one waves much, no one cheers us on to battle. People are quietly walking their dogs in the parks and we stop for some time by some tennis courts and the games proceed uninfluenced by the army passing by. I want to stand up and shout to them 'We're off to France to win the War', to rouse them to action.

It shows how marvellous our security is and how even at this stage the people of Southampton virtually ignore the loading of the invasion force, or perhaps how sensible the citizens of Southampton are.

When we reach the docks, Richards drives the Chev right onto the wharf itself and parks it, and out we get within twenty yards of our pier. The disposal of the car presents no problems either, as Richards espies an attractive Wren, calls her over and gives her the car and the keys, kisses her goodbye, and we stroll coolly down the pier.

We meet Claude Hull, second in command of 6th Green Howards, Claude Hankins and Jackie Bland on the pier, they will do the same jobs as ourselves on King Green Beach. We stroll around, chat and watch some Wrens sunbathing. LCH 267 pulls alongside after about an hour's wait and we are marshalled on to her. Usual tight squeeze on board. Commander Haines (DSOAG) insists on turning the No. 1, Joscyn, out of his bunk for me. I feel very guilty. I share a cabin with Wynn, the Signals Officer, Richards (Naval Transport Officer) and Soo (Navigator). Others on board include the Naval Gunnery Officer Woods, known as the Old Edwardian because of his moustache. We victual up and cast off to travel down Southampton Water to the Solent.

The wind gets up and the sea is about Force 4 even in this sheltered water. It looks as if D-Day may be put back. We should sail tomorrow, Sunday, at 1000 hours and land 0645 Monday morning.

As an indication we soldiers take on board these stores per man:

Compo rations for a week, a composition of various hard-tack foods
6 tins of self-heating soup
2 tins of self-heating cocoa
2 × 24 hrs rations
1 life belt
1 water sterilizing outfit
2 bars chocolate
1 bag of biscuits
1 packet of chewing gum
20 cigarettes
1 emergency ration (chocolate)
plus 2 bags vomit!

This of course is extra to all normal equipment. I have a large pack on my back and things slung all around me. Have a quiet evening going over maps and working out our final plans and positions on the LCH.

Sunday 4th June. Wake late about 0830, ship rolling badly; still Force 4 or 5. Hear that the operation is postponed 24 hours. Glad in a way but we all curse the weather as we want to get on with this now. Pass the day quietly reading and working things out. It seems difficult to realize that we have actually left England for good. A lot of talk here of having to put the whole business off for 10 days.

Old Eisenhower has to take a big decision because we have only 3 days until the half tide (on the flow) comes at the correct time in the morning. Hear in the evening that the party is definitely on. Well, well! hope the sea drops. We shall never do it in this.

Monday 5th June. 0959 off we go down the Solent [Plate 7]. Sea still Force 4 or 5, wind Force 5. We roll. Hastily swallow some pink pills. We turn SE off the Needles heading for Calais just to fox the Boche. Travel beam on to the swell. Sleep and do not eat much. Humphrey and Richards disgustingly fit! Some of the Navy ill though!

We lead our part of G force across the Channel. At dusk we are still steaming south-eastward towards Calais then, as the light fades, we alter course to the south-west. As we do so, our aircraft fly over us, and we can see to our left, on our old course, ripples and ripples of tin foil falling from them. I do not understand it at all, but Wynn explains all about a radar decoy to let German Radar pick up the foil and think it is us continuing south-east. [See Figure 1.]

That evening after dark the Navy has a mix up on the minefields. The Yanks have got to our port instead of starboard! I hope they sort themselves out during the night. [They did!]

Have another look at the maps of La Rivière, Ver-sur-Mer, and Crepon before turning in. We know every house and mine in the place by now. So to bed whilst the Navy gets us there.

STEPHEN PERRY

Romsey May 31st near Romsey. Here are the wagons and George Fanshawe strolling up to wish us good luck; it's easy for him to find us in the middle of this mass of soldiery; the old black berets mark us down as the only three gunners in the neighbourhood. He is in grand form and obviously itching to get cracking on the job. Well, now we are off to Southampton. We debus and start on the dreary three mile tramp through the streets, hot, sweaty and loaded down with kit, and arrive more than ready for the hot cup of char and biscuits that await us on the quay. Gosh, if we feel like this after walking three miles, what on earth is it going to be like fighting with all this equipment slung around us!

Hullo! here's the *Lance*, – the 8,000 ton LSI that is to take *us* to France, steaming up the channel. We file up the gangway; I am in the bows this time with a dozen other officers; Corky, our Naval Forward Observation Officer (FOO) is in the next bunk [Captain Corke, who later in Normandy became Major Corke, commanding 341st Battery]. It seems incredible that this is the real thing and not just another exercise. I wonder if everybody else is thinking the same thing. I suppose they must be, but nobody looks in the least excited, strung up or nervous; we might be just going off for a day's fishing, instead of embarking on a venture which will thrill the whole world, and from which very many will never return. I wonder if it's the Englishman's pride at not showing his feelings, or if they do not realise what they are in for, or are they just blasé about the whole thing?

It is a grand day in Southampton Water; ships and craft of all shapes and sizes are bustling about busily on some errand or other, preparing for the great day. We steam slowly to our mooring in the Solent and drop anchor in the centre of a line of LSIs, four or five cables apart (which are carrying the assault troops of 50 Div) and surrounded by LSIs, fleet destroyers, minesweepers, corvettes, and all the peculiar looking craft that worm their way into an invasion fleet. There are some of those floating piers being towed around, and there is the *Kingsmill*, HQ ship with the CO on board.

So far everything has gone without a hitch; loading up to time and no sign of enemy aircraft. Prospects are good; the weather is not too bad, everyone looks fit and spirits are high. It's very comfortable on board, and four days of good food and no work will be a welcome change after the last few days of frantic preparations and rotten grub. What a relief too, to have no worries, after the responsibility of ensuring that sixty men, their tanks, guns, and vehicles are all 100% efficient.

June 1st – 3rd. Life is very pleasant, and the days slip by. Lying in a lifeboat stripped to the waist, basking in the sun with a book, occupies two or three hours every day. The food is really first class, and writing dozens of goodbye letters prevents boredom spoiling this much needed relaxation. I parade my two soldiers every day to inspect their small arms, and test the wireless. They are both in grand spirits and longing to 'have a go'. The hot showers on board are a real luxury, after all the dust of Romsey; I indulge in these excellent ablutions every day, determined at any rate to start thoroughly clean. We hear that D-Day is to be the 5th.

June 4th. There is half a gale blowing today, and all the talk on board is about the chances of the party being postponed. It must be off if the weather continues like this. Heavy seas would completely wreck the operation, however well it were planned and executed; the LCAs would overturn, the run-in shoot would be too inaccurate to be effective, and no stores could be landed. However, it looks as though it's on, despite rumours to the contrary on board, because we can see the LCTs who will take about twenty hours to cross, steaming up the Solent in single file. Two flotillas have passed the *Lance*, and they all go about and file back again in their moorings off Calshot. So it's off after all; and no-one is surprised, because even here, in the sheltered waters of the Solent, an LCM which has ventured out for a trip is being tossed about and buffeted by vicious waves, and looks as though it will capsize any minute. This is very worrying, because if it is postponed for two days more we will have to wait for another fortnight before the tides are right. What a ghastly anti-climax it would be to go ashore again, and live in that filthy dust ridden camp again for another fortnight, unable to set foot outside the camp boundaries; worse than that, the secret would surely get out, now that even every 'Gunner Snooks' knows where we are going to land. It would be too awful; we must pray for fine weather tomorrow.

This suspense is frightful, and a tense atmosphere is becoming very noticeable on board. The naval Lt/Cmdr. gives us a weather forecast every two or three hours, which is not at all promising.

June 5th. The weather looks very slightly better, though it is still blowing pretty hard. At 9 o'clock we are told that the great decision has been taken, and that the landings will take place tomorrow. What a relief, but what a gamble going over in this weather. The LCTs are again steaming up the channel, looking absolutely magnificent, hundreds of them in single file, with pennants flying, carrying a load of tanks or SPs hidden under a vast camouflage net. From the bridge I can make out their numbers through my glasses. At 9.40 LCT 502 passes by carrying 'B' Troop, the chaps I have trained for two years; and tomorrow they will fire in anger for the first time. It would be ghastly if a bomb got them, and the whole troop were to founder before even setting foot on the beaches. Just one bomb and the whole troop would disappear in a matter of seconds.

Sidney Beck and Signaller Jarvis will be on the lookout for my lamp, 'Good Luck "B" Troop' flashes out, and back comes the reply 'Same to you, see you in France', I hope!

At 1200 all officers [on the *Lance*] are summoned for the final conference. The Naval Commander delivers a most impressive and awe-inspiring address, 'Tomorrow, Tuesday 6th June, 1944, is D-Day for the Allied Invasion of Europe'. We all feel that we are important members of a force which is going to embark on the biggest, most important, and most daring operation in history, the success of which depends, very largely, on the establishment of the initial bridgehead, by *us*! H hour is to be at 0725. Maps are issued and final instructions from Col. Richardson, CO of the 7th Green Howards, given, and that is that.

On deck with Meyer my Observation Post Assistant (OPAck) and Barker my signaller, I go over for the last time where we are going and how we do

PLATE 7. *LCTs loaded in Southampton Water and setting sail 5 June 1944. In foreground 13th/18th Hussars of 8th Armoured Brigade. Other LCTs in background.*

it. We study the photos of the beach, the maps, the route up which we will advance if all goes well, and most important the position of mine fields. We go over the code words, most of which we know by heart now, we take a last look at the wireless, on which everything depends, and trust that we will not be too sick, and that the landing will be a shallow one.

At 1845 hours the *Lance* slowly gets under way and takes its place in the single line of LSTs steaming up the Solent towards the Needles and the beaches of Normandy. Everybody is on deck to see the last of England, and the gigantic air battle which we are told to expect. We pass LSTs, flying balloons, corvettes, concrete piers, LCTs and many other types of craft, all waiting to be given the word 'go'.

At 2020 we pass the Needles; this really is goodbye to England. Our convoy of LSIs is headed by a motor launch (ML) which guides us. The *Kingsmill* is just ahead of us rolling very heavily; I will bet the CO is getting a bit green about the gills. I cannot really see very much of the vast fleet that must be on its way, because we are in single file with just an odd corvette or motor launch (ML) swanning along on the flanks. I can just make out another convoy similar to ours appearing round St. Albans head to the west; probably the Yank assault Division who are landing on our right, coming from Weymouth.

We are all feeling fine on our vast hulk of a ship, which is very steady, but those poor devils on the LCTs, who have being going since 0900, must be having a hell of a time. I hope the men of 'B' Troop will not be too ill to shoot straight at 6.45 tomorrow morning.

Still no sign of the German airforce; they must know we are on the way by now. I will bet those Germans 'standing to' in their pillboxes on the beaches are feeling pretty miserable; but do they know *where* we are coming from or where we will land – that's the important thing; a couple of Panzer divisions sitting on the beaches waiting for us would create the biggest massacre in history. Anyway, we will know tomorrow, so why worry. There seems to be nothing to see tonight, so to bed, and get some sleep; the last night in pyjamas and a comfortable bed for heaven knows how long.

SIDNEY BECK

June 3rd. The guns and tanks move to Southampton Water and load on to LCTs. Skippers, crews and gunners are all familiar with each other and the craft, and the loading goes through without a hitch. A detachment of REs comes aboard, and a huge 'roly-poly' is lowered into the bows by crane. Six days' compo rations are stored. Compasses are swung in the harbour and we anchor in Southampton Water. Secret maps which have been entrusted to the skipper are now produced, and for the first time I learn of the Normandy Coast.

The Solent is choc-a-bloc with ships of all shapes and sizes, ranging from Mulberry Harbour components to Destroyers and Cruisers, all straining at the leash, waiting for the starting pistol. Tension is apparent on board, aggravated by frequent and depressing weather reports and unsettling forecasts.

June 4th. At last, to everyone's relief, D-Day is announced for June 5th. On board maps are distributed and final briefing carried out, the LCTs up anchor and begin running down the Solent passing the great LSTs. Waves are running high. Off the Isle of Wight the convoy stops and hangs around until a signal runs through the fleet. We turn round. Postponed! The suspense aboard all ships is almost unbearable.

June 5th. The great decision is taken. Once again the Armada sets sail despite most unfavourable weather reports. The LCTs weigh anchor at 0900 hrs, once more passing the great LSIs and once more the waves are running high. Capt. Perry and Capt. Hall flash signals by lamp 'Good Luck' to 341 Battery's LCTs as they steam by.

As we pass the Needles Lighthouse and feel the first Atlantic swells, we know that there is no turning back and many begin to take their sea-sick pills. I take the sealed envelope with me to the shelter under the bridge, which is large enough to hold 10 men at a time. Here I spend several hours briefing the men of my troop and the REs, in batches of 10, and reading the messages from the King, Eisenhower, Montgomery and 50th Division's Commander [Major-General D. A. H. Graham]. In the confined space of the shelter, with the noise and fumes from the engines below, and the pitching and tossing of the ship causing the chains and shackles holding the guns and tanks to grind and strain, at the end of the several briefings I am feeling decidedly queasy.

Getting out into the open air does not help much, as I can see a number of the men producing vomit bags, so I take my own sea-sick pills. Before going up to the bridge I check that everyone is wearing a Mae West (life jacket), that everything is fastened down, and the ammo secure and dry. All of us try to snatch some sleep in our vehicles. The skipper, taking pity on me, offers me a sailor's hammock which he has had slung fore and aft up on the bridge in the open air, away from the fumes and the engines.

Spray and waves are washing over the sides. The wind is dead against the bows, the boat heaving and swaying, engines revving at high speed against the high wind. There is little comfort for anyone.

'B' Troop's LCT is towing a fast motor launch to save its fuel. Three times before nightfall the towing cable snaps with the strain of the constant buffeting of the waves. In the end it is cast adrift to come along under its own power. It is almost dark before we finally see that land is out of sight.

Unbeknown to the Germans, we hope, the greatest Armada in the world is assembling off the coast of France in the very face of the enemy. Silently, in the wild darkness of that stormy night, darkened ships, no lights showing anywhere, plunge and toss their way across the Channel. Peering in the darkness from the bridge of the LCT in my hammock, I imagine I am alone under the sky.

3
D-Day Dispositions and Objectives

The various objectives and tasks of the Allied Forces. German troop dispositions. The particular objectives of the 69th Brigade of 50th Division whom the 86th Field Regiment supported.

ALLIED PLANS AND OBJECTIVES

Once the decision had been taken to launch an Allied Second Front in Western Europe, there were really only two possible areas in which to do so: the Pas de Calais and the north Normandy coast. The north coast of Brittany is very rocky, and exposed, and Brittany could be sealed off by the Germans. Anywhere in the bay of Biscay was too far for air cover and a long sea journey. Holland too was easily defended with its water obstacles. North Germany, Denmark and Norway all had similar problems.

Normandy had these great advantages. It was close enough for air cover. The sea distances were reasonable. A major port, Cherbourg, was available. The river Seine on the east and the river Loire on the south formed two natural barriers to any German reinforcement. If the bridges on the Seine were destroyed between Paris and the sea and those on the Loire between Orleans and the sea, then almost all reinforcements, particularly tanks and heavy guns, would have to be funnelled to Normandy via the sixty-mile gap between Paris and Orleans.

The original planning for operation 'Overlord' was carried out during 1943 under the Chief of Staff to the Supreme Allied Commander (COSSAC) Sir Frederick Morgan, before the Supreme Commander himself had been appointed. COSSAC had chosen Normandy for the invasion, but it was Montgomery who, in January 1944, enlarged the original landing area in Overlord from an assault on three beaches to an assault on five beach areas. This required a greater number of assault troops, three US seaborne divisions and three British seaborne divisions, plus three airborne divisions with additional numbers of Rangers, Commandos and Armoured Brigades. There is no doubt that Montgomery's insistence on this increase posed an enormous strain on the Allied resources of shipping and aircraft and that there would not have been available additional back up to land, say, an extra assault division, either by sea or air.

The Allied landings in Normandy were under the control of General Montgomery, who was answerable to the Supreme Commander, General Eisenhower. The chain of command was as follows:

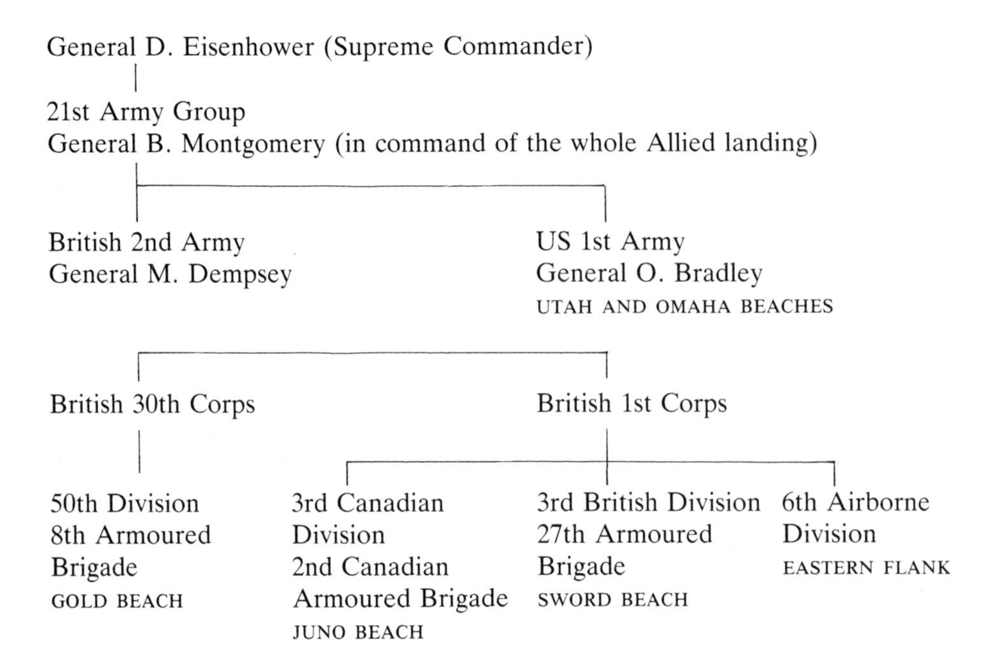

The 21st Army Group plan was to seize two bridgehead areas on D-Day; the first at the base of the Cotentin peninsula, and the second from the mouth of the river Vire eastward and south-eastward to include Bayeux and Caen and the N13 main road through those towns. The Contentin bridgehead was to be some eleven miles deep to Pont-l'Abbé and some twelve miles in width. The larger bridgehead was nearly fifty miles wide and five or six miles deep at its west end, but deepening to eleven miles to include Caen (Figure 2).

After D-Day these bridgeheads would be joined and extended. The D-Day bridgeheads were to be seized by landings in five beach areas, two US, two British and one Canadian. The US 1st Army landed on the two western areas: Utah at the base of the Cotentin Peninsula, and Omaha south-east of Utah. From west to east the British 2nd Army's beaches were Gold, east of Arromanches, Juno, centred on Courseulles, and Sword, centred on Lion-sur-Mer and Ouistreham.

The beach landings were to be preceded by airborne troop landings by parachute and glider on the US front inland from Utah, around Ste-Mère-Église, to clear and secure the exits from Utah and north of Carentan. This was the strategic position between Utah and Omaha. Two US airborne divisions, the 82nd and 101st, were used, one for each task.

On the British front the 6th Airborne Division was dropped on the extreme left of the front, that is to the east, to secure the line of the river Orne and the Ship Canal between Caen and the sea, and to make a bridgehead to the east of it.

The British and Canadian assaulting divisions from west to east were: 50th (Northumberland) British Division, assaulting Gold from Arromanches to La Rivière, 3rd Canadian Infantry Division, assaulting Juno at Courseulles, and the 3rd British Division, assaulting Sword at Lion-sur-Mer and Ouistreham. Each of these infantry divisions was supported by an Armoured Brigade of tanks. The 8th Armoured Brigade was with the 50th British Division. In addition to these were several Royal Marine Commandos: 47 RM Commando landed on the west of 50th Division. 50th Division comprised four infantry brigades, as against the normal three brigades. This was due to them having 56th Infantry Brigade under command for the landing.

The various supporting beach groups and special troops added to the numbers, so the total British and Canadian forces in the seaborne landing were really the equivalent of at least five divisions in all, plus of course 6th Airborne Division. This totalled a force of approximately 80,000 assault troops.

The US force of three seaborne divisions, augmented by Ranger battalions and supported by two US airborne divisions, totalled just over 60,000 assault troops in all.

GERMAN POSITIONS

The positions of German divisions in or near Normandy on 6 June are shown on Figure 2. In essence, there were three infantry divisions in a static coastal defence role between Cherbourg and the mouth of the Seine; 709, 716 and 711. These were reinforced by a mobile and higher quality division, 352, who had moved to the coast between Carentan and Arromanches for a training exercise. It was this division that was to cause so much trouble to the US landing at Omaha and to 50th Division at Arromanches.

On the west side of the Contentin peninsula was a further static coastal division and a mobile one, 91st Division. In Brittany around the mouth of the Loire were five more static coastal divisions, plus one first-class division, 3 GAF (Paratroops) and two further divisions refitting. These formed the German 7th Army.

In the British Sector the German 15th Army had under its command the 21st Panzer Division, just south of Caen, 12th SS Panzer Division between

Caen and Paris, and Panzer Lehr between Chartres and Le Mans, seventy miles from Caen. North-east of the Seine as far as Belgium were seven coastal divisions, five mobile infantry divisions, two Panzer divisions, 2nd and 116th, with two more Panzer divisions in Belgium and Holland, 1st SS and 19th respectively. Both German armies formed Army Group B, since January 1944 under the command of Field Marshal Rommel, once again facing his desert enemy Montgomery.

In the south-west of France the 1st German Army had one front-line infantry division and three others, plus two partly formed Panzer divisions. In the German 19th Army along the Mediterranean coast there were some six infantry divisions, and in the rest of France two infantry divisions and two Panzer divisions, 2nd SS and 9th. Discounting coastal divisions, the position was that west of the Rhine the Germans had eight Panzer divisions with two more reforming.

Apart from the static coastal divisions and 352nd Division, the main reinforcements available to reach the US sector were therefore two first-class infantry divisions, the 91st and 3 GAF, plus the two refitting 5 GAF and 275 Divisions. There were no Panzer divisions in the German 7th Army sector. The British were faced by three Panzer divisions, plus three more Panzer divisions if we include 1st SS and up to seven infantry divisions from north-east of the Seine. The divisions from the south and south-west of France were too far away to interfere until later. For example, 2nd SS Panzer arrived on 29 June from Toulouse and 9th Panzer on 6 August from Avignon.

50th DIVISION'S ASSAULT

The arrangement of 50th Division for D-Day was as follows:

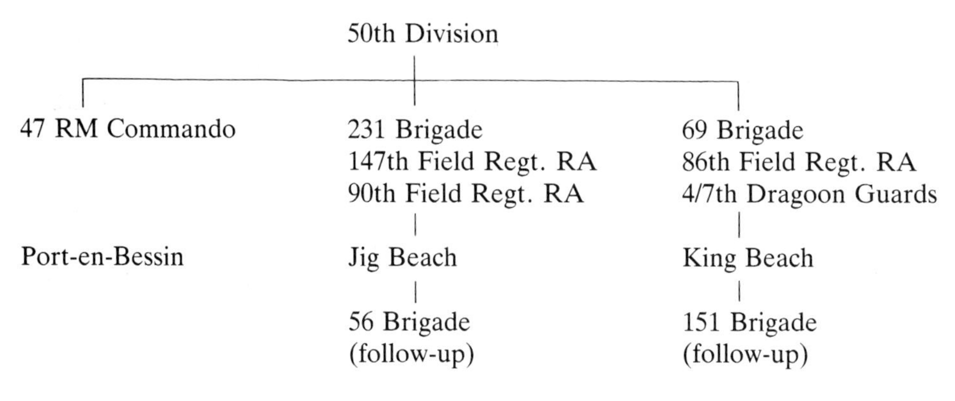

If you look at Figure 3 you will see that the 50th Division's objective for D-Day was to land and to advance westwards to Port-en-Bessin some ten miles away to link with the US forces landing at Omaha and at the same time to advance inland about seven miles to capture Bayeux, secure the line of the Bayeux–Caen road and link with the Canadians on that road about six miles east of Bayeux. To achieve this would require a bridgehead some ten or twelve miles in width and seven miles deep. The troops who would form this bridgehead were to land on Jig and King Beaches in the Gold Beach area, between the 3rd Canadian Division, two to three miles east at Juno, and the US landing at Omaha some thirteen miles to the west.

Figure 4 shows 50th Division's assault with 231 Brigade and 47 RM Commando on Jig Beach on the west side, and 69 Brigade on King Beach on the east. The only part of the Gold Beach area suitable for a landing was between Le Hamel on the west and La Rivière on the east, as there were rocks and cliffs on either side.

Jig Beach stretched about 2000 yards eastwards from the high ground of Le Hamel, a strongly fortified cliff on its western side. There was then a gap of some 1500 yards before King Beach, which stretched 2000 yards eastwards to other strong points at La Rivière and was also exposed to positions further inland around Ver-sur-Mer.

The 50th Division had two follow-up Brigades, 56 Brigade behind 231 Brigade, and 151 Brigade behind 69 Brigade, with the 8th Armoured Brigade in support.

The first objective, shown on Phase 1 on Figure 5, was the capture of Le Hamel, Meuvaines, Ver-sur-Mer and Mont Fleury; features which occupied a semicircle of high ground encircling the beaches at a distance inland of 2500 yards from the centre. Once this high ground was held, the Germans could not observe the beaches nor could they bring any direct fire on the beaches.

Having achieved their initial assault, 231 Brigade were to move westward along the coast, capturing the little port of Arromanches. Arromanches was to be the site of the British Mulberry harbour, an artificial harbour through which our main supplies were to be unloaded. Its early capture by 231 Brigade was therefore vital. After that the Brigade was to advance south and westward to link with US forces and 47 RM Commando, which had been detailed to bypass Le Hamel and Arromanches inland and move across country some nine to ten miles to capture Port-en-Bessin. This was a small fishing port with a sheltered harbour, about three and a half miles from the nearest part of Omaha, where the US forces would link up with them on D-Day. These moves are shown on Figure 3.

Port-en-Bessin was to be the Normandy terminal of a pipeline laid across the Channel to supply petrol to the whole of 21st Army Group. This imaginative project, called Pluto (Pipe Line Under The Ocean), was vital to the

Allied supplies, and therefore the early capture of Port-en-Bessin had a high priority.

As shown on Figure 3, 69 Brigade were to move directly inland in a south-south-west direction, to cut the Caen–Bayeux road near a fortified German radar station on the high ground near St Leger, some four miles south-east of Bayeux. They were to make contact with the Canadians on their left. The 56 and 151 Brigades were to follow inland between 69 and 231 Brigades and to move south-west to capture Bayeux and the high ground to the south and to link up there with the US 1st Division from Omaha.

The task of the 8th Armoured Brigade was to support the 50th Division's assault, but it had an additional objective once 50th Division's bridgehead was established, which should be mentioned at this stage. On D+1, or as soon as possible, the brigade was to advance southward through 50th Division's line to capture the high ground just outside Villers Bocage, some twenty-two miles inland, and to form a pivot or strong point there (Figure 6). This advance was to be led by its follow-through regiment, the 24th Lancers, and the reconnaisance regiment of the 50th Division. These regiments were to land during the late morning and afternoon of D-Day and to form up at Martragny, just behind the Bayeux–Caen road.

69 BRIGADE'S D-DAY TASKS AND DISPOSITIONS

Figures 4 and 5 show 69 Brigade's assault on King Beach, the eastern part of Gold, with La Rivière on its eastern side. King Beach was itself divided into two halves, King Green on the right, in other words the western half, and King Red on the left or eastern side. The 86th Field Regiment was under the command of 69 Brigade assaulting King Beach.

If you refer to Figure 4 and Plate 8 you will see the village of La Rivière with its sea walls and fortifications on the east, with guns and machine guns able to sweep the beach to the west. No landing was to be attempted in front of the sea wall or to the east. To the west of La Rivière the beach was mud, sand and shingle, with sand dunes behind gradually rising to the low hills of Mont Fleury with a lighthouse, and Ver-sur-Mer village to its south-west. Behind the beach, about 2000 yards west of La Rivière, the ground became damper and marshy, with numerous small streams and ditches, and this continued for another 1000 yards towards Le Hamel. The sand dunes and these ditches made the exit from the beach difficult in any area, but impossible in this centre section, which lay between King and Jig Beaches.

The country behind the beach, once one had cleared the marshes and dunes, rose, quite steeply in parts, to the semicircle of hills of about 150 ft described above. Beyond that the country was very like Kent or Devon.

There were trees, hedges and small fields. It was mainly dairy country, but there were lots of apple orchards and potato fields, with small winding lanes and little streams, interspersed with stone farm houses, barns and stone-built villages. The solid stone buildings and walls made perfect defence positions.

The German beach fortifications, as we knew them, consisted of the La Rivière fortifications and numerous pill boxes along the beach. There were heavy minefields at the back of the beach, and supplementing the natural ditches were anti-tank ditches and barbed wire entanglements. In addition the beach below high water was covered in an assortment of concrete blocks, iron stakes and hedgehogs (underwater iron spikes two rows deep), and many of them were mined.

Our information had been obtained partly from aerial photographs of the area, partly from intrepid observers who had actually landed on the beaches from submarines to find out whether they consisted of firm sand or shingle, and also from pre-war postcards, holiday snaps and of course those who knew the area. We were issued with 1:50,000 maps and more detailed 1:12,500 maps of the defences, and low-level aerial photographs of the beach, taken from just out at sea (see Plate 8). By the time we landed everybody knew the terrain by heart, and this intensive reconnaissance and briefing meant that we had few surprises on the day. We all felt that we were landing on a beach that we knew pretty well.

69 Brigade's landing was to be made by the 6th Green Howards on King Green on our right (the west), and by the 5th East Yorks on King Red on our left (the east). Each of the assault battalions would be supported by a squadron of duplex drive (DD) tanks from 4/7th Dragoon Guards, a battery of the 86th Field Regiment, the Armoured Vehicles Royal Engineers (AVREs) and the Centaur 90mm assault guns of the Royal Marines. These would be followed by the third battalion of the brigade, the 7th Green Howards, with a further battery and a squadron of 4/7th Dragoon Guards. The OPs of the three batteries of the 86th were each allocated to a battalion and the line up was as follows:

King Red Assault
5th East Yorks
462nd Battery 86th Field Regt. RA
'C' Squadron 4/7th Dragoon Guards
AVREs

King Green Assault
6th Green Howards
342nd Battery 86th Field Regt. RA
'B' Squadron 4/7th Dragoon Guards
AVREs

Follow Through
7th Green Howards
341st Battery 86th Field Regt. RA
'A' Squadron 4/7th Dragoon Guards
Anti-Tank Battery

PLATE 8. *A low-level aerial photograph of Gold Beach King as issued to Capt. Ash before the landing, taken at high tide. The photograph is composite and therefore the background is highly distorted. On the left the houses and the sea wall of La Rivière with various gun emplacements. Behind and to the right Ver-sur-Mer lighthouse. To extreme right of picture is the centre road exit from the beach past Lavatory Pan*

The main exits from King Beach consisted of three roads or tracks. The first from La Rivière led south-west from the sea past the lighthouse, up into Mont Fleury village and through that to Ver-sur-Mer and on to Crepon. The second ran straight uphill from the centre of King Beach past a house with a circular drive known to us as 'Lavatory Pan House' and up into Mont Fleury village, passing the Mont Fleury Battery on its west side. The third track led from the far west of the beach swinging south-eastwards to Ver-sur-Mer. It was the middle track or road past Lavatory Pan House which became the main exit on D-Day, as the first was under fire from La Rivière for much of the day.

The brigade's objective was planned in three phases, shown on Figure 5 and detailed below.

House, which shows up as a light circular area in a dark field to the right of the road. Behind this, is the wood with the emplacements of the Ver-sur-Mer battery. Ver-sur-Mer village lies in the centre of picture in trees. Note also the ridge of ground behind the beach, the pill boxes on the beach and in many areas behind, particularly in front of the Ver-sur-Mer battery.

Phase I

The objectives of the assault groups were to secure the beach, establish exits, and advance to the high ground of Mont Fleury, Ver-sur-Mer and Pt 52 between Ver-sur-Mer and Meuvaines. In carrying out these objectives, the 5th East Yorks were to bypass then capture La Rivière, to prevent the Germans there from firing on the beach and to capture the Mont Fleury lighthouse. The 6th Green Howards were to advance up the hill past Lavatory Pan House and take the Mont Fleury Battery, then move to the high ground at Pt 52. The 7th Green Howards were to move inland between the 5th East Yorks and 6th Green Howards, to capture Ver-sur-Mer village and the battery to its east. This operation would complete Phase I.

Phase II

The 6th Green Howards would then advance to capture Crepon, a village two miles inland, and then move up across the open country to the main road from Creully to Bayeux overlooking the river Seulles at St Gabriel. The 7th Green Howards would send a flying column of 'C' Company and 'A' Squadron of 4th/7th Dragoon Guards supported by 341st Battery to capture Creully, with its vital bridge over the Seulles, and then would cross the river. The 5th East Yorks' main task was still to capture La Rivière.

Phase III

Once the bridge at Creully was secured, contact was to be made with the Canadians on our left near Creully, and the whole brigade was to advance across the Bayeux–Caen road and hold the high ground around St Leger.

THE BEACH ASSAULT

It was realized that the crucial period was the landing itself, and quick penetration inland through the pill boxes, barbed wire, minefields, anti-tank obstacles, concrete walls, ditches and waterlogged land, while under fire from the defences on the beach itself and from La Rivière and the high ground at Mont Fleury and Ver-sur-Mer.

69 Brigade's H hour was 0725 hours, about two hours after first light at 0515, which allowed for two hours of bombing and observed naval bombardment, plus the fire from our own SPs and the rock-firing craft. It was vital that this bombardment knocked out or at least neutralized the enemy strong points. These are shown on Figure 4 and were known to consist of:

1. 150mm, 75mm and 50mm guns and, of course, machine guns in La Rivière, which could enfilade our beach completely.
2. A battery of at least four 155mm guns west of Mont Fleury.
3. A battery of the same south-east of Ver-sur-Mer.
4. Machine guns and possible further guns on Pt 52 to west of Ver-sur-Mer.
5. A strong point on the beach some 2000 yards west of La Rivière with guns and machine guns.
6. Pill boxes along the beach itself and in several places inland.

Our naval gunfire was concentrated on these strong points. Our own SP target was initially the west side of La Rivière, and then just before H hour we were to lift our fire to the battery behind the beach. The naval fire would also lift to the high ground behind.

As I said, this was the crucial time, and to cover the landing itself we only had naval LCGs which could engage selected targets on the beach which had survived early bombardments. Observers offshore during the actual landing were to do this through the naval gunnery officers, in other words to bring fire on any enemy strong points on or near the beach, which were still in action, and, equally important, to make sure the naval fire stopped when our assault forces were themselves on or close to these strong points.

However well this worked, there would still be a crucial period as the assault touched down, when the assault troops could be devastated by fire before getting up and off the beach itself. To lessen this danger, H hour was fixed for about one and a half hours before high water, so that we sailed over most of the beach obstacles and the infantry had a short beach to cross. This also meant that the naval craft could get away to sea without being left high and dry by an outgoing tide, which was equally vital.

However short the beach, two further things were needed. Firstly, a quick clearance of minefields, ditches, anti-tank walls and obstacles from exits from the beach, and secondly the elimination of fire from reinforced pill boxes.

To achieve this, reliance was placed on the 'funnies', the specially equipped AVREs and the specially adapted tanks of the 79th Armoured Division. These are described in the Glossary and consisted, briefly, of Flail tanks to make paths through minefields (Plate 9), 'Roly Polys' to lay carpets across soft sands, bridging tanks for crossing ditches, and others to blow up pill boxes or concrete obstacles.

Providing covering fire for the infantry and the 'funnies', as they landed and went up the beach, was the job of the DD tanks of the 4/7th Dragoon Guards. All round the hull of the tank was fitted a heavy canvas waterproof side, which could be raised or lowered. When raised the side stood higher than the tank's turret and about six feet or so above the hull. With these sides raised the tank could float like a boat with the tank itself at the bottom, and was propelled by twin propellors on the rear of the tank driven by the tank's engines; the Duplex drive. The crew of the tank sat on the turret, but the driver stayed in his driving seat. They could proceed at a slow steady speed. There were problems of course: the freeboard of canvas was low and with any sort of swell they shipped water, and if the canvas was holed by gunfire or accident, there was little the crew could do but get out and swim before their craft sank – tank drivers kept their hatches open! These swimming tanks were due to be launched some miles out and to swim in ahead of the AVREs and the infantry. Being very low in the water they would present a poor target for the Germans, whose whole attention would be on the mass of ships and craft behind them. Launching was done from a landing craft tank (LCT) through the lowered bow door and into the sea. Launching was difficult, and care had to be taken not to damage or hole the canvas as the

PLATE 9. *To the right a Flail tank of 79th Armoured Division showing chains on sprocket at front of tank to detonate mines as it rotates. Bren-gun carrier on left.*

tank ran down the lowered ramp of the LCT into the water. The tank then proceeded under its own power to the beach.

The DD tanks would stop on the sea's edge, with only their gun turrets showing, and would open fire from their positions half covered by water. They would be followed by the AVREs, particularly the Flail tanks, to clear passages through the minefields. Then the assaulting infantry in their LCAs would land. Once the beach was secure, the assault troops would be followed by the 7th Green Howards, our own SP Guns and the non-DD tanks, anti-tank guns and naval beach obstacle clearance teams, in whatever order they were required on shore. The exact timing and priority of landing would be decided by the naval commanders of the various beaches.

The layout of the landing as proposed is shown in the diagram at the end of this chapter. In practice certain changes occurred. For example, the DD tanks shown on the beaches below high-water mark (HW) were not launched miles out, as our story will show.

86th FIELD REGIMENT'S D-DAY TASKS AND DISPOSITIONS

The 86th Field Regiment's task was firstly, to fire at the defences as our troops sailed in, the 'Run-in Shoot', secondly, to land and to go quickly into action on shore in support of the infantry and tanks.

To carry out these tasks the regiment was split up into different groups, each to sail with different boat loads on various assault craft. These dispositions are shown in the diagram at the end of this chapter. Contributors to this book are underlined below. The major group consisted of the guns. These sailed in six LCTs, one troop to each LCT, each LCT carrying four SP guns plus the GPO's command vehicle, the Troop Commander's tank, his bren-gun carrier and a signal vehicle. These six LCTs sailed together, fired the run-in shoot together and then landed.

Lt.-Colonel George Fanshawe sailed with 69 Brigade HQ on a frigate, HMS *Kingsmill*.

Major John Morgan-Smith, the regiment's second in command, landed ahead of the guns, and had the vital task of organizing their arrival ashore and putting them into action as quickly as possible.

Major George Loveday, commander of 341st Battery, sailed in a motor launch to observe and direct the run-in shoot. Captain Ted Hall, 'A' Troop commander of 341st Battery, did the same, as Major Loveday's back-up. Once the run-in shoot had finished they both landed on foot, waited for their OP carriers, and joined the 7th Green Howards, the follow-up battalion.

Captain Stephen Perry, commander of 'B' Troop 341st Battery, sailed with a small body of the 7th Green Howards on an LSI, and then transferred with them into LCAs for their landing.

Major Kenneth Swain, *Captain Garton Ash* and Captain Geoffrey Street, all of 342nd Battery, sailed with the 6th Green Howards in an LSI and transferred with them into LCAs for the assault landing on King Green.

Major Eric Scammel, Captain Bob Turnbull and Captain 'Pam' Pamphilon, all of 462nd Battery, sailed with the 5th East Yorks, similarly on an LSI and transferring into LCAs, for their assault on King Red.

Two of the three battery captains, Captain Claude Hankins of 342nd Battery and *Captain Robert Kiln*, of 341st Battery, sailed in the LCHs with the naval commanders of King Green and King Red Beaches, as artillery observers and liaison officers. The third battery captain was in charge of our follow-up vehicles in England.

THE NAVAL COMMAND SHIPS (LCHs)

These played a crucial role in the control of each beach. The naval officers in charge of King Red and King Green in their LCHs were to lead the fleet to their beaches, then to stay about 2000 yards off each beach, ordering in the various waves of landing craft, waving them in, so to speak, if all was clear, or telling them to stand by if it was not. On board the LCH was a naval gunnery officer in charge of, or in contact with, the full range of the Navy's fire power, from battleships and cruisers down to small Landing Craft Guns (LCGs).

Also on board each LCH were three Army officers, the second in command of each assaulting battalion, the second in command of the squadron of our DD tanks, and the artillery observer described above.

We all had wireless sets and through these were in touch with our regiments, so that at all times the naval commander would know how the landing was progressing and whether special troops or equipment were urgently needed. The 4th/7th Dragoon Guards officer also had a vital function to perform, which was to decide, with the naval commander, when and how far out the navy would unload the swimming DD tanks into the sea.

The artillery officer's job was primarily to use naval fire on specific targets during the landing, and then, with the naval gunnery officer, to control the naval gun support, once the initial landing was ashore. Through him, OPs ashore could call and direct fire from LCGs, destroyers, cruisers and even battleships. One of the main tasks was to stop ships firing at the wrong targets, or at our own troops, because from the sea it was difficult to see our troops, or to know where they were.

On King Red the naval commander was Commander Haines in LCH 267, and his gunnery officer was Lt. Woods. The three army officers were Major Dixon, second in command of the 5th East Yorks, Captain Richards, second in command of 'C' Squadron of the 4th/7th Dragoon Guards, and myself, second in command of 341st Field Battery.

86TH FIELD REGIMENT'S LAYOUT ON D-DAY LANDING GOLD BEACH KING

KING RED	BEACH	KING GREEN

FOOs in motor launches Major G. Loveday and Captain E. Hall

With Assault Battalion 5th East Yorks	With Assault Battalion 6th Green Howards
Major E. Scammell	Major K. Swann
Capt. R. Turnbull	Capt. G. Street
Capt. H. Pamphilon	*Capt. G. Ash*

LCH	LCH
Naval Command	Naval Command
Capt. R. Kiln	Capt. C. Hankins

With reserve Battalion 7th Green Howards
Capt. S. Perry
(who would be joined by Major Loveday and Capt. Hall
on shore in support of 7th Green Howards)

on HMS *Kingsmill*
Lt.-Col. G. Fanshawe

LCTs with 6 Troops of 4 SP 25-pdr guns
in overall charge Major J. Morgan-Smith

'A' Troop	'E' Troop	'C' Troop
Lt. Cranston	Lt. Eisen	Lt. Mathers
'B' Troop	'F' Troop	'D' Troop
Lt. Beck	Lt. Jamieson	Lt. Geer
(341 Battery)	(452 Battery)	(342 Battery)

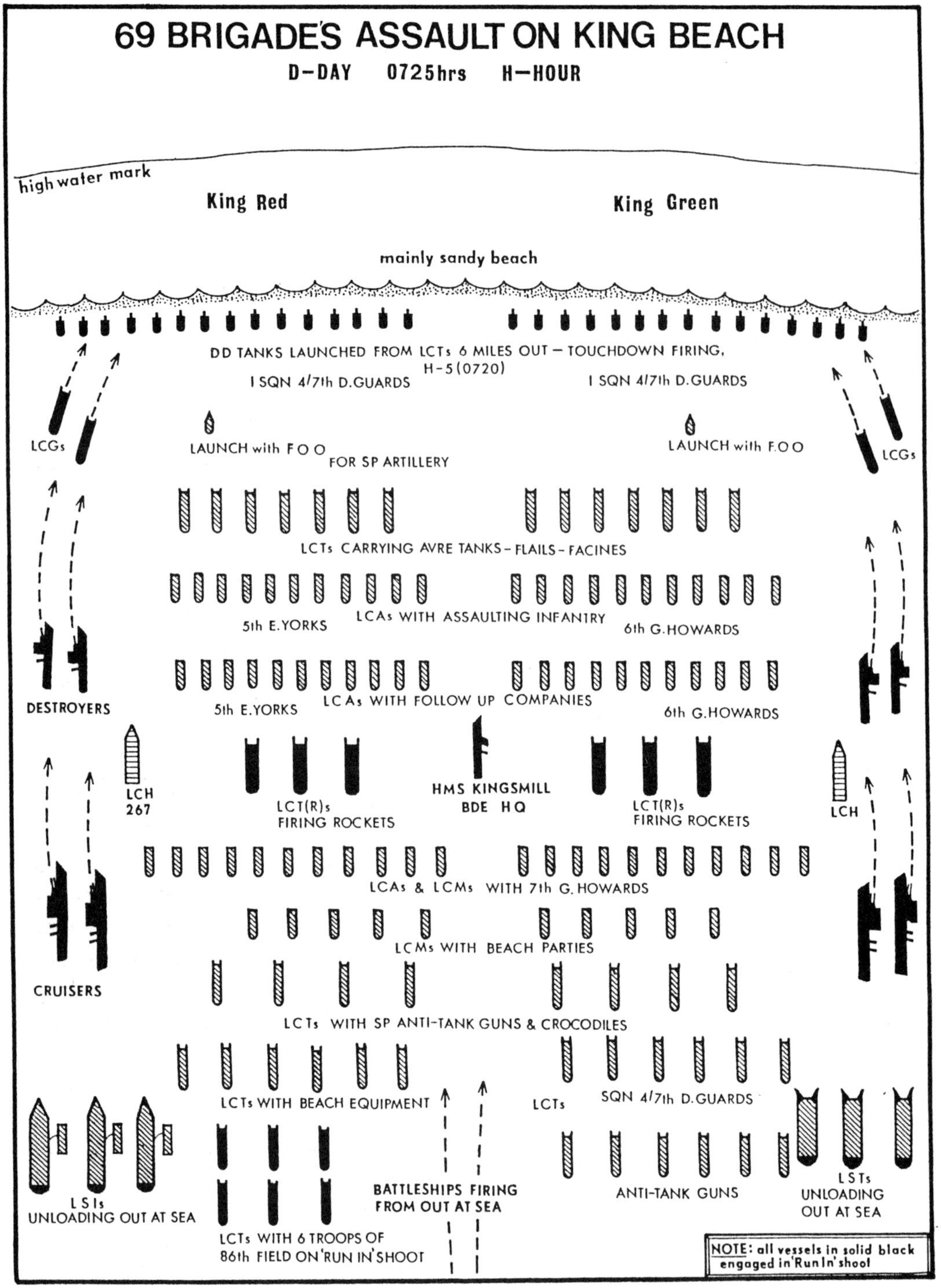

69 BRIGADE'S ASSAULT ON KING BEACH

D-DAY 0725hrs H-HOUR

high water mark

King Red

King Green

mainly sandy beach

DD TANKS LAUNCHED FROM LCTs 6 MILES OUT – TOUCHDOWN FIRING, H-5 (0720)

1 SQN 4/7th D.GUARDS

1 SQN 4/7th D.GUARDS

LCGs

LAUNCH with F O O FOR SP ARTILLERY

LAUNCH with F.O O

LCGs

LCTs CARRYING AVRE TANKS – FLAILS – FACINES

5th E.YORKS

LCAs WITH ASSAULTING INFANTRY

6th G.HOWARDS

DESTROYERS

5th E.YORKS

LCAs WITH FOLLOW UP COMPANIES

6th G.HOWARDS

LCH 267

LCT(R)s FIRING ROCKETS

HMS KINGSMILL BDE HQ

LCT(R)s FIRING ROCKETS

LCH

LCAs & LCMs WITH 7th G. HOWARDS

LCMs WITH BEACH PARTIES

CRUISERS

LCTs WITH SP ANTI-TANK GUNS & CROCODILES

LCTs WITH BEACH EQUIPMENT

LCTs

SQN 4/7th D.GUARDS

LSIs UNLOADING OUT AT SEA

BATTLESHIPS FIRING FROM OUT AT SEA

ANTI-TANK GUNS

LSTs UNLOADING OUT AT SEA

LCTs WITH 6 TROOPS OF 86th FIELD ON 'RUN IN' SHOOT

NOTE: all vessels in solid black engaged in 'Run In' shoot

4
D-Day

The seaborne assault of 69 Brigade of 50th Division. Their advance inland. Their movement to their final objective. Summary of the D-Day achievement.

The 86th Field Regiment (Hertfordshire Yeomanry) was the sole field regiment supporting 69 Brigade on D-Day. The D-Day story is told from original diaries supplemented by later recollections of various members of the 86th Field Regiment. The dispositions of the regiment and those telling the story are shown in the preceding assault formations plan. Figures 3, 4 and 5 cover the landing and D-Day advance.

Our storytellers were positioned for the landing as follows. Firstly myself, *Captain Robert Kiln*, on board the Naval Command Vessel (LCH) controlling the landing of the 5th East Yorks on the left or easterly beach, Gold King Red. Secondly *Captain Garton Ash*, Troop Commander of 'D' Troop, 342nd Battery, who landed with the 6th Green Howards in the initial assault on King Green. Thirdly *Captain Stephen Perry*, Troop Commander of 'B' Troop, 341st Battery, whose battery was with the follow-through battalion the 7th Green Howards. Fourthly, *Lt.-Colonel George Fanshawe*, Commanding Officer of the 86th who sailed with the Brigade Commander of 69 Brigade on HMS *Kingsmill*, a frigate, and then transferred to an LCM off the beach to land on King Green behind the assaulting infantry of the 6th Green Howards. Fifthly, *Lieutenant Sidney Beck*, GPO of 'B' Troop of 341st Battery who sailed with the four guns of his Troop in an LCT with five other LCTs carrying the remaining five troops of the regiment's guns. They fired their 'run-in shoot' together, but once on shore, 341st Battery supported specially the 7th Green Howards. Sixthly, *Sergeant Reg Munt*, Signal Sergeant of 342nd Battery, also in an LCT with the four guns of 'D' Troop. I start with my account of the landing.

PHASE I: 0300–0900 HOURS

Captain Robert Kiln

Our LCH 267 under Commander Haines is leading the force into the most leftward or easterly beach of the 50th Division's assault, Gold Beach King Red.

Those that slept are awake by 0400, and after a hasty breakfast move to action stations. Dixon, Richards and I establish ourselves just aft of the bridge and flag deck. We have a superb all round view and are in close contact with the Commander and the Naval Gunnery Officer. It is still not properly light and we are out of sight of the coast. Soon afterwards dawn begins to break upon a cloudy day with a strong wind – around Force 4 or 5 – and with a really choppy sea, again 4 or 5. It is a distinctly cool dawn for a summer's day.

As we sail in, leading our fleet on its eastern flank, we can see behind us and to our right the whole sea covered with boats and ships pitching up and down. The sky lightens over the coast away to our left and the dawn as it comes is cloudy but a wonderful red and yellow glow. We continue sailing on with our following fleet to our right and the heavier cruisers on our left hand, away from the landing craft.

At 5.30 the cruiser *Belfast* 'opens the party' by firing star shells at the Ver-sur-Mer battery, the RAF bombers come in at that time too, and we break wireless silence. The other cruisers join in as we continue shorewards. Nothing from the shore at all, all the way from Arromanches to Courseulles it is extraordinarily peaceful, with just a whomp of shells or bombs now and again.

At 6.30 the destroyers open fire from our left.

At 6.50 off go our own SP guns on their run-in shoot. By now our LCH is only 2000 yards off the shore, and taking up station to control the landing. I have a perfect view of our shells falling on their target of La Rivière, and over the wireless I can hear George Loveday and Ted Hall on the air observing and correcting the firing from their speedboats in front of us. Wireless perfect, weather bloody, no DD Tanks launched.

Landing craft are now sailing past us. The LCTs of the assaulting Royal Engineers with their funnies to clear obstacles, closely followed by the smaller LCAs carrying the assaulting infantry of the 5th East Yorkshires and with them the LCTs still carrying the unlaunched 'DD' swimming tanks of the 4th/7th Dragoon Guards.

Today Richards and Commander Haines had an agonising talk about this. Richards, to his great credit, maintained that the sea and wind were too great for an early launch, and if they launched well out the tanks would be overwhelmed and would sink. The Navy, on the other hand, had the problem that bringing the LCTs in close would increase the congestion and expose the LCTs to mines and German gunfire. Anyway, the DD tanks are not launched but are taken in close to the beach with their LCTs among the REs and the infantry LCAs.

Note. In my view this was absolutely right, as the tanks of 4th/7th Dragoon Guards, along with the rest of 8th Armoured Brigade, went ashore with few losses, and their presence on the beachhead during D-Day and the days that followed played a major role in the success of 50th Division's assault. If half or more had gone to the bottom before H hour, then the story might well have been different. Even the sight of the DD Shermans with their 'skirts' still on them was to be a wonderful reassurance in the Normandy lanes in the days to follow. The US assault divisions at Omaha to our right, with slightly less rough weather, launched theirs miles out and lost 90% of them to the bottom.

It is now just before 0700, and from our vantage point we have the most superb view of the whole beach. The weather is still chilly with an overcast sky with low cloud in places, but the visibility is excellent. The wind is still very strong and squally and the sea has white horses up wind and down wind. It is a typical English 'summer' day when, if you are on holiday, you know it's going to be too cold on the beach, and a cliff walk with windcheaters and sweaters looks the best occupation. At least it is not raining, though the odd shower looks likely.

To our left we can see the low rocky coast stretching away to the East, beyond which the Canadians will soon be landing at Courselles, about 3 miles from us. To our front is the small town of La Rivière with a solid stone sea wall 1000 yards or so long, with stone houses behind it and the rows of buildings rising 50 feet above the sea. On the right hand or west side of the village is a slipway, and we can make out the German pill boxes and gun emplacements facing westward and covering the beaches west of the town itself. The sea is already pounding against the sea wall as we watch, no landing there! To the west of the town and right ahead of us the beach starts, with low dunes behind, and this stretches away in an arc some 2½ to 3 miles and we can see the high ground at Le Hamel and Arromanches away to our right.

Behind the beach just west of La Rivière we can see the ground rising in an arc behind the beach all the way round to Le Hamel. Firstly, there is the Mont Fleury lighthouse and the Mont Fleury gun emplacements, then behind that the hump of ground near Ver-sur-Mer and then Meuvaines and on to Le Hamel. All exactly as expected!

The whole coastline is now under bombardment from the sea, and above the smoke and flashes of explosions we can see now and then our aircraft flying low inland. By this time their bombing of the beaches has ceased. The bombardment from the sea is quite superb. The cruisers and destroyers are bombarding the higher ground at Le Hamel all the way round this half circle of low hills to Mont Fleury, with each cruiser or destroyer having its own particular target to neutralize.

The fire of our SP guns is falling on the La Rivière causeway and its defences. At sea other craft are joining in. We have two Landing Craft Guns (LCGs) armed with two 4.7″ naval guns, and we are using these to bring accurate observed fire on the strong points at La Rivière and two pill boxes on the beach. We also have a Monitor with two enormous 15″ guns, whose target I cannot work out! It is all so impressive, and with the good visibility, each ship can clearly see its target and is hitting it most accurately.

The bombardment goes on for two hours in all. Most of the German strong points

PLATE 10. *LCT (R) with its rows and rows of rockets pointing forwards to shore.*

are knocked out, and those that survive the bombardment behind their concrete, are clearly being neutralized, and as our whole fleet moves closer and closer, the fire from the land is spasmodic.

Behind us and to our right as far as we can see, stretches line upon line of craft of all shapes and sizes, following in the wake of the LCTs of the Engineers and the LCAs of the 5th East Yorks and the 6th Green Howards to their right.

The fire from the land is simply overwhelmed. About twenty shells come close to us, and we are straddled by a burst of four shells but are not damaged. As our craft approach the beaches, German guns and spandaus come into action, but few of their big guns are firing out to sea.

Closely following the infantry landing craft are three LCT(R)s packed with 60lb rockets, and when they are just behind us they open fire [Plate 10]. The firing is not selective; all the 100 or so rockets on each craft go off together. First one craft, then the other two. They are aligned to land just behind the beach in several great clumps.

We are not prepared on the LCH bridge for this firing and jump about three feet as this enormous 'whoosh' goes off to our right. I follow the flight path of these rockets arching high in the air over the landing craft in front of them and crunching down on the German defences. I do not know the physical effect of these rockets, but the visual and sound effect is awe inspiring. Even if they never hit a German, the mental impact on the enemy must be stupendous, and a great cheer goes up from us all once the initial shock recedes. There is no doubt too that the morale boost to the poor seasick infantry in their LCAs is terrific. We are now coming up to H hour at 7.25.

At 0720, as the infantry are within 1000 yards of the beach, our gunfire shifts from the beach at La Rivière to its second target, which is the area of the Mont Fleury battery just behind the beach on the higher ground, which we suspect to hold guns, machine guns and enemy observation posts. This shift we can clearly see, and we can also hear on the wireless the comments of Ted Hall and George Loveday from their motor boats.

It is now within ten minutes of the touch down of the assaulting infantry in their LCAs, but they are going to be a few minutes late which, considering the state of the sea, is really superb. Commander Haines, after conferring with Humphrey Dixon, asks me to keep our guns firing for another ten minutes. So, for the first time that day, I use my wireless to contact George Loveday and arrange for the Regiment's firing to continue for the extra period, wondering as I do so whether they will have enough ammunition, and hoping that they will have enough time after they finish firing to prepare all the guns and vehicles for landing.

At 0730, as the first craft touch down on the beaches, a smoke screen drifts across the beach. It is not very dense and we can see through it. It looks as if some of the German 150mm guns are now firing from Mont Fleury, and others open fire from La Rivière. Two of the LCT(A)s carrying Royal Marine Centaur guns are hit, or are swamped and sink and we see that one of the Armoured Vehicles Royal Engineers has been hit and is 'brewed up' i.e. on fire on the beach. A sickening mushroom of smoke, and then a second one, goes up. It looks as if a heavy German gun is firing from La Rivière, but it is difficult to spot the gun. And away to our left over Courselles we can see a great mushroom of smoke on the Canadian front.

At 0740. By now we can see the LCAs on shore and infantry going up the beach following thc AVREs and the flail tanks; mixed with them too are the Shermans of the 4th/7th Dragoon Guards. What a superb sight as they swarm up the beach. We watch as they move across the beach, suffering heavy fire from La Rivière on their left. Woods and I bring the two LCTGs into action to hit La Rivière, but the battle ashore flows inland up the low hill. It is going well, but the beach is already piling up with craft. Some are blown up, some stuck, some broadside onto the surf. The German guns now seem to be silent, thank God.

At 0750, twenty minutes after the first touchdown, the 7th Green Howards land and move off the beach to Ver-sur-Mer.

At 0800, the 5th East Yorks take the Mont Fleury lighthouse position. Wonderful!

At 0805, I can see our first SPs ashore on the beach.

Captain Garton Ash

D-Day for me started soon after 0200 hrs. It had been a short night since we sailed past The Needles as the light failed, but some sleep had been possible. Breakfast was a silent affair on the *Lance*, which was taking the 6th Green Howards to launch the assault on Gold King Beach with the 5th East Yorks on our left. [The *Lance* also carried a small body of 7th Green Howards and Captain Stephen Perry.]

Bacon and eggs may not have seemed the ideal start to what looked like being a very rough passage but in true Navy fashion the tea was laced strongly with rum, the taste of which remained with me for much of the day.

Soon after 0300 hrs. the leading companies were called to the disembarkation stations alongside the LCAs slung in davits each side of the *Lance*. The bulkier items, such as our No. 18 wireless set, had already been stowed on the LCA but climbing over the side and down the net into the LCA some 30 feet above a very rough sea, and in the half-light, needed strict concentration. All went well and my signaller and I were successfully in 'D' Company headquarters LCA with Major Ronnie Lofthouse, and lowered into the rough sea and pulled away to take our station with the other LCAs carrying the company ashore.

There then began three hours of slow progress through heavy seas when at times all that could be seen over the side was the top of the waves, whilst as we rose onto a crest other LCAs could be seen disappearing into the trough of the next wave. Many were seasick (some had even succumbed on a training disembarkation whilst anchored in the Solent) but my mind was not really on how I felt.

As it grew lighter we could see more of the surrounding sea, which appeared to be full of ships and craft of all shapes and sizes, all heading towards the beach. It was a most impressive sight. Gradually we came near enough to see the shore line and the ridge behind which was our first objective. Although it was the first time we had been there it was all completely familiar since the features were already well known from the oblique photographs which had been provided by the RAF to show a complete panorama of the shore. Our particular landmark was a house with a distinctive circular drive ('Lavatory Pan House') situated by the road leading from the beach up the hill to Mont Fleury alongside which was the German gun position which 'D' Company had to neutralise.

The RAF bombing of targets ashore and the bombardment from the sea on the coast seemed to envelop the whole area ahead in smoke and flame. A few enemy shells landed near us but drew an impressive response from the Navy with four Hunt class destroyers steaming in line abreast and opening fire together just like a gunner troop.

The Royal Marines were clearly going to land us exactly where planned some 200 yards west of the road and very nearly on time, and shortly after H hour, 0725, we ran straight onto the beach, the ramp went down and along with all the other assaulting infantry we poured ashore.

A number '18' wireless is not the easiest of objects to carry when wrapped in its waterproof bag, especially when one had to handle it carefully to avoid it being thrown off net. My signaller stumbled in the water when carrying the set but between us we got half-way up the beach without trouble. Some mortar fire appeared to be landing in the soft sand at the top of the beach and as it was a slow business to carry the set between us we decided to take it out of the waterproof bag so that it could be carried properly. This only took a few moments but when we then continued up the remainder of the beach I found there was no sign of 'D' Company.

The plan had been to get off the track at the top of the beach, work to the left and up the road leading to Mont Fleury past the house with the circular drive. We followed to the hedge at the bottom of that track quickly, passing a flail tank knocked out when trying to get up the bank at the top of the sand.

My first task was to act as one of three methods of communicating to the Navy to stop firing on the Mont Fleury battery as 'D' Company were ready for the final assault. One method was infantry wireless, which was not thought to be too reliable; a second was the firing of a 'Very' light, with the risk that in the smoke of battle this would not be seen, and the third was for me to pass the order to Claude Hankins on the Naval LCH. He was tuned into our wireless net as station No. 72.

As we were going further up the road I saw the 'Very' light and immediately gave the order to stop firing on Mont Fleury. There was no acknowledgement from Claude and I tried again and again. The thought went through my mind that my very first task in action would prove to be a failure, but after several more frantic attempts the message was acknowledged by another station on the net. The message got through and the firing stopped. It had always been a worry that between the last tuning of all sets on the regimental net in our concentration camp at Romsey and the landings, with the subsequent manhandling down to the docks, on board ship, onto the LCA and across the beach, the number '18' set would be thrown off net so that we would not be in touch with the rest of the stations.

We set off as fast as we could from the garden of the house, across to the south-west behind Mont Fleury and past the battery of guns in their casements, which had by then been neutralised by 'D' Company. The advance continued in open order across the high ground between Ver-sur-Mer and Meuvaines, catching up with 'D' Company and shortly to be joined by the reserve companies 'B' and 'C' and with them my OP Ack. This completed our Phase I.

Captain Perry

June 6th D-Day. Woken up at 0300 and go on deck to see what is going on. I can just make out the ships in front, though there is not a light to be seen. We are still on the move and must be about 15 miles off the French coast now. Bombers are roaring overhead, probably the Sixth Airborne Division going in as well. We have a smashing breakfast – eggs and bacon, toast and marmalade, and a mug of tea primed with a very stiff tot of rum. There is a tense atmosphere at breakfast, nobody talking very much, and everybody's thoughts centred on the hell that will be let loose within the next few hours.

Back to the 'cabin' and pack haversacks. My blue silk pyjamas will have to be left behind for some merchant seaman. I cannot take them because I am already loaded down with kit, all of which hangs somewhere around my person; but still it was worth bringing them for five comfortable nights, the last for some time. Have we got everything: maps, glasses, protractor, water bottle full, rations, gas mask, gas capes, webbing? Right! down to the troop deck. I find Meyer and Barker down in the bowels of the ship, lit only by a few dimmed red lights. It is a seething mass of soldiery, all trying to get vast packages of equipment onto their shoulders. I hope to God they do not drop a bomb on us; the panic and shambles would be indescribably ghastly down here.

Everyone is kitted up at last, and now we have an hour or so to wait until the loud speaker calls us up to load. Thank Heaven, I have got two reliable chaps to start off with. Meyer looks as though he is off for a day in the country, exactly the same as ever, with an enormous smile lightening up his fat red face, cracking a rather doubtful joke. He will keep us all amused whatever happens; and there is Barker, he is quieter, but a good steady type, with bags of guts. An hour's wait down here in this fug is not much fun. I suppose those Germans are waiting on the beaches with their fingers on the trigger, and those two batteries of 155s with guns loaded, feeling safe as houses in their enormous concrete casemates. However, they have got a shock coming to them, 50 planes and 2 destroyers allotted to each of them; that ought to shake them up a bit, though there will still be plenty left for us.

'Load Serial 9', that is us. We get on board LCA 440 and lower away at 0540. The boat shudders as she hits the water and then, for the first time, we realise how rough the sea really is. We are tossed about all over the place; 2½ hours of this is going to be pretty hellish. We form up in three lines, with 6 LCAs in each, and set off to cover the 7 miles to the beaches.

Let us have a look around and see what is going on. Aircraft are continually roaring overhead, but there do not appear to be any dog fights going on, or any bombs dropping around, which is rather surprising.

Over to the West there are three or four fair sized 'brews', and odd thumps are coming from our part of the beach, which indicates that the RAF are on the job. As we steam towards the shore we pass close to one or two destroyers sending up great sheets of flame as their salvos speed towards the enemy batteries, which very soon *we* will attack. We are all feeling that another half hour of this buffeting will be too much for our stomachs, despite the anti seasick tablets which we hopefully devoured. Our worst fears are soon realised, and we all feel we would rather meet the German bullets than spend another hour in the LCA. However, we are not too ill to take an interest in the battle, which is now starting in real earnest. The RAF are dropping tons of bombs on dozens of concrete pillboxes and gun casemates. Cruisers, destroyers and LCGs are all opening up, and at a quarter to seven we hear George Loveday's familiar voice on the air starting clocks for the run-in shoot. The voices of all the GPOs come up, so they have all got so far safely. At 0650 the 24 guns of the Regiment roar, and for 36 minutes our shells pound the defences at La Rivière. By 0700 everything has opened up; we cannot see very much on the beaches except the smoke from shells and bombs. Suddenly a vast sheet of flame shoots up from an LCT(R); it is a batch of rockets going up to add more devastation to that caused by shells and bombs. At 0725 the AVREs touch down, and at 0730 the DD tanks and centaurs.

By 0800 the 6th Green Howards and 5th East Yorks are all ashore and cleaning up the beaches. Judging from reports on the wireless, the battle is going pretty well, although we can see tracer flying in both directions and quite a few shell bursts both on land and in the sea. A few shells send up mushrooms of water fairly close to our craft, though none are near enough to cause any casualties. We are running in now and the beaches seem pretty quiet. 'Prepare to beach', and off come our protective gas capes, and on go wireless sets. We can see the foreshore very clearly now, the poles with mines on the end every 10 or 15 yards, the barbed wire, 2 or 3 LCAs wrecked on the shore holed, and a few LCTs looking very unhappy on the beach, two with holes in the bows, another with a jammed door, and one broadside on. The Mont Fleury battery must still be in action because shells are falling, most of them in the sea, Brens and Spandaus are rattling just over the sea wall, an LCA

PLATE 11. *Infantry landing from LCI with LCTs in background, Gold Beach, 6 June. Note the roughness of the sea.*

goes up just to our right, probably on a mine, and there is our landmark 'Lavatory Pan House', but we are about a quarter of a mile to the right of where we should be. 'Out kedge', and when the bottom grinds on the coast of France 'down doors', and off we go, at 0805. Well, this is it chaps, and the water is waist high. We trudge along the beach until we come to the white tapes marking our exit through the minefields; thank heaven the Sappers have done their job. The 7th Green Howards are getting themselves sorted out, and there are the guns coming in to land. Our little party join B Company of the 7th Green Howards, and we set off inland, passing through the 6th Green Howards who seem to be getting on all right. A wave to Ken Swann as we push on.

Lt.-Colonel George Fanshawe

The Navy woke us at first light. The sight from the deck was the most incredible I have seen. About fifteen miles away was the French coast covered in mist and smoke;

to our right, left and behind us were ships of every sort and size, all stationary, nothing happening and only a very occasional shell from the Mainland.

Turning towards the land the panorama, not surprisingly, was exactly what we had expected. On the right, the high land of Arromanches with the enormous concrete emplacements of the Meuvaines Battery, then going left, a square wood where I had arranged to meet my BCs at 1630 hours that afternoon (I had said it holding my thumbs). Going on left and down to the beach was a *Sign Post* which we had seen on the aerial photos but could not imagine what it was. Further left was the village of La Rivière with its sea wall which was our left boundary and behind that was the lighthouse. To our surprise there was no fire coming from the Meuvaines Battery and none ever did.

Then about an hour before H-Hour the whole fleet came alive: little boats, LCAs and LCMs were spewed out of bigger ones and busily went to other boats. Our frigate got its LCM which came alongside, and the sailors told us it was time to go, in tones that made it clear that they thought they were as good as killing us. Little did they know that the soldiers could not have cared less as long as they got off the sea onto land, any land.

Our LCM chugged off towards the beach and eventually got stuck on a small sandbank some 200–300 yards off the sandy beach. The flap was let down and the Brigade Commander walked off into about 2 feet of water followed by me his Gunner Commander. The sandbank finished, and we found ourselves in 5 feet of water – we waded ashore.

On the way in we passed several iron girders stuck in the sand with uncapped shells tied to them – these were the sea obstacles. We walked out of the water almost exactly opposite the 'Sign Post' which said 'Bus Stop'.

At this moment – about half an hour after H-hour, or 0800 hours – our bit of beach was more or less empty. The leading Companies had landed but the Beach Group had not. I had with me one signaller and an '18' wireless set. The Regiment had done its Run-In Shoot, but was not yet due to land. My signaller tried the '18' Set but having been immersed in 5 feet of water it would not work. The Brigade Commander, John Knox, an Ulsterman, had gone to find his leading Companies.

By the 'Bus Stop' sign was a track leading off the beach through the marshes and into the cornfields beyond, and everyone who had landed was going along it: Infantry, the Specialised Tanks and any other vehicles that had landed or were landing. This track was fortunately unmined, although a flail tank was flailing along just to make sure.

So my signaller and I joined the trail, and I found myself walking through the cornfields with the leading Infantry, the 6th Green Howards. They were walking through the corn in extended order with their rifles more or less at the Port. The only noise was the ping of German sniper rifles hidden in trees, every now and then a soldier fell down hit, the rest just walked on. A most impressive performance. As we were walking past a cottage, an old woman came out of the cellar and offered me two eggs. This was my baptism of fire.

At about 0900 hours my signaller and I returned to the beach. The sight now was very different. The tide had risen and the beach was only half the size, and absolutely

PLATE 12. *LCTs unloading at Gold Beach on D-Day. Note DD tank on left with its waterproof skirts up. In foreground beach party is trying to salvage a sunken vehicle.*

packed with vehicles with more and more LCTs arriving. The Beach Group was there now and in general control, getting vehicles off the beach as fast as they could past the 'Bus Stop' and along the track to the cornfields – it was, in fact, ordered chaos. The Beach Master called in LCTs as space permitted.

The German gun which had been infilading the beach from its emplacement was now silent. The story of its silencing by a Sergeant in the 4th/7th Dragoon Guards is in many of the histories of the landing. [In other accounts this was silenced by an AVRE.]

I watched the LCTs with my Regiment's guns on board unloading, the soldiers looked in surprisingly good nick. An LCT is an extremely unsteady craft in any sort of sea. It has no cabins as such, and the soldiers lying amongst the vehicles suffered very badly during the crossing. The Gunner Regiments recovered during the Run-In Shoot when they had excitement and a lot to do.

I found my Second in Command, John Morgan-Smith, who came ashore ahead of the Regiment's LCTs, and whose business it was to take charge of the guns and get them into action. In fact one LCT had landed its guns and was in action on the beach and firing. John was clearly and very efficiently in charge, and I was only in the way, so I waited until my tank, with two 19 Sets inside, landed and returned to Brigade HQ.

Lieutenant Beck

Reveille for us is at 0430 hours. It is still dark and cold as the men stow blankets, snatch a hasty breakfast, prepare ammo and check the guns. Wireless silence, which has been maintained for more than 10 days, is broken at 0530 as sets are switched on and communications checked. Just ahead of our LCT are the small LCAs of the 7th Green Howards, and on either side are long lines of DUKWs or amphibious lorries. From my position on the bridge I see each gun crew fall silent as they report 'ready for action' and the ship goes strangely quiet except for the engines. At 0645 I pass on the order to fire, and the run-in shoot begins while we are still 7 miles from the coast. H-hour, the time for the first troops to set foot on Gold Beach, is 0725. Our run-in shoot is extended by nearly ten minutes, but as soon as it finishes preparations begin for landing. I shake hands with the skipper, thank him for my hammock and wish him a safe return to England, while he, in turn, wishes us luck and promises us a safe and smooth landing in shallow water! I make my way to my Command Post tank in the bow of the craft behind the REs' roly-poly, and prepare to be the first vehicle ashore from our craft.

As we steam up and down, waiting to land, from my vantage point in the tank turret I can see over the top of the ramp to the beach, where the first half of our regiment has already landed. At 0755 'A' Troop go straight into action on the beach with water lapping round their tracks, and fire in support of the 7th Green Howards assaulting up the hill to the Ver-sur-Mer battery. On the beach all seems confusion, with men and vehicles moving in all directions. Our skipper is finding it difficult to locate a clear spot on the beach. The strong wind and tide have made the first ships ground almost sideways to the coast, while ships which should have pulled away after unloading have been damaged or stuck, and the beach is fast becoming jammed.

As we steam nearer the beach, I see in front and to our right a small craft with about six persons aboard breasting a wave, when it suddenly disappears from sight as a column of water shoots into the air – a mine or direct hit, I do not know. Our craft comes in alongside an LCT which has already beached. The first vehicle off its ramp has stuck in the water, and none of the other vehicles can get off, nor can the ramp be closed. But it shelters our craft for a perfect beaching.

At 8.45 we go into land. As the ramp goes down in shallow water the RE detachment unrolls the roly-poly, a long hessian carpet strengthened with iron bars to form a firm trackway, over the wet sand, now a narrow strip between the high water mark and the tide, and crammed with boats and men in seeming confusion. Rolling clouds of smoke from burning buildings and grass form a fitting background. As my tank runs down the ramp and begins to cross the beach, an Officer waves me towards a single file of vehicles making for an exit from the beach marked as clear of mines. The guns follow me off, dragging behind them flat 'porpoises' full of ammunition. My first sight of the enemy is a batch of German prisoners standing dazed and bewildered amid all the activity. One of them lifts a wounded Tommy out of the path of the vehicles. The track from the beach leads on to a road, where my tank and the column following me are photographed by the Army Film Unit! Such is fame!

Captain Hall is there on the beach to welcome and guide us, and he sees all the guns safely off the beach, through the minefield and on to a narrow road. This leads uphill past the Mont Fleury Coastal Battery, which has suffered a heavy bombardment and looks really devastated, and I receive orders to site my guns alongside the casements. My Troop Command Post is established in a bomb crater. Three Centaur tanks manned by Royal Marines also occupy the area, giving me a 7-gun troop for the first (and last) time in the campaign. When I report the Troop ready for action, 'A' Troop, who have been in action on the beach, move up to occupy a position alongside, forming our first Battery position. [Later we were to learn that the German gunners who had survived the bombardment were still underground in their casement shelters, and only surrendered a few days after D-Day.]

Sergeant Reg Munt

We had completed our run-in shoot, and were steaming off the beach preparing to land, when our LCT was hit by either a mine or a shell from a German gun which was still firing from over to our right towards Arromanches. The bows of the ship were hit, and the landing ramp blown off, leaving us no bows and no ramp! The skipper somehow made towards the beach and the first tanks literally plunged headlong into several feet of water. D Troop guns and the Shermans all made it safely. I was in the last vehicle to leave the LCT, which was our signals half track vehicle. By this time the captain of the LCT was having a hell of a job holding his craft on the beach and had drifted out. Our driver, Driver Stark, drove hard off the LCT, but into several feet of rough sea about twenty yards from the beach. I was in the back of the vehicle operating the wireless during the landing. Wearing headphones, I did not hear Lt. Dovey, our GPO, or Stark shouting at me to get off.

Our signals half track (M1) was being tossed about, with water pouring into the back around me. I tied the waterproof cover around the wireless set, pushed the headphones through the roof and climbed out myself. Everyone was shouting at me to jump but I was too scared, and stayed put and prayed. All of a sudden the half track, with me on top, was pushed ashore by a bulldozer. The Beach Master shouted 'Get that bloody vehicle out of the way'. Driver Stark jumped in, pulled the starter and off she went first time – he did his waterproofing well.

Completion of Phase I

Readers will recall that once the beach had been cleared, the plan was that the two assault battalions, the 5th East Yorks on the left and 6th Green Howards on the right, with 4/7th Dragoon Guards in support, would move swiftly inland to capture the high ground stretching behind the beach from La Rivière on the sea to Mont Fleury, Ver-sur-Mer and Meuvaines. This would complete Phase I of our plan.

Mont Fleury lighthouse, as reported above, was taken by 5th East Yorks by 0800 hours, the Mont Fleury battery by 6th Green Howards soon after, and Ver-sur-Mer by the 7th Green Howards moving through the 6th Green Howards before 0900 hours.

By 0900 hours, therefore, Phase I, the capture of this high ground overlooking the beach, was complete. La Rivière had been neutralized but not yet captured. The 86th Field Regiment were coming into action at Mont Fleury, and the 7th Green Howards were moving inland through Ver-sur-Mer. The beach exits were clear, and the Beach Party firmly in charge.

To accomplish all this in about ninety minutes was an incredible achievement by 69 Brigade, and it was not bettered anywhere else on D-Day.

PHASE II: 0900–1400 HOURS

Once Phase I was completed the plan was for the 7th Green Howards to move through Ver-sur-Mer and to seize the vital river bridge at Creully on the Seulles, four miles or so inland, as shown on Figure 5. Stephen Perry describes this action:

We pass through Ver-sur-Mer, I wave at Ken Swann with the 6th Green Howards looking very cheerful, and we push towards Crepon. There is a lot of small arms fire flying about, heaven knows where it is coming from. There is a platoon of enemy infantry running across the field; we will have a go at them. We 'brass them up', with a few rounds of gunfire, then crawl along the ditches to the Company Commander to see what is going on. Everything seems to be going fine, but we have got to push on and capture the bridge at Creully. In the outskirts of Crepon, spasmodic small arms fire and gunfire knocks out three or four of the infantry, but a few rounds of gunfire on the enemy seems to quieten them down. At 1030 we bypass Crepon on its east side, and form up the flying column to capture the bridge, 'C' Company, 7th Green Howards and A Squadron 4/7th Dragoon Guards. My carrier has not turned up, but another carrier 'B' Troop Leader eventually rolls up to our relief, and off we go for the bridge. Small arms fire crackles just ahead; nothing to worry about, just a couple of Jerry cars; they are out of action now and the crew are prisoners; that was easy. There is a patrol going down to the bridge now, and I will go along with them. We can see the bridge now, and a lot of Jerries appear to be having a crack at us from the houses over the river; well here goes; 'Troop Target', and a perfect shoot comes down slap on top of them; 'Just the job' says the Company Commander.

We are over the bridge, our objective. Creully is a hotbed of snipers, but we get through all right, and get into position in the southern end of the village. Blimey!

there are a couple of 88s sitting on top of the next crest, we range on to them after a rather shaky start and 'brass them up' with a couple of rounds of gunfire before they eventually disappear over the horizon.

At 1500 the rest of the battalion come up, and we have time for a bite of chocolate and biscuits, and a quick 'drum-up' of tea goes down very well. We push on again, and attack a network of slit-trenches, where a company of enemy are proving rather tiresome; however we get through and 30 prisoners eventually emerge from them.

This somewhat laconic account summarizes a remarkable little action. While the flying column captured Creully and the river crossing, the 6th Green Howards with Captain Garton Ash in support had a tough time clearing Crépon of Germans:

The advance of the 6th Green Howards continued astride the road from Ver-sur-Mer towards Crepon, but was held up short of the village. 'B' and 'C' Companies were told to bypass the village while 'D' Company cleared the way through. My Bren carrier had by then joined me, having landed from the troop's LCT, with the Naval Liaison Officer who was to accompany us during D-Day to assist in directing supporting fire from the Navy. I told them to go with 'D' Company through Crepon whilst I continued on foot with the other Companies bypassing the village on its west side and going ahead across the open ground past Bazenville towards the road running from Bayeux past Creully. The Green Howards paused on this line which was on the higher ground before it dropped down to the river Seulles. By that time the carrier had joined us again, my signaller, Bombardier Croxford, proudly displaying his tea mug holed by a sniper's bullet. The Green Howards' Phase II had been successfully completed and we paused on the line of the road.

The remainder of the early afternoon passed quietly except for the appearance of German guns on the far horizon to the south-west, and which I saw going into action off the road over the hill on the skyline. I ordered my first troop target and corrected the fire until it was too hot for the German gunners and they retreated out of sight.

I now resume my own account from the LCH controlling the landing of the 5th East Yorks on Gold King Red.

Back at sea, we were still steaming up and down. And while the battle streamed inland during the rest of that morning, stiff resistance was being met by the East Yorks in La Rivière. They had already suffered heavy casualties in house to house fighting along and behind the sea wall.

The Navy bombard 'Desk', the code name for the centre of La Rivière, with destroyers to help the East Yorks, and Lt. Woods and I use the two LCGs to bombard the pill boxes along the sea wall.

I am through on the wireless to Eric Scammell, the Battery Commander of 462 Battery, in support of the East Yorks. One of the problems from the sea is to locate exactly where the front line of our own troops is. We solve this problem using yellow recognition signals.

Note. Before D-Day it was realized that our own aircraft and at times our own artillery might strafe our troops unless there was some easy means of recognition. Thus all ground troops were issued with yellow smoke canisters and yellow silk squares, which could be displayed horizontally in front using both arms so that a yellow square showed skywards, or vertically for ground recognition. They worked well on land but often there was a problem from the air in that either the pilots had not been told about them or just did not see them.

I tell Eric to get his forward troops to hang out their yellow squares over the sea wall and to release yellow smoke. We can now see where they are, which is the first step, and it is easier then to locate the enemy strong points.

Woods and I relay Eric's targets to the LCGs who then engage the targets. We help a bit and soon after midday the East Yorks clear La Rivière of German troops, but not of German mines and booby traps, at a cost, we learn, of around 100 casualties to them.

The beach itself is now an appalling mass of grounded craft. Three or four more LCAs or LCMs have gone up on mines, and the weather is still bad. Commander Haines is clearly worried, and he has to divert a troop, or is it a flotilla, of DUKWs (amphibious lorries) to King Green because of mines and the congestion.

We are now out of the battle, as it has moved inland, and we relax, have some food and a drink, and listen to the one o'clock news all about ourselves!

PHASE III: 1500 HOURS ONWARDS

By 1500 hours the 6th and 7th Green Howards had moved up in force to the Phase II position at Creully and along the river Seulles. They still had over four miles to advance, over enemy occupied country, to reach their final D-Day objectives across the Bayeux–Caen road at St Leger. The country between them and the beaches still contained Germans in villages, and strong points which had been bypassed in their advance. No contact yet had been made with the Canadians on our left, which was therefore exposed. The delays on the beaches meant that reinforcements and follow-up tanks of the 8th Armoured Brigade were not yet ashore.

By this time too everyone was getting tired. However, the advance continued, with Stephen Perry now joined by Major Loveday and Captain Greig. They had shelled two 88mm guns just to the south of Creully, as reported above, an ominous sign that soon they would meet greater resistance. The advance continued until 1730 hours when, as Stephen Perry records, they came under machine-gun fire with a lot of bullets flying around, and then three of the 4th/7th tanks were hit and 'brewed up' in quick succession by a wood 400 yards in front of them at Fresnay-le-Crotteur.

PLATE 13. *Gold Beach King, 7 June. Cromwell tanks of the 7th Armoured Division coming ashore up main exit past Lavatory Pan House which lies off picture to left. Note LCTs massed on beach centre right with LSIs and LSTs at sea.*

Captain Perry and Major Loveday engaged this target with the eight guns of the battery firing six rounds of gunfire, the enemy retreated. At around 1800 hours they came under murderous fire, with salvo after salvo of heavy shells falling on them. They soon realized that these were naval shells. George Loveday contacted me on the LCH by wireless and, as I will record, we stopped the firing, but not before they had suffered several casualties.

Pushing on again, they were then held up by enemy infantry, who were swiftly overrun by the 4th/7th Tanks. Over fifty German prisoners were taken. The left-hand column of the advance, the 7th Green Howards, moved towards the small village of Coulombs, but just to the south of Coulombs they came under very heavy fire from Nebelwerfers, spandaus and 88mm guns. These were again effectively engaged with our 25-pounders, but by now it was dusk and the 7th Green Howards moved to the high ground to the west of Coulombs village and dug in for the night. They finished around 0200 hours after a hot meal at midnight.

The 6th Green Howards on the right continued their advance in the evening, moving south from Villers-le-Sec, passing a German armoured car with engine and wireless still operating but no crew, as they had been holding up the advance from a ditch nearby with a spandau, but had been effectively dealt with by one of the supporting tanks. They crossed the river Seulles just north of St Gabriel and with our guns shooting a prearranged plan on the villages of Brecy, Rucqueville and Martragny, advanced in open order through the fields on the north-west of all those villages. As the light failed, burning buildings lit their way, but by then everyone was very tired and eventually the advance halted on the line of a long hedge in open ground just west of Martragny about a thousand yards short of their final objective, the main Bayeux–Caen road.

The OPs settled down for two or three hours sleep with the tanks and infantry until stand-to at 0500 hours on 7 June. At least most of them did. The three Battery Commanders were called to a conference at Regimental Headquarters at St Gabriel. Major George Loveday proceeded back on his own on a motorcycle at around midnight. He arrived, but on his return journey he ran into four German soldiers and was shot through the lung and left for dead. He was not found until dawn when one of our signal sergeants heard him, still alive, and signalling by sounding his horn. He was a lucky man. As Stephen Perry remarked: 'The Regiment's first officer casualty, and a lesson learned: do not swan around on your own in the middle of the night on a motor bike when the battle is fluid.' George was attended to by the 7th Green Howards' Medical Officer, and taken back to England on a stretcher early on 7 June.

After the initial landing 'A', 'C' and 'E' Troops were in action on the beach. 'B', 'D' and 'F' Troops moved inland to Mont Fleury, to be joined by the others later. At noon they moved forward. Lieutenant Beck records:

> Without having fired a shot from the Mont Fleury position we are ordered forward, and on our way I see the bodies of some dead Germans lying in the fields beside the road. Soon after we pass three civilians who wave gaily at us. By 1230 our guns are deployed in an area just north of Ver-sur-Mer and we are called upon to fire in support of the flying column of the Green Howards in their attack on Creully. The Battery remains at this position for the remainder of the day, engaging a number of targets as the infantry advances until dusk. During the afternoon some shells land in the Battery area; fortunately no damage is done. Some British tanks engage snipers in the woods around us. During the day we have only seen our own aircraft but at night we hear the rattle of AA guns from the beaches come under attack from enemy aircraft, I am relieved to be well inland.

In the meantime I was still lying off the beach, and for long periods of the afternoon, once La Rivière had been cleared, there was little I could do. The battle had passed inland, and I listened in to its progress over the wireless with mounting excitement. I was ready to fire a cruiser or battleship if required, but that day none was wanted. On the bridge of the LCH, which took up station about 1500 yards offshore on the left or eastern side of the beach, the whole panorama of the landing could be seen. As the side turned, the mess of wreckage on the beach grew. I could see twenty or more landing craft blown up or piled sideways on the beach. The upper part of the beach was littered with wrecked tanks and vehicles. The naval engineers were busy blowing up beach obstacles, and explosions went on continually. The procession of craft to and fro on the beach continued through and round the chaos.

The weather got no better; in fact by the afternoon it was worse. Landing Ship Tanks (LSTs) were unloading tanks from their bows out at sea on to 'rhinos', great self-propelled rafts, which then made their way to the beaches with two small engines, but many rhinos had broken loose and the seas made it impossible to hold them close to the ships' ramps. We envied the US beaches to the west, particularly Utah, which was protected from the westerly weather by the Cherbourg peninsula, and we wondered how the two landings to our east were coping. There was no doubt that Commander Haines and the Navy were as worried as hell, but on and on it went, with always more and more craft to take the place of those wrecked by mines and weather.

We could see the beach quite clearly, and through glasses the steady procession off it up through Ver-sur-Mer. The beach groups of 54 Division, including the Hertfordshire Regiment, looked as if they were coping well. Delays became inevitable, and all day the Commander had to keep craft out at sea until he could see an opening for them on the beaches. By 1800 hours we were two to three hours behind schedule, according to the Navy. In my view, considering the weather, this was a remarkable achievement by the Navy. What it would have been like if we had had major air raids, I tremble to think. As it was, we only had one small incursion by daylight, and that plane did little damage.

We continued to man our wireless set in case naval fire was wanted. When the call came, it was unexpected. At around 1800 hours George Loveday came through on the wireless calling me direct and obviously with great urgency, reporting that he and our own infantry and tanks are being heavily shelled by naval fire. Woods and I hastily scanned the sea behind us to see who was firing, and lo and behold, only one ship, a cruiser, was firing. Woods called them at once and they ceased firing. My recollection was that it was the cruiser *Belfast*, but it was, I now think, the *Orion*.

I reported to George Loveday, whose relief was very audible, as also were

PLATE 14. *Gold Beach infantry landing with 25-pounder SP gun of 90th Field on left (broken down). LCI wrecked in foreground.*

his caustic comments. Woods then contacted the cruiser to find out who ordered them to fire. After an acrimonious exchange, all we can elucidate is that 'the target is a map reference', but I am sure in my own mind that a naval aircraft was responsible for engaging our own troops. At least our wireless network and my presence on board saved us heavy casualties. As a result of this, Commander Haines decided that I should remain on board for the night in case of further problems, and also to be available in case the Germans mounted a counter-attack during the night or early next morning.

By nightfall things became a little more sorted, with our riding lights shining across the water guiding more craft shorewards.

We were preparing to go to bed, and just opening tins of self-heating soup in the Operations Room shortly after midnight, when a stick of bombs straddled the ship. One hit the ship's bows and holed her above water, causing casualties. Two men were killed, including the Naval Medical Orderly, and Commander Haines put me in charge of the casualties, of which three were serious and four less so. We were of course still on station about 2000 yards off the beach, and displaying red and green lights to guide the shipping ashore. One of the German bombers out that night had a perfect target, and we were extremely lucky to escape as lightly as we did. My record of it at the time was:

I brew up a tin of self heating soup in the ops room at midnight or maybe one o'clock. Suddenly whoomp, whoom, whoom, whoom, then CRASH. A bomb hits forrard. Out comes the Commander in his pyjamas, up I go. Someone shouting and groaning above me. A sailor in a large pool of blood making a hell of a noise. I have a look at him, bleeding a bit. Have to rip off his trousers and see his tummy gashed, patch him up and give him morphia. Lash him to a stretcher. He looks bad but wrap him well up and hot tea comes up. Refuse him that. I think that's right with a tummy wound. Bleeding stops but he has a good 3″ hole in him.

My first introduction to war! L/Bdr Child has shrapnel in hand and leg, though not bad. Have a devil of a job evacuating these chaps onto an LCA in the pitch dark and a heaving sea. Well now I know that I shan't mind the sight of blood – much!

Before all this happened, during the afternoon and evening of D-Day reports came in of the progress of the invasion.

The 6th Airborne Division had secured the left flank. The 3rd British Division's landing was successful, they were moving on to Caen and had linked up with the Airborne Division, when they were counter-attacked by German tanks, suffered heavy casualties, and halted north of Caen. There were reports that the German tanks had reached the sea at Lion-sur-Mer beyond Courselles and the Canadians.

We heard that the 3rd Canadian Division's landing had gone well, then later that they had moved inland and captured Carpiquet airfield just west of Caen. Later still it was reported that they had retreated.

The news of the American landing at Omaha on our west flank was ominous. Firstly we heard that the landing was failing; that they had launched their DD tanks six miles out and lost nearly all of them; that their bombardment had only lasted half an hour and fell behind the defences; that having no 'funnies', such as flails, fascines or bombards, their infantry were pinned on the beach and unable to clear any exits. There was even talk during the afternoon of D-Day that their reinforcements would come ashore on our beach, but by the evening they were ashore – just; the beach more or less operating, and its exits cleared.

The Utah landings had gone well, there were wild reports of their airborne troops being dropped all over the place, but as night fell the seaborne divisions had met the airborne troops and linked up behind Utah.

A sad report came through about a flying column of Royal Engineers mounted on half-track vehicles, which had been given a special role of advancing with explosives to blow up bridges well inland to prevent German counter-attacks. They had made good progress to a crossroads five miles south-south-east of Bayeux, known as Jerusalem Crossroads. This was an amazing advance some eleven miles inland, but then disaster struck. They had halted, when they were attacked by Allied fighter bombers, in spite of all their yellow squares and yellow smoke recognition signals, and their explosives went up, wiping out the entire force.

On the rest of 50th Division's front, 231 Brigade's assault had been successful; they had had a tough struggle at Le Hamel, had captured Arromanches that afternoon, and had moved on west and south. Their story at Le Hamel was outstanding and as successful as ours. 56 and 151 Brigades had been delayed on the beaches by a combination of weather, mines and congestion, but had moved rapidly inland against light opposition, to enter the outskirts of Bayeux on the evening of D-Day. 47 Royal Marine Commando had covered their ten miles to Port-en-Bessin, which turned out to be more like fifteen miles on the route they had had to take. They had occupied high ground outside the town on D-Day evening. (They took the port and linked with US patrols on the next day. It was an outstanding feat.)

69 Brigade, with the 86th, whose final D-Day objective was the high ground across the Bayeux–Caen Road near the German radar station at St Leger, had stopped within sight of it at Coulombs and Martragny, as we have noted. They were 12,500 yards inland as the crow (or shell) flies, just about seven miles, and had travelled and fought more like ten or more miles across the Normandy countryside to get there.

D-DAY IN RETROSPECT

The Navy

Any review of D-Day must start with a huge compliment to the Navy, who got us there on time and plumb in the right place in poor weather; whose ships hit their targets accurately and who continued to land men, tanks and equipment in atrocious conditions, and all done with great calm and humour.

Air Control

The complete mastery of the air by the RAF and USAF was a major factor on D-Day, not only in the bombardment but in bombing and strafing all German troop movements made to reinforce their defences. In addition the cutting of German communications reached a crescendo; bridges, railways and roads were continually attacked. The Luftwaffe were neutralized so that there were no real air attacks on the landings. Not only that but German aerial reconnaisance failed to notice the build-up in the Solent, the crossing itself and the arrival in France. It seems in retrospect quite incredible.

The Weather

The weather during the whole of May and right up to 3 June had been warm and sunny with calm seas. On 3 and 4 June the weather broke, bringing cooler stormy weather, and our landings on the morning of 6 June were made in a brief lull on that day. There is no doubt that an enormous gamble was taken by General Eisenhower. We have recorded the havoc caused by the weather on Gold Beach, but it also caused delays to the 3rd Division's advance on Caen and to the Canadians, and was a major factor at Omaha. Utah was luckier as it was sheltered by the Cherbourg peninsula itself. However, the weather gave us the enormous initial advantage of surprise.

There is no doubt that the Germans had daily been awaiting our invasion all during the fine May weather. When the weather broke, they relaxed. Rommel himself took the chance and went on leave to Germany on the 5th for his wife's birthday. Several senior officers were also on leave, and some went off to attend a conference at Rennes. No doubt, too, there was a general relaxing of tension by the Germans. We therefore achieved a surprise which we would not have done had we attempted to land, say, a fortnight earlier. Our disadvantage was the havoc the weather inflicted on our ships, landing craft, and above all, the landing itself from the morning of D-Day onwards.

Omaha lost nearly all its DD tanks. The 3rd British Division's follow-through brigades were not ashore early enough to help with the drive on Caen. Had 6 June been a calm, sunny day, and if (it's a big if) the German reaction and resistance had been the same, then it is quite likely that Caen, or most of it, would have fallen on D-Day.

D-Day Objectives and Achievements

The Allied objectives have been described: generally they meant an advance of around ten miles inland, because this line could be covered by naval gunfire. One purpose of setting objectives is to give troops and their commanders something to aim at, but more importantly, it is to make sure that troops do not go too far. If things go well in one sector it is important that those troops do not advance out of phase with the rest of the operation. In addition, the Allied airforces would know the maximum advance line of their own troops.

I doubt very much whether Montgomery, or any Allied commander, expected anything like 100% achievement of this objective. As Figure 3 shows, only 50th Division nearly achieved their objectives, with the Canadians getting over half way to theirs. The Utah forces and the British 3rd Division and 6th Airborne achieved about 50% and the Omaha forces 10%.

To land on a beach and then walk or drive ten miles as the crow flies across country does not sound an impossible task, particularly as on 6 June there were fifteen hours or more of daylight. Ten miles as the crow flies is more like fifteen miles, so an average speed of one mile per hour is required. It does not sound difficult until you consider the factors prevailing on D-Day. Troops were carrying heavy equipment; the weather caused delays on landing; troops had had a long sleepless sea crossing, and then there was the enemy! Even if enemy opposition had been light and spasmodic and had not halted the advance, it would have caused delays and casualties. Two or three spandaus behind Norman stone walls could hold up an infantry advance by an hour or so. So can an 88mm gun which knocked out two leading tanks of a squadron.

Even given that things went reasonably well, the maximum realistic penetration possible on D-Day must have been around six or seven miles: ten or eleven miles was not possible except in exceptional circumstances, such as calm weather, no enemy resistance on the beach or inland, and no other hold-ups. The capture of Bayeux was, therefore, possible and almost achieved. The capture of Caen on D-Day could never have been more than an outside chance with odds of about ten to one against.

Therefore, to talk about 'the failure of the British to capture Caen on D-Day' is stupid. The real and only failure on D-Day was the American operation at Omaha, and the effect of this was, in my view, to be the crucial problem of the first few days ashore. The probability of capturing Caen on D-Day could only have been improved by the landing of airborne forces on the outskirts of the city to the west or south. If, for example, a division or brigade of paratroops and gliders could have taken Carpiquet airfield and a crossing of the Orne south of Caen, then the Canadians' tanks and armoured cars who reached Capriquet and then withdrew would have linked up, and could have moved tanks and guns to their support.

Presumably, Montgomery would have done this if he had had the aircraft available, which he did not. Obviously he gave priority to the 6th Airborne's task of securing the Orne bridges north of Caen and eliminating the Merville battery: without this his left flank might have been grievously exposed. 6th Airborne were only able to land two brigades initially due to shortage of aircraft. Priority was given to the two US airborne landings behind Utah; both of these had vital jobs to do, one to secure the inland end of the beach exits from Utah across the marshes and the second to move on Carentan, the vital road and bridge link between the two US landings.

In the event, the 6th Airborne landings and the 3rd British Division's advance from Sword beach were met by the only armoured German counter-attack on D-Day. This attack was made by the 21st Panzer Division, who were moving up the Falaise–Caen road by 0800 hours on D-Day. By 1630 the attack was launched, but although a few tanks reached the sea, the

PLATE 15. *A Sherman Firefly landing direct from LST, Gold Beach, 7 June. Note the long barrel of the 17-pounder gun.*

German attack was a failure and they lost over sixty Mark IV tanks out of the original 120 used. Even if the 27th Armoured Brigade, supporting the 3rd British Division, had made a dash for Caen, I have no doubt that they would have been driven out by 21st Panzer and by the 12th SS Panzer who were moving up in support.

By the next day (D+1), 21st Panzer and Panzer Grenadiers were dug in, and Caen could never have been taken by the 3rd British Division. An outside chance had not come off, but it was not a failure. To have secured the bridges north of Caen, a bridgehead to the east and a bridgehead six miles deep around the north of Caen, and then to have defeated the counter-attack by 120 tanks of 21st Panzer, was by any standard a very substantial success for the 6th Airborne and 3rd British Divisions. Even without Caen, the east end 'hinge' of the Allied bridgehead was established and firmly held, and never in serious jeopardy after D-Day. It would hold because the Germans would find it impossible to launch an effective attack on it. To do so they either had to eliminate the bridgehead east of the Orne and north of Caen, then assault and bridge the ship canal and the Orne itself, or alternatively, any attack had to be launched through the streets of Caen. Our bombings and congestion would have ruled this out.

To turn now to the Canadians. In my view they achieved all that could be expected of them. They actually reached the outskirts of Carpiquet airfield, but their tanks and armoured cars withdrew as they had outrun their infantry. The Canadians were five to six miles inland by the end of D-Day.

At Omaha the US 1st and 29th Divisions had failed to advance more than a mile or so. All D-Day morning their invasion was touch and go, but by the afternoon and evening of D-Day they were just firmly ashore, but a very long way from their objective, and they had left a huge gap to the west of 50th Division.

Why was Omaha so nearly a failure? There were a number of causes. Firstly, they had a difficult beach with cliffs and a steep shingle bank in front. Secondly, their beach was manned by elements of the German 352nd Division, a first-line field division, as well as by part of the 716 coastal defence division. Therefore, they met greater opposition than on any other Allied beach. But there were two US Divisions assaulting Omaha, and although the opposition was more formidable than on Utah or Gold, there were other reasons for the US difficulties. These were:

1 They allowed less than an hour of daylight for their naval bombardment. Their H-hour was 0630, ours on Gold 0730.
2 This bombardment was ineffective, not observed closely, and mostly fell behind the defences. It was only later in the morning that US and British ships came in close and did a pin-point bombardment.
3 The pre-invasion bombing also seems to have been too far inland, due to low cloud.
4 They launched their DD tanks too far out, and lost nearly the lot.
5 The US commanders had refused to use the Hobart 'Funnies', other than DD tanks, offered to them by the British. Thus they had no 'flails', 'fascines, 'petards' or 'bombards', nor flame-throwing 'crocodiles'.
6 Their assaults were made directly opposite German strong points on the cliffs and not between them and to the west, where the cliffs were lower.

We always had the feeling in Normandy and in the UK beforehand that they did not make the meticulous reconnaisance and detailed planning that we carried out, and without the 'funnies' they had nothing to achieve the vital, quick break through minefields and strong points. That Omaha survived at all must be due to the sheer guts and drive of some of their infantry and engineers.

As regards Utah, this was successful, and the three US divisions, the 4th Infantry from the sea, the 82nd Airborne behind them and the 101st Airborne north of Carentan, were firmly ashore, or down and linked up.

Therefore, by the end of D-Day there was 80%+ success. Four assault forces, Utah, Gold, Juno and Sword had achieved their task, though not all had reached their final objectives. Only Omaha was a partial failure, but at least they were ashore and, protected by us to their east, they would have had time to recover without a German counter-attack. Montgomery was fully justified in having five beaches. A 20% partial failure was containable, but had Omaha been one of three beaches only, or been subject to counter-attack by 21st Panzer on the afternoon of D-Day, as was Sword, the story of the invasion might have been very different.

50th Division's D-Day Assault

To end this chapter it is right to comment on 50th Division's assault as it has been little recognized by commentators and historians, who concentrate on the comparative failure of the US landing at Omaha, on the airborne forces' battle or on the failure to capture Caen. In my view, 50th Divison's actions, including those of 8th Armoured Brigade and 47 Royal Marine Commando at Port-en-Bessin, were among the outstanding achievements of D-Day. They were successful because of very careful planning and use of firepower and 'funnies' on the beach. But all this would have failed had it not been for the superb performance of the infantry, particularly of the two assault brigades, the Green Howards and East Yorks of 69 Brigade, and the Devons, Dorsets and Hampshires of 231 Brigade. Their *élan* and dash in storming ashore and inland was quite breathtaking. Anyone who is interested should read their regimental histories, as this is not the place to describe their heroic actions in detail. The casualties suffered were severe, but would have been much greater had they faltered and not advanced, regardless of their losses. Their actions were recognized by the award of many medals for gallantry, including a large number of Military Crosses and Military Medals, and one Victoria Cross to CSM Hollis of the 6th Green Howards.

The support too of the 8th Armoured Brigade, and the AVREs of the Royal Engineers was superb. We in the Hertfordshire Yeomanry were lucky on D-Day to fight alongside the best division and the best armoured brigade in the Allied armies.

By midnight on D-Day the division's four infantry brigades and the 8th Armoured Brigade were firmly entrenched in positions near their objectives.

More importantly, the next morning they moved forward to occupy Bayeux fully and then moved south of Bayeux to capture the St Leger position and the high ground on the Bayeux–Caen road. By 0800 hours on 7 June, twenty-four hours after landing, we had established a front seven miles wide and eight miles deep into Normandy. Contact with the Canadians on our left was not firm, and contact with the US troops to the west of Bayeux on our right had not been made. They were still stuck at Omaha. We were soon to realize that the Canadians and the British 3rd Division had not taken Caen.

We were the only Allied division to establish such a front and our achievement became vitally important. Our position across the Bayeux–Caen road denied the Germans the possibility of attacking the US 1st Army at Omaha, as the country to the south of Bayeux had no easy east to west roads and they would be subject to attack by us. In reality, the pattern of the Normandy battle was already set, with the German armour being concentrated against the British sector, leaving the US armies comparatively free to advance inland without serious armoured opposition. This pattern was to continue for the next ten weeks or more.

5
First Week

Allied objectives. The fighting of the first days ashore. 8th Armoured Brigade's projected advance to Villers Bocage. German counter-attacks. Occupation and battles at Pt 103 at Audrieu. Our advance with 7th Armoured Division and 56th Brigade on Tilly-sur-Seulles. Stalemate.

A successful landing having been made, the next tasks of the Allied forces were:

1 To enlarge the bridgehead, and to link up all the beaches into one continuous front. In doing this a large enough area had to be enclosed to cope with the Allied build-up of troops, stores, ammunition and close support airfields. A bridgehead roughly ten miles deep and fifty miles wide would be enough for this. Whether it included Caen or not made little difference, provided that this eastern hinge was securely held.

2 To repulse any German counter-attacks, particularly that of the three Panzer divisions around and south of Caen. Therefore, the Allied perimeter must not be too large, nor too far from the sea, otherwise it would lose the support of naval gunfire. These counter-attacks, particularly of German armour, must not be made against the US forces for three reasons:
   a Because of the situation at Omaha.
   b Because of the necessity for Omaha and Utah to link up by capturing Isigny and Carentan, both in very difficult country with lots of rivers and marshes.
   c To allow the US forces to break out from Utah, overrun the Cotentin peninsula and capture the vital port of Cherbourg as early as possible.

   Therefore, everything had to be done to draw the German armoured forces to the British Sector and especially to Caen, as far away from the US forces as possible.

3 To keep up the deception of another landing in the Calais area so that the Germans would not move their considerable forces from there to Normandy. The double threat of an advance from Caen and a landing

in the Calais area would deceive the Germans into not attacking the US forces while Cherbourg was captured.

4 To reinforce the assault divisions with new divisions as quickly as possible. The allied build-up across the beaches had to be quicker than the German build-up by land.

By D+1 it was obvious that Caen could not be captured by the 3rd British, 6th Airborne and the 3rd Canadian Divisions. They did of course try, and by doing so kept the Germans tied down there and absorbed the attacks of 21st Panzer and the newly arriving 12th SS Panzer Division.

The advance was therefore to be led by the 8th Armoured Brigade supported by the 50th Division and is the subject of this chapter, but before this I will describe the position of our guns and OPs and my own arrival ashore.

D-DAY+1 (7 JUNE)

Our guns remained for the night of D-Day at Ver-sur-Mer within a mile from the beach, but at 0530 hours on 7 June advance parties went forward to reconnoitre a new position just south of St Gabriel, over four miles inland. During the night the battery position had been troubled with small arms and spandau fire, so early in the morning the woods behind the battery's position were attacked by flame-throwing tanks, and over 200 German soldiers winkled out and captured.

Our infantry were still fighting to clear Crépon and the villages to the south of it. By 0800 this was achieved, and the road through Crépon and Creully lay clear and open. The regimental guns then advanced by 1000 hours to a position forward of St Gabriel, to the south of the river Seulles. The new gun position 5000 yards behind our forward troops allowed the guns, with their range of 13,000 yards, to cover if necessary the whole front, from Bayeux in the west to the outskirts of Caen in the east (see Figure 7). The guns in this position also provided a very valuable anti-tank defence, guarding the river Seulles bridges against any possible German counter-attack.

At our OPs on 7 June, 'stand to' was at 0500 hours, but there was no German counter-attack. At 0815, the 7th Green Howards, with Stephen Perry and Dick Greig (but no George Loveday) in support, launched their attack on the fortified and barbed-wired radar and wireless station near St Leger. The Shermans of 'A' Squadron of the 4th/7th Dragoon Guards were in support, and the battle was short and sharp. We suffered four tanks lost, mostly on mines, and twelve infantry casualties, in capturing the strong point and taking sixty Germans prisoner.

The 6th Green Howards had moved forward across the road to Duoy-Ste-

Marguerite by 1000 hours, but had come under heavy mortar fire. The 7th Green Howards had also crossed the road to the outskirts of Brouay, linking with the Canadians on our left.

Meanwhile, still at sea on board the LCH, having spent several hours evacuating our casualties, I had not slept, and was up before dawn and tuned in by wireless to all those ashore. Dawn came and went, and by 0800 hours no German counter-attack had materialized. Bombardier Childs, my OPAck, could not walk so much to his chagrin he had to be evacuated as a casualty that morning.

I was ordered ashore to take command of 341st Battery at their command post now being established at St Gabriel. Having said farewell to the Navy, I went ashore in a passing landing craft. It was coming up to high water and the beach was littered with craft, but landing was going full ahead and vehicles, equipment and troops moving inland all the time. I started walking on my own with a pack, a wireless set and my revolver, up off the beach to Ver-sur-Mer. I soon thumbed a lift as far as Crépon, where I had to make a left turn, and my transport was going straight ahead. So on a peaceful June morning I started walking through the outskirts of the village, past the deserted church and alongside a stone wall. The road and village were calm and peaceful, a chicken crossing the road and a cow mooing in the distance, then 'crack', and then a second shot ahead.

Hastily drawing my revolver and retreating to a convenient doorway, I was frightened. Fear is a curious thing and it takes people different ways, but that morning, in that quiet, peaceful lane, all by myself, two shots scared me, and the thought of walking four miles on my own was too much for this brave Captain, so I slunk back to the main road and waited until a jeep with a Medical Officer and his orderly turned my way and gave me a lift to St Gabriel.

All was well with our guns, so I picked up my OP tank and crew and we proceeded to the St Leger position across the Bayeux–Caen road. (This is our Phase III objective captured that morning, as described above). By the time I arrived, fighting was over, the radio location station captured and all the Germans made prisoners. Stephen Perry and Dick Greig were brewing up tea and preparing to move forward having established OPs. The main problem concerned the German guard dogs, about a dozen really ferocious alsatians by this time both ravenous and highly excited, and running wild in the compound. It is curious in war how small things cause problems, but all us brave soldiers who would happily kill Germans, were terribly reluctant to kill their dogs. We argued for a long time until someone was badly bitten.

Stephen, Dick and I had a relaxed picnic lunch at St Leger and compared notes. For the first time we began to realize what had been achieved. We are eight miles inland, firmly ashore with OPs established, and targets in front of us registered against a German counter-attack. 69 Brigade are in position across the main road, with the 6th Green Howards in Cancagny and Duoy-Ste-Marguerite, and the 7th Green Howards have linked with the Canadians at Ste-Croix-Grande-Tonne and Brouay.

The plan now was for the 8th Armoured Brigade to form up behind the road and advance on two centre lines to capture Villers Bocage, fifteen miles away to the south (see Figure 6). This advance had been planned to start on 7 June, but the 24th Lancers, who were to lead one column, were not able to land on the afternoon of D-Day and only came ashore on the 7th, so the attack was put off until the 8th. For the rest of 7 June we dug in and rested. During the afternoon we heard a lot of gunfire to our left and I went off down the main road to Caen. Just past Ste-Croix-Grande-Tonne I halted, having seen nothing, and all seemed eerily quiet. I felt decidedly nervous, if not downright frightened, so I returned. Later that day we heard that the Canadians had been attacked by German tanks, so there is little doubt that I was very lucky to return in one piece.

8th ARMOURED BRIGADE'S ADVANCE (8–9 JUNE)

8th Armoured Brigade were assembling just behind us at the St Leger position. The advance was to be in two columns (see Figure 6). The left-hand or easterly one, led by the 24th Lancers, was to advance some two miles down the Caen road and turn south through Brouay and Putot-en-Bessin, then through Fontenay, proceeding south-westerly to Villers Bocage and the high ground (Pt 213) just to the east of the town. The right-hand column's route was via Audrieu and Juvigny to Villers Bocage, led by 61st Reconnaissance Regiment of 50th Division. The main gunnery support would be provided by the Essex Yeomanry. We, the Hertfordshire Yeomanry, would support the follow-up infantry of 50th Division, as the advance continued.

On the morning of 8 June, Stephen Perry went off after breakfast with the carrier platoon of the Green Howards to establish contact with the Winnipeg Rifles down the main Caen Road at Ste-Croix-Grande-Tonne. He had a frustrating day as the 8th Armoured Brigade and the Canadians were held up at Putot-en-Bessin and the advance was stopped.

In the morning I remained at the St Leger position; and we engaged several targets to our west around Nonant and then to our south towards Audrieu. In the afternoon I advanced southwards with the 4th/7th Dragoon Guards, bypassing Duoy-Ste-Marguerite, towards Audrieu (Figure 8). However, the two advances of 8th Armoured Brigade were halted. The 24th Lancers suffered heavy casualties at Putot-en-Bessin and Brouay, and the other column was stuck and under heavy fire just south of Loucelles.

I was ordered to support this column at Loucelles (see Figure 9). I arrived to find the column halted, with three tanks knocked out by German 88mm guns, one of them the OP Tank of Chris Sedgwick of the Essex Yeomanry. We helped to get him out of his tank, which luckily had not caught fire, patched him up and sent him back.

The problem was that we had to cross about 300 yards of open ground across a valley to the station and the first houses in Audrieu Bas village. This section was wide open to German gunfire from the village, and also from the higher ground to the south-east. This high ground rose about 200 feet or so to Cristot and woods between Cristot and Brouay, and German 88mm guns were firing from the edge of these woods, about 800 to 1200 yards away.

The column commander told me to silence the German guns, and to fire on the station and village while the infantry and then the tanks crossed this open stretch of ground. I found a superb OP in a field above the road to the west with a very high Norman hedge, from the top of which I had a good view of the station and the high ground to the south-east. We shelled the German gun positions first using two batteries of our guns, sixteen guns in all. Then I switched one troop of our guns onto the station and village, only 300 yards ahead of us. After half an hour's firing, the infantry and tanks moved forward and successfully took the station, then moved through the village southwards, house by house. I continued firing away to the south-east, towards the high ground south of Brouay. Darkness came and I stayed in my field that night.

My OP team and I 'stand to' at dawn on 9 June ready to fire but with no visible targets. In the middle of breakfast I was joined by my Colonel, George Fanshawe, and Arthur Fayre, CO of the Essex Yeomanry. The plan for the 8th Armoured Brigade's advance had been changed: they had withdrawn from Putot-en-Bessin and Brouay on our left, leaving the 50th Division's infantry to hold the line. The whole of the 8th Armoured Brigade was to move across the open country to our west and occupy a pivot or strong point at Pt 103, the high ground just south of Audrieu village, about two to two and a half miles south-south-west of us, overlooking Tilly-sur-Seulles, the village of St Pierre and the ground towards Fontenay (Figures 8 and 9). Major artillery support was to be given right away to our troops at Brouay and to the whole operation, and we all sat down in my field with George Fanshawe saying 'Well this seems a good spot, Arthur, and the wireless works, so let's do it from here.'

I survived that morning in a haze of exhilaration. I fired the whole of the 86th Field Regiment on the woods and on the Germans south of Brouay. Arthur Fayre used the Essex Yeomanry and a medium regiment, and George Fanshawe directed the fire of several naval vessels. A whole succession of targets was selected from the map to bring down a massive bombardment on

PLATE 16. *British Piat anti-tank infantry weapon. Note spare bomb in foreground.*

all likely German positions and forming-up areas, all the way from south of Putot-en-Bessin round through Cristot, Fontenay and Tilly.

Our wireless networks and system of gun controls need a word of explanation. A Troop Commander could call for fire from his troop of four guns by calling for 'Troop Target'. A Battery Commander with his eight guns could do so by calling for 'Battery Target'. A Regimental Commander wanting concentrated fire from all twenty-four guns would call for a 'Mike Target'. A division's artillery target was an 'Uncle Target', and a corps target a 'Victor Target'.

If I, as a Battery Commander, needed all the regiment's 24 guns, I had to clear this with the Colonel or Regimental Headquarters (RHQ). If my target was big and important I might be allocated the whole division's artillery consisting of three field regiments of 72 guns plus the heavier guns of a medium regiment. Of course, at times priorities had to be decided, and the various artillery commanders had to switch guns, troops, batteries, or regiments between the targets of OP officers, depending on these priorities.

In Normandy a great deal of this firing was done by the map. We knew when a German attack had started, so we used some guns for the immediate visual targets, and other guns were fired at likely German positions, forming-

PLATE 17. *German Panzerfaust anti-tank infantry weapon. Notice larger bomb than Piat. Both weapons used at Tilly and in the hedges of the bocage with considerable effect.*

up places and mortar or gun positions. We therefore had to be able to read the map with great skill and imagination, and to put ourselves in the German commander's shoes to work out where the enemy would advance, be it along the edge of a wood or along a sunken lane, whether their HQ would be in that farmhouse or in a château, where their guns would be in that belt of trees. We would bring down our fire on the appropriate map reference at the best time, and then switch the guns to a new target. Heavy concentrated fire in short bursts on a variety of targets was usually the most effective. With good communications, the speed and weight of our response could be overwhelming and there was no doubt that that morning from Loucelles it was devastating to the Germans.

During this bombardment our column moved south through Audrieu village up on to Pt 103 which had been occupied that morning by the main body of 8th Armoured Brigade with Stephen Perry. My diary records:

Once my job is finished I am ordered forward to Pt 103, so we pack up our OP and take the tank forward across the 300 yards of exposed ground. Just as we start, a

German gun from away to our left opens fire. If he is firing at us he misses us. Now we have a convenient bank along the road to our right, and I think, let's get over that and we will be in shelter. So ordering my driver to the right we crest the bank, to see to my horror a veritable canal on the other side. Hastily correcting, we come to a halt on the top of the bank, with one track over the water. We all think we are done for as we present a sitting target to the Germans. One more shot misses us and then my driver somehow rocks us out and we speed for the railway station and the safety of the cover of the village.

We proceed slowly and cautiously up through the village, and then the tank breaks down with engine trouble. We limp slowly forward with urgent demands through the wireless for me to rendezvous at once at Pt 103. Eventually I make it, on foot ahead and the tank crawling along behind.

I report to Brigade HQ and meet up with Stephen, who is doing a marvellous job in his carrier, under considerable mortar and shell fire. His driver and signaller have both been wounded in the face and head by mortars and are evacuated.

Stephen and I, together with the Essex Yeomanry, find OPs looking south, and bring down fire on St. Pierre and Tilly sur Seulles. Pt 103 is under very heavy fire from 88mm and 155mm guns and German mortars, and we keep under cover and pray.

In the meantime, I get through to the battery position and order up another tank to replace mine. I give them careful instructions as to the safest route to our position. Lt. Mackie brings the tank forward with a bren-gun carrier 'TLB', and nothing more is heard from them.

We hold Pt 103 firm all that afternoon and evening under heavy fire, and firing back very heavily too. Come nightfall, I am ordered back to Regimental Headquarters and we limp home in the gathering dusk, leaving Stephen Perry at Pt 103.

The crew stripped the tank and repaired it all night as I had been detailed off to join our new advance down the west side of the river Seulles on to Tilly-sur-Seulles first thing on the morning of 10 June. We learned later that my replacement tank and carrier had run into the Germans. Lt. Mackie was killed by a grenade thrown at him in the tank turret, and the others were all captured. This was a disaster for which I blame myself. Did they take a wrong turning and go straight into enemy lines, or did the Germans make a foray into Loucelles or Audrieu? Either could have happened, as the Germans were on all three sides of Pt 103. In fact, Stephen Perry described it in his usual laconic way as 'not too healthy'.

During the morning of 9 June our guns had moved forward and westward to a new position at Martragny, just north of the Caen–Bayeux road at St Leger. This enabled them to fire with a shorter range and thus greater accuracy in support of Pt 103, and in support of any advance on Tilly-sur-Seulles (Figure 7).

9 June will always live in our memories as the first day of real German opposition, when we realized from intelligence reports that we had the fanati-

cal German 12th SS (Hitler Youth) Panzer Division, and the even more formidable Panzer Lehr Division, attacking our front. For the first time Tiger tanks had been in action against us at Pt 103. That morning we had reports of a major German tank advance to our west, by Panzer Lehr moving up on Bayeux from the south. In the afternoon we heard that it had been halted by gunfire, including heavy naval fire at Ellon, and instead of pushing forward, it had withdrawn south to Tilly-sur-Seulles. At the time we did not realize that this German withdrawal was made because of the threat our own attack at Pt 103 posed to them. Nevertheless, it was obvious to us all that evening that all the way from Caen to Tilly, the Germans were opposing us in force with their superb 88mms, and more ominously, their superior tanks, and that now any advance in that area would be very costly. In fact, it would be hard to hold all we had gained (see Figure 10).

But what was happening to the west, and where were the Americans from Omaha, who should have been up alongside us two days ago and who still had not arrived? Had the German tank attack at Ellon pushed forward to the west of Bayeux, they would have encountered little opposition, and would then have run into the US troops from Omaha. The result might have been disastrous. Alternatively, had that force succeeded in taking Bayeux or had bypassed it on the west, they could have swung east behind our lines and caused enormous damage to our supplies, the Pluto terminal at Port-en-Bessin and the Mulberry harbour at Arromanches. Once this German force withdrew, it appeared that there was much less German armour west of Tilly-sur-Seulles, and none at all in the US sector. All this appears to have been realized 'on high', and whoever could fill this empty space first could make a significant advance. The Germans' attempt had failed and we were now to make ours.

First, I should finish with 9 June, which had started so well and ended so badly for me. The seizure of Pt 103 by the 8th Armoured Brigade had been accomplished, and turned out in my view to be one of the most significant battles in the Normandy campaign: I will analyse its importance at the end of this chapter. One of the nastiest facets of war is always the killing of prisoners. The Château of Audrieu, which had been used by the 12th SS (Hitler Youth) Panzer Division, yielded a grisly story when we captured it – in the courtyard a number of Canadian POWs had been shot in cold blood.

TILLY-SUR-SEULLES (10 JUNE)

On the evening of D+3, 9 June, George Fanshawe had pulled me out from Pt 103 on the east bank of the Seulles river, and told me I was to support an attack the next day by a mixed column of 7th Armoured Division and 56

Brigade, down the main road on the west side of the river, to capture Tilly-sur-Seulles and push south to Juvigny. This was quite something! The 7th Armoured Division were the famous Desert Rats, Monty's crack armoured division. They had started coming ashore on D+2, but were not all ashore by any means, so 56 Brigade of 50th Division were 'lent' to them.

Early on 10 June, a lovely day with the sun shining and grass gleaming, I took my repaired Sherman tank, and with Dick Greig and Ted Hall to support me, we reported to the column commander, a colonel of the 7th Armoured Division, on the road south of Jerusalem crossroads, just north of Buceels, a small village, itself two miles north of Tilly-sur-Seulles. Feeling very young and inexperienced, I find the column drawn up on the road itself in splendid gleaming order. The colonel, nattily dressed in desert boots and breeches, with a paisley scarf in lieu of a tie, is sitting languidly on the top of his armoured car. I hastily tuck my tank well out of sight behind the usual Norman hedge, and approach on foot. The tanks of the 7th Armoured's column are supported by the 2nd Gloucesters of 56 Brigade, with artillery support from us and their own Field Regiment. Apparently, the advance has temporarily halted, and the Colonel is planning to attack a little hamlet called Pont-de-la-Guillette in a valley about 400 yards to our south. Behind this rises a hill, and a mile beyond that lies the village of Tilly-sur-Seulles, out of our sight (Figure 12).

I am briefed on the plan, which is that the Gloucesters are to be deployed on the east side of the road, to advance and capture Pont-de-la-Guillette. The tanks are to advance to support on the right. I am given the job of shelling the hamlet on the far side of the bridge as the attack goes in. In the morning sunlight the whole thing seems unreal. I know that the Germans are across the Seulles river under a mile away to our east, and yet the whole column is pulled up along the road in bright sunlight. Anyway, the sartorial elegance of the 7th Armoured and their superior confidence is most inspiring. Nevertheless, I leave my tank well hidden and crawl on foot down the ditch by the road until I have a perfect observation post over Pont-de-la-Guillette and the hill on the other side. We do a little excavation, just in case someone fires along the ditch, and settle down to register our target. I fire one ranging round, which goes over the village into a field as planned, and am correcting the range to bracket the target when there is movement in the village below – a German half track coming towards us? We hastily prepare for action, sending a message back via the wireless to my tank for the sartorial Colonel. Feeling very foolish on my own in a ditch, I peep over the bank and unconcernedly up the hill comes a British bren-gun carrier. Eventually it comes near enough for me to recognize one of our own signals carriers reeling out a telephone line.

No Germans anywhere! So I hail the bombardier, much to his surprise, and ask him where he has come from. He points down to the village. Apparently, one of our OPs is ahead of us on the right and has sent the carrier back to the guns via our Pont-de-la-Guillette target. On enquiry, the bombardier says that Pont-de-la-Guillette is deserted except for some nuns with a party of children sheltering in the hamlet's barns – my very target. The nuns report no Germans there; there have been, but they have moved south at dawn, so I pluck up my courage and walk down the ditch into the village. No Germans, only nuns, children and one farmer, and all is very quiet, so post haste back to the column commander to report, so that the attack can be called off. Not a bit of it, he refuses point blank, and we wait another two hours until all is deployed and ready, then the set piece attack goes into an empty hamlet.

I am not going to fire on nuns and children, so ignoring orders I choose my own target up the hill where the Germans are likely to be waiting for and watching us, and for good luck, put down some smoke shells too, to screen our advance. The morning is now well advanced and we move through the hamlet and up the hill on the far side without a shot being fired against us, but not before I get a real dressing down and a threatened court martial for not firing on my given target from the sartorial 7th Armoured. At least none of the French children were killed.

As we advance over the brow of the hill, the ground flattens; suddenly there are reports of German tanks ahead. A hasty conference and I am asked with the other gunner to bring down fire on them. I drive my Sherman tank very gingerly up the road. Round the second bend and hell! 250 yards ahead in the centre of the road, two German tanks! We back very hastily and squash the Company Sergeant-Major's bicycle, luckily missing the Sergeant-Major himself. So into the ditch again, and very gingerly forward until I can see the German tanks quite clearly.

One tank is disabled, the second, a Panther, is waiting beside it and helping to repair it. They had not fired at us because their gun was traversed to our left and is only now swinging our way. Anyway, for the next twenty minutes or so I fire a precision shoot, using one gun only and ranging carefully as our forward troops are within 200 yards of the tanks. I use 'cap on' high explosive shells on these two tanks, as leaving the cap on the shell delays the fuse, and the shell should penetrate the tank armour more effectively. It is a lovely little pin-point shoot and I register quite a number of hits and near misses. At the same time the infantry advance along ditches, and one sergeant with a Piat hits the tanks too (see Plate 16). We both claim them as our kill, no time to argue, as we soon pass them. I think we must have caught the German crews when they had dismounted to repair the second tank.

We are now in sight of a belt of trees and orchards behind which lies Tilly-sur-Seulles. The road runs straight ahead, with the wood or orchards on either side of it. The plan this time is for the tanks to do a right hook and come into the town from the west side, and for the infantry to attack from the front. We are to support the infantry.

We advance. The Germans are there this time. Still, we make the wood and the edge of Tilly under heavy fire; Ted Hall and Dick Greig are on foot with the infantry, and I am going up the road behind them in my Sherman feeling very isolated in a lone tank. As the road enters the orchards, we come over a slight rise and I can see, from the top of the tank, clear down the road south through the village of Tilly, past the crossroads and down a long wooded avenue towards Juvigny. As I watch, I can see German reinforcements, vehicles, half-tracks, tanks and guns, coming up the road into Tilly from the south.

I take up a position in the middle of the road with only the very top of the turret showing (I hope) to the Germans, and proceed to range my guns onto the target. This is very difficult. All I can see is the tree-lined road running south (Plate 18), I cannot pick out my shell bursts, and distances are very deceptive. I get it in the end, using smoke shells which I can see as markers. Even then it is not easy. I order 'Fire' directly a German vehicle appears, but by the time the shells arrive the vehicle has turned off the road into the woods. Dick and Ted report increasing resistance, so I fire as much as I can, but for once I cannot get the use of the whole regiment, let alone other regiments or the Navy. I knock out two vehicles and hopefully more in the woods. I even call for the Typhoon aircraft with their rockets, as the German vehicles would make a perfect target, but none are available. I am both exhilarated and frightened, as my Sherman is in a terribly exposed position, even though I withdraw and advance in a slightly different position all afternoon. All the time I expect a 88mm shell to come sailing up the road, dipping over the crest, and hit us head on.

Both Ted and Dick are in the thick of it and firing too. The Gloucesters capture the northern half of Tilly, but then things become bogged down. The Germans are reinforcing hard and our attack is stuck. French civilians, some of them bleeding, and one man on crutches, are streaming back past us down the road. There is no sign of our tanks from the right. We hear that they have advanced one behind the other up a narrow hedged lane, three or four have been shot and all lost, thus aborting any tank support just when the Gloucesters need it most.

The infantry has to withdraw eventually, having had pretty nasty casualties. If only we had not wasted three hours earlier that morning at Pont-de-la-Guillette, Tilly might have been ours by midday. So we pull back across the open field under the cover of the hedges. I report to the Gloucester HQ just down the road.

Now it is late afternoon, the sun has gone in, and a sense of foreboding

PLATE 18. *Tilly-sur-Seulles. Centre of village looking south after its capture. The avenue looking south towards Juvigny described by author is clearly seen.*

sets in. The tanks of the 7th Armoured are conspicuous by their absence, the Gloucesters are in almost their first battle. Our position is actually pretty safe, but we have a wooded river valley, the Seulles, to our east, another stream to our west, and Tilly with the Panzer Lehr Division or at least quite a lot of them, to our south.

My report of the reinforcements that I have observed has not helped morale much, I imagine. Anyway, the optimism of a 'swan' of the morning changes dramatically, and we start to experience the extraordinary feeling of fear spreading. Rumours circulate that we are surrounded: 'The Germans are coming up the valleys on either side of us.' The fear is triggered by the officer commanding one of the Gloucester's forward companies who seems to have had some sort of breakdown. His company starts to stream back down the road. His Company Sergeant-Major does his best, but once the contagious fear spreads, it is very difficult to stop.

I keep the gunfire going, and wireless back to Dick, who is half a mile down the road up a tree, using it as an observation post, to get his bren-gun carrier across the road. I tell him to get out a sten-gun and turn any retreating infantry back. He does. Then I am grabbed by the second in command of

PLATE 19. *Capt. Hall with his bren carrier on road to Tilly-sur-Seulles with evacuees from that village, 11 June, three days before Capt. Hall was killed at Verrières.*

the Gloucesters, who says 'You and I are going to walk up and down this road, smoking our pipes and talking, to show these bastards that there is nothing to fear.' I reluctantly climb out of the ditch, and we do exactly that. We talk about rugby and the games we have played for what seems like hours; it is probably half an hour!

Nobody actually shoots at us, though we are mortared severely, and the amount of steel flying around is considerable. Neither of us are touched, which I regard as a minor miracle. Having discussed the intricacies of rugby scrummaging, we gradually chat up those cowering in the ditches: 'It's fine up here – ping – no problems – whoosh.' Their fear subsides, I could feel it ebbing away with the evening light. The Gloucesters soon recover their nerve, to their great credit. They dig in there for the night, and we arrange plenty of artillery fire on Tilly and the Germans to help them.

PT 103 (10–11 JUNE)

While we were so engaged at Tilly with the Gloucesters, the rest of the 7th Armoured and 56 Brigade were fighting south on our right with a similar story to ours. The whole advance halted, retreated a bit and then steadied along a line north of Tilly towards Bernieres Bocage to the west (Figure 11). Pt 103 still held. It was subject to German counter-attacks but our tanks and infantry pushed forward to the little village of St Pierre at the foot of the hill. During 10 and 11 June, German tanks overran Pt 103, but were driven out again and again. This vital pivot position held – cut off and surrounded it may have been but it survived, and the Germans retreated to the valley below. Stephen Perry's diary describes it thus:

[10 June]. Resistance is very stiff in St. Pierre. The 6th Durham Light Infantry (DLI) go into St. Pierre with a squadron of tanks, but three tanks 'brew up' in the cornfield in front of us, and the DLI return badly mauled.

We've got a good O.P. with Lyle (Essex Yeo), but we're spotted and an 88 ranges on us. They've got a bracket on us; as soon as the next round has fallen we'll shift further down the hedge; I'll drive. Bang! 15 yards away. Right, off we go; we tumble into the carrier, and I drive off just in time to miss the next shell, which knocks our 38 wireless set for six; Just in time! We'll be more careful to conceal ourselves this time; I can see four smoke rings coming up out of the wood over the valley every time they fire. So I order Mike Target and down come our shells on them, although a bit spread out. It's shut them up anyway.

We put a regimental concentration down on Tilly crossroads, while Bob, Dick and Ted advance on the town with 56 Brigade. They reach the crossroads, but come out again rather more quickly than they went in; our Forward Officers Dick and Ted have a sticky time, but get out safe and sound.

Another short and noisy night! We get a couple of hours sleep when off duty from the wireless, but shelling all night from German 155mm guns causes too many rude awakenings for peaceful slumber.

[11 June] Barker and Burns have come up in place of Butcher and Whitelock who were wounded yesterday. We man the O.P. from stand to at 0500, and get a good 'shoot' at a troop of enemy tanks that come out into the open; also we have a shot at a sniper whose bullets are getting unpleasantly close, we cannot see him but we put a few rounds from the rifle through a likely tree.

At 1700 all hell is let loose, and the pivot is the scene of a first class tank battle. Enemy tanks counter attack from the south and east; three Shermans are 'brewing up' i.e. on fire, before we realise what is going on. AP shot is whining all around us; all soft vehicles withdraw to the north going like scalded cats; anti-tank and tank guns are firing for all they are worth. Everything seems confusion, but the Brigadier is cool and confident, and has the situation under control; later everything is quiet and the counter attack has been driven off.

PLATE 20. *A German special Mk IV tank with 75mm gun knocked out by Durham Light Infantry near Pt 103, 10 June.*

At 1900 we get orders to return to the gun area. Which is the way back? Turn left at the 'brewed up' armoured car, and then right just past the crashed Spitfire, we are told. We pass the Cromwells of 7 Armoured Div. moving down to Villers Bocage, on the way back, and get into B Troop position near Jerusalem Crossroads just as it's getting dark. Report to Bob Thornton, the Regiment adjutant, and then round the Troop while grub is being cooked. It really is grand to see everyone for the first time, and in very high spirits. Everyone is hard worked, but not a single shell or bomb has troubled them down here.

Meyer and I are just about flat out and settle down to a long and undisturbed sleep, the first since D-Day.

Like Stephen Perry, I also returned to the gun end on the evening of 11 June, to be told that the command of 341st Battery was to be given to Major Corke, 'Corky', who had been attached to the 86th since D-Day as a Naval Forward Observation Officer (FOO). 'Corky' was older and senior to me and rightly deserved his promotion, so on the 12 June I reverted to my original position of Battery Captain. I returned from the 'sharp end' to the comparative calm and peace of the gun end.

It is curious how fate works. At the time I was disappointed, but the fighting at the sharp end was just about to enter its bloodiest stage. 'Corky' himself was killed in the advance to Antwerp in August 1944. The casualty rate of OP officers, like the infantry officers they served, was over 50% in three months and the greatest toll, as we shall see, came between 12 and 20 June.

Whilst Stephen was battling at Pt 103 Garton Ash was moved to the west in support of the Devons of 231 Brigade, who were to move south from Bayeux to conform with Monty's proposed right hook by 7th Armoured Division, moving down the boundary with the US Army and then wheeling left towards Villers Bocage. He passed through Bayeux on 11 June on a glorious sunny Sunday morning and joined the 2nd Devonshire Regiment moving south. On 12 June they advanced to the crossroads at La Belle Epine well into the bocage country. Captain Ash established a forward OP behind a hedge some 200 yards south of the crossroads only to have a German tank come up the road from the south and stop on the other side of the hedge. The enemy tank opened fire on an anti-tank gun of the Devons. After a few tense moments the tank withdrew and Ash and his crew smartly withdrew to La Belle Epine crossroads.

RETROSPECT: PT 103 AND TILLY

The 8th Armoured Brigade's advance on Villers Bocage was halted almost at its start. However they seized Pt 103 at Audrieu. This and our threatened advance on Tilly and Juvigny brought down on the brigade not only the 12th SS Panzer Division but the formidable Panzer Lehr Division. The seizing and holding of Pt 103 represented a threat that the Germans could not ignore. The Panzer Lehr thrust west of Tilly to Bayeux was halted at Ellon on 9 July. Instead of pushing forward into the US sector towards Omaha, they were recalled to deal with our threat at Pt 103.

It is interesting to speculate what might have happened had the 8th Armoured Brigade captured Villers Bocage by 8 June. This might well have been the case had the 8th Armoured Brigade's advance been made west of Tilly. The German advance by Panzer Lehr on 9 June would have cut them off. As Villers Bocage was outside the range of most of our artillery and beyond the range of accurate naval fire, and there were no US troops on their right to support them, they might well have been eliminated. Without 8th Armoured Brigade and without US support, 50th Division would have been hard pressed to hold Panzer Lehr and 12th SS Panzer Division. In my view it was a mercy that the 8th Armoured Brigade were stopped at Putot-en-Bessin and Loucelles, as described.

The seizing of Pt 103 as a substitute was a brilliant stroke, as this pivot forced the German's hands and had these vital consequences. It made the Germans recall their attack on Bayeux and prevented any German armoured move against Omaha and the US Sector, and also caused heavy losses on Panzer Lehr.

Along with the securing of the hinge at Caen, Pt 103 was therefore the vital battle of the first few days ashore, and it continued the whole pattern of the Normandy battlefield, which was to be the engagement and containment of the German armour by the British and Canadians, leaving the US forces free of armoured attack while they recovered at Omaha, captured Cherbourg and then launched their offensive southward.

6
The Killing Fields

The 7th Armoured Division's advance to and withdrawal from Villers Bocage. The bloody fighting with 50th Division and 8th Armoured Brigade against the German Panzer Lehr Division west of Tilly-sur-Seulles. Lingevres, La Belle Epine, Verrières, Tilly, Hottot and Le-Lion-Vert. The role of the infantry and the casualties of 50th Division. Mulberry harbour at Arromanches and the storm of 19 June.

By nightfall on 12 June, the Germans had taken up a strong defensive position based on a string of villages, wooded orchards and farmhouses from Cristot in the east through Tilly to La Belle Epine in the west (Figure 11). The Norman stone walls and massive stone farms and houses made superb defensive positions. Their line of defence from the northern outskirts of Tilly-sur-Seulles ran westward along the road from Tilly to La Belle Epine, with the villages of Verrières, Lingevres, La Schaudière and La Belle Epine as its strong points. It was a natural defensive line, because to the north of these strong points the country was fairly open cornfields and fields of new potatoes, divided by thick hedges and interspersed with apple orchards rising gently to the south. This provided open fields of fire for the spandaus and the German 75mm and 88mm guns and their formidable Panther and Tiger tanks.

To the south of this road the country was much closer, with small grass fields, woods and high hedges with sunken lanes and tracks between banks five or six feet high and the same width, typical 'Bocage' country. It was ideal country for camouflage and for siting the German mortars. This continued to Hottot and Le-Lion-Vert two to three miles south of Lingevres.

This then was the terrain over which 50th Division and the 8th Armoured Brigade were to battle against the German Panzer Lehr Division and remnants of the 716 Division, with the 12th SS Panzer (Hitler Youth) Division to their east. Before describing some of this fighting, one battle must be mentioned.

The defended German front extended to La Belle Epine to the west, but beyond that there was no German armour and little German resistance. The boundary between us and the Americans began just west of La Belle Epine. Six days after D-Day the US troops from Omaha had advanced alongside us. In fairness to them I must say that their priority was to capture Isigny and

Carentan and to link with Utah, but there was little German opposition to them on our right, and their failure to advance earlier was inexplicable to us.

After their initial failure against Tilly on 10–11 June, the 7th Armoured Division were withdrawn, and reformed with their troops who had landed on the 9th and 10th. They then advanced westward of La Belle Epine through the US Sector, and south to enter Tracy Bocage late on 12 June and Villers Bocage on 13 June. This was a marvellous piece of news which raised our morale, but on 13 June much of their forward Armoured Brigade were wiped out by the Tiger tanks of SS Hauptsturmführer (Captain) Wittman of the Panzer Abteilung 101 Heavy Tank Battalion of 1st SS Panzer Corps. Villers Bocage was evacuated, and the 7th Armoured withdrew westward to Tracy Bocage. A new division, the 2nd Panzer Division, attacked them there, but were heavily repulsed by the 7th Armoured Division with the help of US artillery fire (Figure 13).

The 7th Armoured Division's 'failure' at Villers Bocage has been described many times, and that division's poor performance in Normandy was undoubtedly the main part of the problem. However, historians have been unduly critical, in my view, as the division's advance made considerable gains. The US troops advancing with them captured and held Caumont and the British line stabilized in front of Livry to its east. This represented a salient some twenty miles deep into Normandy.

The blunting of the 2nd Panzer Division by the 7th Armoured at Tracy Bocage on 14 June, with US artillery support, continued our successful strategy, as it meant that 2nd Panzer Division were prevented from moving west to the US sector, and like 21st Panzer, 12th SS Panzer and Panzer Lehr before them, were all committed piecemeal against the British. There were therefore four German Panzer divisions east of Caumont and not one against the US forces. Also, one should not forget the heavy Tiger tank force of Panzer Ab 101 which was also committed against the British.

On our front a series of attacks was ordered in support of the 7th Armoured Division's advance. These attacks were launched against experienced and well-armed German troops occupying strong defensive positions, and were bloody affairs, undertaken with great courage but at great cost.

The first of these 'killing field' attacks was carried out by our old comrades of D-Day, 69 Brigade, on Cristot just to the east of Tilly. They attacked from Pt 103 on 11 and 12 June. The 6th Green Howards, I believe, lost 25 officers and 250 men at Cristot. Our guns were continually firing in their support.

Following the massacre at Cristot, assaults on the German defensive line west of Tilly was planned for 13 and 14 June, again to help the 7th Armoured Division. 151 Brigade, consisting of the 6th, 9th and 10th battalions of the Durham Light Infantry (DLI), were to attack Verrières and Lingevres. On 13 June Stephen Perry was with one of the leading companies, 'A' Company of the 6th DLI east of Verrières, and reported very heavy fighting; the company captured their objective but then had to withdraw. He put 'A' Company's casualties that day at 35%. All day he was firing our guns in support. On the same day too Captain Bob Turnbull of the 86th's 462nd Battery was with another leading company of the Durhams. Every single officer was killed or wounded and Bob took command, only to be shot through the head himself and killed outright.

On 14 June a set battle was laid on for 151 Brigade to capture the rest of Verrières and Lingevres. The 6th DLI on the left would clear Verrières and then advance south to the Lingevres–Tilly road. The 9th DLI would attack Lingevres direct from the north. The brigade would be supported by the 4th/7th Dragoon Guards of 8th Armoured Brigade.

If you refer to Figure 14 it clearly shows the outline of the battle, and Plates 21–3 illustrate some of the Lingevres action. I am using the accounts of Stephen Perry with the 6th DLI on the left or east side, Garton Ash with the 9th DLI on the west side and Driver Bullen in his tank with the 4th/7th Dragoon Guards in the middle to tell the story of a typical bloody day in the Bocage. Let Stephen Perry start.

By 0900 we are on the start line with 'A' Company of the 6th DLI, I am on my feet with the Company Commander, an enormous tough Spike Galloway wearing the MC and Bar. I have given orders to Meyer to follow in the carrier, keeping one hedgerow or field behind me. The barrage starts and 120 guns pound the country in front of us unceasingly for half an hour, but the infantry cannot keep up and the barrage rolls away.

Now the fun starts, mortars, anti-tank guns, SP guns, Spandaus and rifles all open up on the infantry advancing now over flat wheat fields. Galloway orders a halt, and we are all very relieved to be able to lie down, at any rate out of sight in the corn, and bury our heads in the ground when the moaning minnies whine over. This really is a rough battle; everything on earth seems to be landing in our fields, and if we poke our noses above this corn the Spandaus in those farm buildings will knock us down like ninepins. We cannot get the guns onto them because Ted and his company are coming round the right of the farm. We lie in the open for about half an hour while the Battalion Commander sums up the situation. Then we get orders to advance. It seems suicide to stand up in the corn with a dozen Spandaus just in front, ready to knock us down, but Spike Galloway is a grand chap, and with a cheerful 'Come on chaps', we all get onto our feet and start walking forward; the Spandaus open up and a dozen of our chaps go down. After 100 yards down again into the corn and get ready for the assault; as we go down there is a shout from Spike; he is shot through the shoulder; we help him back to the stretcher bearers and oh Hell, the wireless has packed up. We will have to dash back and get another. I walk back to the carrier thinking that every moment will be my last, but for some reason nothing opens up.

I hop into the carrier and off we go for a new set. As soon as we start moving, bullets from a Spandau thud on the outside but to our relief bounce off, then a rifle bullet through my control box, three inches from my head. We go like hell, and find the CO who gives us a new '38' set, and while that is being netted [tuned in] a cigarette and a cup of tea are a great relief. Then back again to join the Company. This is not going to be much fun; a 75 SP fires at us, luckily with HE and the nose cap hits the wing, knocking the carrier back on its sprocket, but no damage is done. We rejoin 'C' Company and hear that Ted has been killed and Mitchley his assistant badly shot up in the leg; however he keeps his set going, sending back information, and the BC calls for Meyer to go back with the carrier to fetch him out. Meyer goes over, strides across the open with Mitchley on his back amidst a hail of bullets, and gets him back to the safety of Battalion HQ. [For this and a number of brave actions Bombardier Meyer was awarded the Military Medal.]

Meanwhile we are going into assault; the Durhams go like mad with fixed bayonets, and we are in the farm building at last. No wonder we have had a tough time getting here. In this farmyard alone there are two 75s, three SP guns, a half track and seven Spandau positions dug into the bank of a sunken lane. As we are going in a bullet whistles through my battle dress but does no more damage than a graze on my shoulder blade. The battalion consolidates around the farm, with just a few odd shells coming over, but casualties are so heavy after the battle that two composite companies have to be formed from the whole battalion. By last light we are all dug in, and ready for anything. We get ordered back to the guns for the night. What a day! But what magnificent troops these Durhams are; it was just sheer guts that got them into Verrières. 9th DLI were successful at Lingevres, but had an equally bloody battle, where 'Sloppy' Harris (4th/7th Dragoon Guards) saved the situation by knocking out 5 Panthers.

Garton Ash tells his story in support of 9th DLI on the right flank:

Early on June 14th, Kenneth Swann gave me orders to join the reserve companies of 9th DLI for a set-piece attack on the village of Lingevres whilst, as Stephen Perry has reported, 6th DLI on our left were to take Verrières. The start line was in the line of a hedge some 500 yards north of a wood. The land in between was open fields with standing corn some three feet high. Some 600 yards the other side of the wood lay Lingevres. The leading companies struck very considerable resistance, particularly from machine-guns dug into the wood, but in spite of heavy casualties they made progress and eventually the reserve companies moved forward and, although held up on the left, were able to work forward on the right and eventually, with support from the 4th/7th Dragoons to get through the woods and across more open ground into Lingevres itself.

The village had already been heavily damaged but I was able to work forward in the carrier towards the eastern end of the main street, just short of a dip in the road leading down to a stream south from Verrières. When there I kept the carrier under cover and tried to find the Company Commander. I found the 6th Durhams in the line of a short hedge overlooking the dip in the road (I later discovered they were the remainder of 'A' Company) but there was no sign of any of their officers. A

PLATE 21. *Centre of Lingevres village after the battle showing Sherman tank of 4th/7th Dragoon Guards with one track blown off. Church to left.*

German tank was spotted on the far side of the stream close against the side of farm buildings, and thus protected from shellfire. The crew were just scrambling into it. The whole village was full of dust and debris and I searched round the back of houses to try and find anywhere to provide a decent OP looking south, but this was impossible because of the bocage.

Returning to the main street I found Kenneth Swann's tank, the crew showing me the large gouge in the side where a shot from an SP gun to the east had given them a glancing blow and put their main wireless out of action. I searched again for an OP, and saw one of the Shermans near the War Memorial with a hole through its front transmission and a large pool of oil underneath. I remember an infantry carrier on fire towards the eastern end of the main street, its ammunition exploding in all directions, and later getting the carrier back under cover near the Church.

Late in the day, two or three German tanks tried to get back into the village, it was no place to keep the carrier, so we took this down a steep bank behind the Church into the field to the north.

From a ditch on the north of the field I heard a shout and found Kenneth Swann and his crew with some Durhams, Kenneth having been firing DF tasks from the map on counter-attacks to the south of Lingevres. Kenneth told me to try and work back into the village to report what was happening. I took the '18' set and a signaller

PLATE 22. *Centre of Lingevres with disabled German Panther tank, one of Sloppy Harris's five.*

and started back on foot up the road leading into Lingevres from the north where we had advanced earlier in the day. When we were about 100 yards short of the main road, I heard gunfire from the west and looking along the road was horrified to see three Panthers advancing up the road into the village. We took cover in the ditch beside a small building and I radioed the information to Kenneth. Shortly afterwards there was a loud crack from immediately behind us, followed by two more. I looked round and saw what appeared to be a Firefly of the 4th/7th Dragoons on fire, but in fact it was only their camouflage netting lit by their own muzzle blast and looking back I realized that all three Panthers had been knocked out [Sloppy Harris stopped five that day]. Shortly afterwards a reserve battalion came through to take over the village. We cheered them on and went up to inspect the Panthers. My carrier driver unerringly delved into the leading Panther which had finished near the Church, and unearthed an old shirt in which was wrapped a bottle of Calvados. After that we returned to the gun position and Hall gave me a glass of the Calvados, and after that I slept much better than expected.

Gunner Chick Bullen, driver of X Tank of Major Kenneth Swann, BC of 342nd Battery, described his dramatic escape at Lingevres on 14 June. This account is extracted from *Panzers in Normandy – Then and Now*.

PLATE 23. *Two more blown-up Panthers. Looking up road to Lingevres village centre.*

Our Sherman tank had had its main 75mm gun removed and substituted by a dummy gun barrel. This was to enable the gun turret to contain a plotting table and various other items for pin-point bombardment and an extra wireless set. We also carried a 'walkie talkie' wireless. Without that Lingevres might have taken a little longer to eliminate.

At dusk on June 13, our Commander, Major Kenneth Swann gathered the crew of 'X' tank and told us that we were to join a squadron of 4/7 Dragoon Guards immediately. We moved off and before complete darkness fell had met up with our 'big boy friends' . . . a term used largely when units were in company with armour.

While the skipper was away at Commanders' briefing, we prepared a cold meal. Fires were not allowed but the cans of self-heating soup were a blessing, as they proved to be on several occasions. While we ate our meal, the skipper gave us crew briefing. Although every detail was covered, it simply meant that at first light several flights of rocket-firing Typhoons would loosen up the enemy, who were holding Lingevres. While the Typhoons were attacking the armour would advance, giving close support to the infantry, to capture and hold the village.

The main road at Lingevres was of secondary standard only, both in terms of width and surface. The village square is bisected by the main road and again by a single track road leading from Longraye to Verrières. Another, even smaller track, led off to the north-west.

'Stand to' at first light on the 14th was no different from previous ones. It was possible to discern black from grey but not men from shrubs and trees and the tanks in 'league' could have been mistaken for buildings. As the sky lightened and turned to sunrise, it was apparent that the previous day's hot and sunny weather was to continue.

Breakfast, maintenance, checking of guns, ammunition, the wireless nets and dozens of other personal and tank daily checks were done almost in silence. Probably everyone shared the same thought: 'I wonder if . . .'

Around 8 o'clock we heard the RAF arrive and minutes later the familiar sound of rockets came to us. 'Mount . . . start up . . . driver advance . . .' and we were off. We went up a slight rise in the ground, through a hedge and had our first sight of Lingevres. From the angle we were at, it appeared to be a fairly large village, complete with a church and a few outlying farms, situated about half way up a small hill. One or two small fires were burning but it wasn't possible to say where as we were still about 2000 yards away. We did, however, have a good view of the Typhoons going in. My own thought was that we would only have the sweeping up to do.

We were now advancing across a large field of corn in company with eight other Shermans in a rough line abreast, with each tank well separated from the next one. As a driver I was getting many changes of direction, unnecessarily I thought, until I realised we were advancing through our own infantry who were invisible to me through my periscope. The corn was almost eye level!

About 500 yards from the village I saw a Dragoon tank hit way over to our right. Suddenly one to our left stopped and the crew baled out. That, too, was hit. Then, quite suddenly, all hell let loose. Small arms and machine gun fire was exchanged across the cornfield. The main armament of tanks fired at targets I couldn't see and the wireless sets which I could hear in the background were constantly receiving and sending messages. I can remember one in particular: 'Mike target . . . Mike target . . . Mike target . . .' followed by a map reference. This was from my own Commander and seconds later a barrage of shellfire burst upon the village. It seemed to go on for an hour or more. In reality it was only a few minutes.

We were now at the end of the cornfield facing a typical Norman hedge. My instructions came over the intercom: 'Go through and turn left.' This was unusual. We had seen tanks defeated by such rows of hedges before and, of course, the thin armour of the belly of the tank was exposed. I engaged low gear and went through, made a left turn and continued ahead. I can remember seeing a car, motorcycle and machine gun crew all knocked out. We were in a very narrow road and about a hundred yards ahead was the church where some infantry chaps of ours were digging in.

As we got closer I could see more infantry setting up machine gun positions. Then I turned into the village square and found far more destruction. The church, houses and shops had obviously been caught in the Typhoon raid. A few dead German and British soldiers were scattered about. A Sherman was positioned by the entrance to the church and, on the other side of what I call a square but was in fact just a road junction, a Firefly stood with its gun pointing up the road to the north-west.

I was told to stop by a Sherman and wait, engine running. The Commander called a greeting and waved. In answer to a request from our skipper he pointed to the Firefly. Our Commander ran across the road, climbed on the Firefly and pointed to something out of my vision. I didn't have a chance to wonder what he was pointing at. Our own wireless operator shouted into the intercom: 'Driver reverse, right-hand down and go like ****!' I didn't hear the last word – I was already going!

The tank lurched, a building to our right collapsed, followed by a loud explosion and pieces of flaked enamel came flying around inside the driving compartment of the tank. For a minute I couldn't gather my thoughts. I remember saying to the co-driver: 'Christ!' His reply was something to the effect that his wireless had gone 'diss'.

When the Major rejoined us he gave me directions and guided us across a small field behind the church, we broke through a low hedge and parked in the corner of a field. We found a stream running down one side of the hedge with a culvert about three feet deep in the corner. Taking cover there were about a dozen of the Durhams, most of them wounded. We gathered what might have been useful – grenades, Stens, a Browning, first-aid box and a No. 18 wireless, which the operator extracted from the bowels of a Sherman – and joined the infantry. From our new position we had a good view of the crossroads and saw that our friendly Sherman had been knocked out. We couldn't see the Firefly. Apart from spasmodic small arms fire and the occasional thump of a tank gun, it was reasonably quiet.

We learned from the skipper that he had seen an SP gun that required the attention of the Firefly's 17-pounder. While he was directing the fire he spotted a Panther up the Tilly road bringing its gun to bear in our direction. He shouted to our operator to 'move'. The shell, an HE, took us on the right-hand side while we were in reverse. It ricocheted off and exploded in the shop we were going behind for cover. When we examined the damage sustained outwardly there was not too much to see. The shell had left some score marks about a foot long and about an inch deep. The side of the tank was slightly concave for about two feet. Inwardly, the front set was out of commission, as was the forward Browning. Flakes of white enamel covered the driving compartment.

The infantry officer and our own quickly exchanged views on the situation, which wasn't very comforting. Our tanks had come up against a strong armoured force of panzergrenadiers and several of the 4/7 Dragoon Shermans had been knocked out. Our own infantry had lost a great many men and those remaining were engaged in house to house fighting. About half a dozen tanks on the enemy side were knocked out, along with some SPs, but two or three were still roaming about. This was particularly disturbing as we had previously seen shots from the Shermans bouncing off the enemy armour.

After about half an hour in the one position, our officer took the No. 18 set and went off to the village to see what was happening. The ground was higher there. Judging by the artillery barrage that arrived shortly after, he must have found things a little sticky as he was bringing shellfire down on or very close to his own map reference. He arrived back shortly afterwards and said he had seen a Panther coming from the west in our direction. A few minutes later it arrived and stopped about twenty yards from our position. Only a hedge separated us. We were relieved when

PLATE 24. *2nd Essex of 56th Brigade moving into Tilly-sur-Seulles on 19 June past knocked out German Mk V Panther tank. Typical Norman road.*

it moved off again but our relief was short lived. It stopped at the crossroads and started traversing its gun in our direction. Whether it was going to fire at us we didn't know. Fortunately a Firefly of the 4/7 Dragoons, which looked as if it had been following the Panther, stopped where the German tank had originally halted. It fired two quick shots of AP at three hundred yards. The Panther had no chance with two 17 pounders up its stern!

These attacks were successful but at an enormous cost in lives and tanks. The cornfields were filled with bodies and burnt out tanks. The new potatoes, ready to cook, lay bloodstained in the fields. The grotesque dead cows inflated to the size of elephants, with four feet pointing skywards, and overall the smell of dead cow mixed sometimes with overripe camembert from deserted cheese factories on the farms. There was never a moment without the rattle of spandaus or the crack of guns, and the wail and whomp of the Nebelwerfers.

The battles in these killing fields were all so similar – great determination and heroism by the veterans of 50th Division and the tanks of 8th Armoured Brigade. They fought on south. La Belle Epine was cleared by 15 June, and then Tilly was finally cleared by 56th Brigade on the 19th and 20th (Plate 24).

PLATE 25. *'B' Troop 341st Battery's Command Post camouflaged in hedge near Jerusalem crossroads, 13 June 1944. Lt. Sidney Beck GPO on left sorting mail from home.*

Then by 20 June both sides were exhausted and a new front was established in the depth of the bocage either side of Tilly and just north of Hottot which was not itself to fall until mid July.

The cream of 50th Division's infantry died on these fields. The 8th Armoured Brigade lost over 100 tanks, and we had lost Ted Hall, Bob Turnbull, Ken Swann, Pam Pamphilon (a little later), all killed outright, Geoff Street evacuated and George Fanshawe wounded; 50% of our OP officers casualties in ten days.

The Germans too were broken. Panzer Lehr, the finest Panzer division in Normandy, started with 200 tanks – 100 Mk IVs, 90 Panthers and 10 Tigers – and ended with only about 65: two-thirds lost in ten days' fighting.

Montgomery in his messages to us called it 'Keeping the battlefield alive', but at what a cost in unalive men and dead tanks!

Our CO, George Fanshawe, was wounded on 18 June by a mortar which lodged pieces in his head and hand. He was evacuated and sent back to the Field Hospital, and was ready to be flown back to England when the weather broke around 19 June and no planes could fly. George wanted to stay, so he told the sister he was returning to duty; she must have been an understanding woman and she agreed. George then got a message through, ordered up his 'Z' Car and returned to the regiment. He lay on his bed for a week with a

PLATE 26. *'A' Troop 341st Battery's Command Post near Jerusalem crossroads 13 June 1944. Lt. Kalbrier on left, next to him bareheaded with glasses Lt. Craston, GPO.*

blinding headache and a high temperature. On the seventh morning he awoke to find his pillow soaked in sweat, blood and pus and a large piece of mortar on his pillow. He recovered rapidly, and was snapping around at us again, as nasal as ever, in a very short time – the character of the man shines through.

I took no part in this holocaust except to go forward most evenings with the rations, Calvados, and any mail to the OPs. My time was taken up at the gun end, and in particular keeping supplies going. One of my tasks was to keep a watch out for our support vehicles landing at Arromanches and to make sure we got ammunition. Petrol and food were never a problem. Our guns were close to Jerusalem crossroads (Plates 25 and 26).

The first evening I had free I called on my opposite number in 342nd Battery, Claude Hankins, and we went into Bayeux to have dinner at the Lion d'Or hotel. There was little to eat, and we imagined this was because they had no food. We learned later that they had been eaten out of house and home by the war correspondents who were billeted there! We dined on good wine, cider, Calvados, artichokes and Camembert.

I remember my first sight of the Arromanches Mulberry harbour from the top of the cliffs above it. It was quite literally stunning; a vast semicircle of

PLATE 27. *The Mulberry harbour at Arromanches looking towards land along the unloading road from the pierhead where ships docked under shelter of the outer breakwater of sunken ships. Taken on 14 June before the great storm. Arromanches village to right of roadway. The high cliffs to the left lead towards the German strongpoint at Le Hamel stormed on D-Day by 231 Brigade. Gold Beach lies further to the left.*

ships and concrete blocks filled the whole bay, and inside it vast straight roadways floating out to the docks with ships being unloaded by big cranes, and a stream of lorries proceeding shorewards and up the hill past us (see Plates 27 and 30). A huge new road made of steel wire mesh had been bulldozed south out of Arromanches east of Bayeux and ended near our gun position (Plate 29).

By 17 June new divisions were ashore, notably 49th Division, who took over the area east of Tilly around 13 June, captured Cristot and advanced gradually south to Fontenay. Supplies had been coming ashore well now the weather was better. The guns were firing intensely during this period using large quantities of ammunition. On 16 June 341st Battery's eight guns fired 144 rounds per gun in support of 49th Division's attack on Cristot, on 19 June 200 rounds a gun in support of 50th at Hottot and Tilly and another 170 rounds a gun the next day. The 1600 rounds fired on 19 June, for example, represents about eight three-ton lorry loads of ammunition in one day. It was no easy task to keep them supplied, and no easy task to hump over twenty tons by hand.

PLATE 28. *Arromanches. Similar view taken on 24 June after the great storm.*
PLATE 29. *The Bayeux bypass laid across open country on east side of Bayeux from Arromanches to Jerusalem crossroads.*

PLATE 30. *DUKWs going ashore unloading across beaches. Mulberry harbour in background. June 1944.*

The weather broke on 19 June with a major storm, the US Mulberry harbour at Omaha was destroyed, and our own harbour very badly damaged (Plate 28). I watched it being lashed and buffeted on the 19th or 20th, but it just survived. However, our ammunition supply was badly disrupted, and by 21 June I had to ration it to thirty rounds per gun per day, about a fifth of what we had been firing on a busy day up until then.

In the days before the storm broke I used to travel on my journeys on a 125cc motorcycle, which was a marvellous way of getting about; the beach-head at this time was stupendous. There were guns, stores, airfields, Montgomery's HQ at Creully, the whole place was buzzing with activity. But the contrast between the front line and the rear areas will always live in my mind. I quote here from a letter to my father at the end of June, which best describes my feelings.

I have never realized it before Dad but the only people who see any war at all in this party are the chaps up the front i.e. mainly the infantry. They have a hell of a time, how they stick it I don't know. It seems easy to say that our infantry took up a position and all was quiet except for sniping and enemy mortar fire. They live, even at a quiet time, perpetually in trenches and perpetually getting gradual casualties. They are the only people who deserve your thanks and thoughts. The RASC, RAOC, most of the RA, RE and all the oddments have just one big picnic. Ensa shows and anything else that's going.

I feel very strongly on this as I have been with the infantry most of the last three weeks and lived and worked with them. Then we have been back down here and have seen the rest of the army just enjoying themselves anyway comparatively speaking. I wish the Press would stop talking nonsense about the organization and so forth and go and shoot a line for the people that really fight for all of us.

Did any of you hear the one o'clock news today? They gave the gunners a piece of praise for once. For we have won this battle so far, of that there is no doubt.

On 21 June I was summoned to Regimental Headquarters and promoted to the rank of acting Major, to be Battery Commander of the 342nd Battery in place of my old friend Kenneth Swann, who had been killed north of Hottot on the 19th. So I went back to the sharp end with an experienced tank crew of Bdr Williams, signaller, Driver Bullen and my new OPAck Hunter. My X tank bore the scars of the Lingevres battle described earlier in this chapter by Chick Bullen. I had little time to settle in before we were ourselves sent forward towards Hottot.

7
A Month in the Bocage

The static warfare from 21 June until 19 July interspersed with the major battles of 'Epsom' and 'Charnwood'. The regiment's stay in a 'rest' area south of Bayeux from 20 to 28 July. Some poetry and personal feelings of war and fighting. The Normandy campaign in retrospect.

'Bocage' consisted of small fields and sunken lanes both lined with huge banks ten feet wide and as high in places, with woods and apple orchards interspersed with small stone farms. The Camembert and cider country.

By the time I became Battery Commander of 342nd battery on 21 June, both sides on our front had settled down and dug themselves in on a line which stretched from south of Tilly north of Hottot and on to Le-Lion-Vert, and then south-westward to link with the US forces near Caumont (figure 11). Our particular piece of the bocage, at the end of June, was between Lingevres and Hottot.

We soon established a rota of duties at our OPs: twenty-four hours on, twenty-four hours off, unless any attack was expected either by us or the Germans. OP was a misnomer, because in this country you were lucky to be able to see 200 yards. It was an infantry war, and we gunners lived in trenches next door to the infantry command post, who sent out patrols, usually at night or dawn. We fired defensive targets on suspected German positions, and were ourselves periodically fired at, particularly by Nebelwerfers (Plate 31). When these opened up at us, two or three OPs would take a bearing on the mortars, exchange bearings by wireless and locate their positions, and then bring down a 'stonk' of shells onto them. We became quite expert at this, and often the mortaring stopped. We never knew whether we had hit them or just caused them to move, but it raised our morale and more importantly that of the infantry.

My recollection of this period is one of dreary wet weeks with casualties occurring regularly. The real battles were occurring elsewhere. The US forces had made slow progress, and it was a week after D-Day, on 13 June, that the two bridgeheads of Omaha and Utah were joined near Carentan. Then they started to move, and drove westward fast across the Cotentin peninsula to Barneville on the west coast, cutting off Cherbourg from the rest of France.

PLATE 31. *Captured German Nebelwerfer, six-barrelled mortar with wheels for mobility. A devastating weapon in the bocage known also as 'Moaning Minnies'.*

On 22 June they opened their attack on Cherbourg, and the vital port fell on 27 June. The capture of Cherbourg had taken the US forces three weeks of hard fighting in difficult country, against determined German opposition but without a single German Panzer division to oppose them. It was a major landmark, not only because it was the capture of our first port, but also because it freed the US Army and enabled them to come into line with us to our west and to fight southwards with us in the main battle.

'EPSOM'

The reader will remember that the great storm of 19 June had gravely restricted our supplies, particularly ammunition and reinforcements. Montgomery's next major attack, codenamed 'Epsom', was therefore postponed for a few days, and took place on 26 June. This battle took place to the east of our front and was conducted by the British 8th Corps, consisting of three divisions, 43rd, 15th and 11th Armoured all newly arrived in the beachhead. They were to strike southwards, halfway between Tilly-sur-Seulles and Caen, across the river Odon. 49th Division of our own 30 Corps would also attack south on their right flank, just to the east of Tilly (Figure 15).

Our part was limited to firing in support of 49th Division's attacks. We laid down a series of barrages, and fired numerous Corps and Army targets (with up to 700 guns at Epsom). Our OPs remained locked in on our own front.

On the evening of 25 June our guns were busy preparing for a barrage in support of a major attack by 49th Division, near Cristot, east of Tilly-sur-Seulles. Running ahead of my narrative of 'Epsom' below, I give here the next three entries in Lieutenant Beck's diary.

June 26th. The barrage begins at 0415 hrs and we fire 128 rounds per gun. Later the CRA reports 'Barrage was a tremendous success'. As the attack progresses we fire another barrage of 110 rounds per gun at *lunch* time, cursing as always at the frequency with which meal times coincide with a period of hard firing. We are called upon to fire many opportunity [unforecast, mainly moving] targets, and firing continues all night with harrassing tasks. Just before dusk 'F' Sub gun has a premature, fortunately outside the bore, and no one is injured. During the day, which has been overcast, 5 MEs [German Messerschmitts] fly over the gun position and cause quite a stir. The bofors gun, about a quarter of a mile in front of our guns, opens up and joins in the general noise.
June 27th. It rains and blows all day and we feel sorry for the infantry. 49th Division is still progressing and reaches Cheux and Rauray supported by several fire plans and giving us considerable firing [Plate 32]. In our exposed position there is little shelter from the elements and our canvas bivvies give little comfort to the resting gunners. We are cheered however by two sackfulls of mail, but the letters speak of more buzz bombs and create some uneasiness of mind.
June 29th. We are cheered by the news of the capture of Cherbourg by the Americans and we all begin to speculate when it will be ready for use as a port for supplies and reinforcements. The Big Plan must be going well! Our work during the day consists mainly of fire plans in support of patrols of the 1st Battalion Hampshires near Hottot. In the night we fire on a number of targets giving a warm welcome to two SS Panzer Divisions arriving on our front. Monty himself sent the order and told us to 'Give it to them hot'. We did!

The Hertfordshire's Yeomanry contribution to 'Epsom' was limited, but in my view this was one of the decisive battles of Normandy. Three British divisions advanced south through Cheux, against very fierce opposition, crossed the river Odon south of Tourville, and advanced south to Pt 112 near Esquay. They withdrew a little way on 30 June to Baron and the Odon bridgehead. To describe 'Epsom' like this may make it sound like a failure,

PLATE 32. *German casualties of Epsom. A Tiger tank knocked out by Sgt. Dring MM of Nottingham Sherwood Rangers Yeomanry in 49th Division's attack on Rauray, 27 June. In background a Mk IV.*

but on the German side it was seen very differently and was in fact a major British achievement. To appreciate 'Epsom' we need to set the scene.

By 17 June the British and Canadian fronts had stabilized from Caen to Caumont; four German Panzer Divisions and the heavy Tiger group were all facing that front (Figure 16). The US forces had crossed to the west coast of the Contentin peninsula and Cherbourg was cut off. Our landing and reinforcements were coming ashore well enough. Then on 18 and 19 June the great storm arose and destroyed the US Mulberry harbour, stopped new divisions arriving, and cut down all our supplies. This delayed the US attack on Cherbourg, and it also put back Montgomery's next British attack which was to have coincided with or preceded the attack on Cherbourg. The delay caused by this storm was very serious to the Allies and advantageous to the Germans, as they, with no sea problems, could reinforce more quickly than we could, and did so.

On 12 June, a German Panzer Corps of the 9th and 10th SS Panzer Divisions had left Russia for Normandy, arriving there around 20 June. The 1st SS Panzer Division was coming from Belgium and the 2nd SS Panzer

Division was moving up from Toulouse. These four new Panzer Divisions, once ready and concentrated, would be a formidable striking force. 2nd SS Panzer were assembling at St Lô, south of the US forces, but part of it came up to face the British sector as a result of 'Epsom'.

On 25 June, Cherbourg surrendered to the US forces. On that day the newly arrived British 8th Corps carried out their attack across the Odon, 'Epsom', four days late due to the storm. The attack drew into it the 9th and 10th SS Panzer Divisions, part of the 2nd SS Panzer and the 1st SS Panzer as they arrived, as well as part of 21st Panzer, 12th SS Panzer and 2nd Panzer. Panzer Lehr remained to the west of Tilly.

The objective of 'Epsom' was to outflank Caen from the west, as the Germans realized. They were not prepared to have Caen surrounded and reacted very determinedly to prevent it. Had 'Epsom' succeeded in outflanking Caen, it would have been marvellous. In fact, it could only have succeeded if the 10th SS, 9th SS, 1st SS and 2nd SS Panzer Divisions had not countered to stop it. Had some of these divisions been used elsewhere, for example if some of them had moved west against the US sector, 'Epsom' would have succeeded in encircling Caen, but at considerable cost to the US forces, as they were still busy at Cherbourg and were thus unable to face southwards with all their strength.

By 29 June then, the seven German Panzer divisions, or major parts of them, were involved at 'Epsom'. The British withdrawal on 30 June to defensive positions was perfectly timed and done deliberately. The German counter-attacks on 30 June and 1 July were beaten off with the help of intensive artillery, naval fire and air bombardment. One Panzer division (9th SS) was almost annihilated by artillery fire alone.

The result of 'Epsom' was therefore to draw German armour to Caen, and then to destroy that armour, and it represents one of the most important British military successes. 'Epsom' ensured the success of the Normandy campaign, and after this victory, the end for the German armies was inevitable. They were never again able to mount an effective major Panzer attack in Normandy after their losses at 'Epsom' and the US armies remained free, without major armoured opposition, to prepare and mount their offensive 'Cobra' in July.

We, sitting in our slit trenches, were very well aware of its success and significance, because as a result of 'Epsom' the only Panzer divisions available to be moved west to hit the US forces in early July were our old enemies Panzer Lehr, now with only sixty tanks. It was not until 8 July that the units of 2nd SS Panzer engaged at 'Epsom' moved west across our front to the US Sector.

We remained holding our lines west from Tilly in support of 50th Division. On 6 July the regiment's guns moved up to La Belle Epine, some five miles west of Tilly, and we at the OPs moved down to Livry and the high ground west of Caumont, in many cases sharing OPs with the US gunners. In early July, as part of the 2nd SS Panzer Division moved westward, the Germans mounted a series of attacks against us to the east of Caumont. By this time we were well organized to repel them.

In June, soon after taking command of 342nd Battery, I came to the conclusion that our three OP officers needed a forward HQ to provide a meeting place and a resting place close behind us. In addition, the forward HQ could provide spare equipment, especially spare wireless sets, and a spare OP officer. One of our junior subalterns was brought forward with a half-track and a jeep to form this 'Tactical' HQ. This worked very well and saved the OP teams going back to the gun end for supplies. In a battle situation, our Tactical HQ would be with me alongside the headquarters of the battalion we were supporting. In advance of us would be one or two OPs forward with the front-line infantry. I will relate one such action in early July.

We were holding a section of our front line and knew from aerial reports that a German attack was expected. I had one forward OP, Garton Ash, to give me warning of any German build-up, and a second officer, in this case our subaltern Tony Dorling, forward with the advance company. With my Tactical HQ, I was dug into a ditch alongside the infantry battalion headquarters. My fire plan against a German attack was carefully worked out.

Using maps only, I had put myself into the position of a German commander attacking our position and marked out as our targets the routes he was likely to use to attack us: this sunken lane, that belt of trees; where his mortars would be sited; where his forming-up position would be behind that hill or this wood; where his headquarters must be put in that farm. Each of these positions was prerecorded as a target. Of course, we could not see these positions, and could not record them directly with observed fire, but we registered a known feature on the map close to our lines that we could see by firing our guns on it and recording its range and bearing. Using that recorded target as a base, we recorded all the other targets indirectly.

Once the German attack was under way, I tried to visualize where the Germans would be, and brought down the regiment's guns on forming-up places, then the approach routes, with a switch to their presumed headquarters. My OP could use one battery of eight guns if he could see a target, but his view was limited. Tony Dorling, with the forward infantry, also fired a battery once the Germans approached our front line, which was along the edge of a wood.

The defence plan was simple: if the Germans reached the wood, our troops would fall back several hundred yards to prepared positions in the wood itself, alongside six Churchill flame-throwing tanks. Once our infantry had withdrawn, we would shell the edge of the wood, then the infantry and

PLATE 33. *Churchill flame-throwing tank, 'The Crocodile', in action attacking occupied farm buildings.*

Churchill tanks would counter-attack (see Plate 33).

It was similar to many such actions and memorable to me for its complete success. We fired as we planned, and the action ended with few casualties on our side and the Germans flung back and being chased in a horrible fashion through the trees by the flame-throwing tanks.

Over 100 prisoners were taken, and while one of the captured German officers was being interrogated the battalion information officer called me over and said 'Bob you ought to hear this'. The German officer told how his infantry division had moved up to Normandy from near Bordeaux, partly by rail, but mostly by night on foot, and how they had been put in to attack our positions. I quote (in translation):

> It was terrible, we formed up to move forward, and your guns shelled us so we moved to a little wood and the shells followed us. Even our headquarters in the farm was shelled. Then we moved forward down a lane and the shells followed us, and then when we got to your positions, you had gone and more shells came down on us. Then the few of us that were left were chased by horrible flame tanks. It is enough! We lay in a ditch and then surrendered. I have had enough of war.

This was perhaps one of the nicest compliments I have ever been paid as a gunner, and we had the verbatim report posted up on our gun positions for all to read.

'CHARNWOOD'

All through July our orders were to hold our line and keep the pressure going to relieve the US forces on our right who were to make the breakout. We waited and waited, wondering what delayed them. Then on 15 July the regiment moved back east of Tilly to support a major attack, 'Charnwood', on the same front as 'Epsom'. This time we supported 33rd Armoured Brigade and 59th Division. The following extract from Sidney Beck's diary describes this action well.

July 16th. Our new gun position is just south-east of Fontenoy-le-Pesnel, about 3 miles south-east of Tilly. Dawn comes in quietly under cover of a thick mist and we awake to find all around us in the cornfield, Shermans and Churchill flame-throwing tanks, waiting silently for the attack. They belong to the 33rd Armoured Brigade who are supporting 59th Division in the attack on Noyers railway station which bars our way into Villers Bocage from the East [see Plate 34]. The attack begins at 0530 hours when the air suddenly becomes alive with shells from the massed guns. A colossal barrage. In the first two hours we fire over 1500 rounds from the Battery, and the noise is terrific. We eat our breakfast as we fire. Firing continues all day. By teatime we have expended over 2000 rounds and by midnight our total expenditure is 3370 rounds, over 400 rounds per gun. Cordite fumes swirl around the guns, and in the evening hang low over the ripening corn. A very hot, tiring day, not relieved by any good news. 177th Brigade on our left has a very bad start when 12 Shermans run into a cunningly concealed minefield. Despite this, they reach their objectives, but being too weak on the ground, are counter-attacked before they have time to consolidate and are driven back almost to where they started. 197th Brigade on the right reach the station and the church at Noyers after some bitter fighting, but owing to the failure on their left, have to withdraw again to prevent exposing themselves to a flank attack. At 2300 hours, just after it has got really dark, the whole area is raided by German bombers. Bombs and flares are dropped over Caen away on our left. The AA fire is terrific, and we lie in our slit trenches watching the patterns woven by the tracer shells. Anti-personnel and oil bombs are scattered over a wide area, but fortunately, none land near the Battery.

July 17th. The attack is resumed at 0500 hours, but owing to heavy and effective enemy fire on our forming-up areas, the attack does not really get going until midday. We then fire a quick barrage to cover the advance of flame-throwing tanks, then targets follow in quick succession. We have five OPs in action, and orders for Mike and Uncle targets rain upon the Command Posts. By evening a certain amount of progress on our front has been made and our troops consolidate for the night. Almost

PLATE 34. *Tanks of Northants Yeomanry advancing across open fields in 59th Division's attack towards Noyers on 16 July. In centre of the picture with trees in background is 'Z' tank of Lt.-Col. Fanshawe, CO of 86th Field. Col. Fanshawe in turret.*

immediately afterwards the division on our immediate left flank is severely counter-attacked. From 2000 hours onwards the whole divisional artillery fire DF tasks in rapid succession, and the roar of the gunfire thunders over the cornfields. At 2200 hours the situation has not improved and 59th Division artillery join in with harrassing fire (HF) tasks. For two solid hours until midnight we keep up a rapid rate of fire on several targets and the whole area, as far as the eye can see, is trembling under the roar. In the middle of all this confusion, German raiding aircraft again visit the area. The AA fire is even more intense than last night and, to give the lie to the person who said 'It's one of ours', a plane drops huge orange flares directly overhead. Night changes instantly into day and our faces take on ghastly hues in the unnatural light. A rain of AP bombs crackle down away on our left; a stick of HE bombs falls on either side of the roadway about 300 yards behind the guns, and a farm to our right rear goes up in flames. Every man stays at his post and the guns keep up their murderous rate of fire. Then at midnight a hush falls over the great gun area as the guns cease firing. Except for the noise of weary gunners picking their way through piles of cartridge cases and ammunition salvage, and the crackling of the burning farmstead, everything becomes unbelievably quiet. We turn in to our blankets with a feeling of triumph.

July 18th. Those of us who have been on night duty see an unforgettable dawn. The eastern sky is filled with every conceivable shade of red, from rose-petal pink to vivid scarlet, with great feathery clouds extending over the dome of the heaven. Into this beautiful scene a long black stream of Lancaster bombers comes in from the coast, circles south of Caen, drops its bombs and wheels for home. For over an hour the long procession winds its way against the background of scarlets and yellows and gold. Later, as the sun rises, another stream of bombers, Liberators and Fortresses, flies overhead further inland, to keep up a most intensive bombing of the areas supplying the German front line. This is a prelude to a hot and dusty, but quiet day, and we relax from yesterday's excitement. We learn that the station at Noyers is in our hands, but that most of the town is still strongly held by the enemy. The CO congratulates the regiment on its fine performance yesterday, especially during the raid in the evening.

My own recollection of this battle with 59th Division is hazy, not so much because my memory is poor, but because the whole three days passed in a haze of dust and a cacophony of noise.

Stephen Perry, with 341st Battery, and myself and Garton Ash with 342nd Battery, were advancing with the 33rd Armoured Brigade in our Shermans. The country here was rolling, with more open fields, and the weather had cleared up. We did not take part in the fighting on the 15th, but joined the tanks for their advance on the 16th and 17th. On the 17th we formed up at about 0600 hours, moved forward and then stuck. Then we moved forward later in the morning through areas covered with shell craters and burned-out Shermans, carriers, German tanks and guns. We could see little as the dust obscured everything, and we fired mainly from the map. The battle went on all that day and half the night, as we too were bombed. Early the next morning we were bombed again; this time by our own bombers!

On the 18th things sorted themselves out somehow, and we advanced and captured Noyers, or at least the northern part of it. The battle then quietened down, we laagered for the night close to our tanks, and were bombed again. I remember I was returning on foot from our order group, and was caught in the open. I dived promptly under the nearest lorry, snuggling my head and body as close as I could to its large tyres and wheels. However, we had few casualties, and the next morning, 19 July, we were ordered back to our old front west of Tilly.

SUMMER HOLIDAY AT ST ANDRÉ

From 20 to 28 July the regiment was moved out of the line into a rest area at the little hamlet of St André, in peaceful country a few miles south of Bayeux; the first time we and the guns had been out of action since D-day.

Directly we were ordered out of the line on 19 July, I arranged to meet my Battery Captain, Claude Hankins, at St André, and drove there ahead of the battery. The regiment's rest area was in a typical Norman high-hedged field, next door to a small hamlet and just across the road from the 'Château'. Actually, the Château was a modest country house with a French family in residence, who had two charming daughters.

Regimental headquarters was naturally housed in the Château, but Claude had done well, he had taken over two small cottages; one for an Officer's Mess, one for a Sergeant's Mess and best of all, a large barn as a general Battery Mess Room and shelter. He had even got to work and collected tables and benches.

We discussed our plans, and decided that we would have a real slap-up lunch on our first day. Claude then went off to organize supplies. Various vans and lorries disappeared, to come back with good Norman beef, eggs, butter, cheese and barrels of cider. Our first lunch was to be a real treat after six weeks of tinned food, and accompanied by cider for every man.

We all settled into our area on a fine evening and slept well. I was up at 0630, with our first parade of all troops scheduled at 0800, to start maintenance and cleaning of all our guns and equipment. There were grim grey skies that morning, and a persistent wetting downpour. At 0730 I called a conference with my Troop Commanders and the Battery Sergeant-Major (BSM), and decided that we would postpone the 0800 parade until the rain lifted. I could see little point in unwrapping guns and weapons only to get them wet. So all members of my battery stayed in their tents or bivouacs and I retired too to have a second cup of coffee.

At 0830 my BSM rushed in and informed me that the Colonel was approaching. Out I went, saluted smartly, and got a right old dressing down. Why weren't you on parade? He would have no slackness in his regiment. Maintenance was our first job, and if I wanted to keep my job, I had better smarten things up pronto. George Fanshawe then stormed off to the next battery to deal out the same treatment to them.

So, out with the troops into the rain and off with the covers. We cleaned and maintained as ordered, with grumbles rising in the rain. Everything was soaked, but orders are orders.

I asked Sawyer, my BSM, to post sentries and runners to warn us of any further visitations. The first arrival was Eric Scammell, the Battery Commander of 462nd Battery. He was bright red in the face and boiling over. 'Bob, have you had that bastard Fanshawe chewing your balls off too? I'm standing no more.' We eventually simmered him down and decided on a protest to the Regiment's second in command. So we contrived a quiet session with John Morgan-Smith and let him know that we were both seething at being dressed down by the Colonel in front of our own men and officers.

John was sympathetic and we left it to him. He was a great diplomat, and the only person capable of talking to George Fanshawe about such a matter.

Back to my own battery and I wondered whether I was wise to go ahead with our plans for lunch. I stuck to my plans, and at 1230 everyone stopped maintenance and cleaned themselves up for lunch. The barn was beautifully laid out with tables and seats, food all ready and rows of barrels of cider. As the troops filed in, they collected their cider and food, and the officers and sergeants moved around helping and serving. Just as it was getting under way, up came Sawyer and whispered 'The runner has just reported that the Colonel is on his way.' Hell! I thought, that is the end of my reign as Battery Commander. I met George at the entrance with a smart salute, and in he strode. Dead silence while he strolled around, looking at the cider and the roast beef. He strode over to me and said, 'Bloody good show Bob, best thing I have seen today.' I had the courage to offer him a mug of cider, which he drank, and then went off with a beaming grin to talk to my officers and men. The sun broke through, actually and metaphorically.

I remember little of the rest of those seven days at St André, except that it gave me a chance to meet and get to know the officers and men of my battery, which had been impossible on the battlefield, as I was always away from the gun end up at an OP. We also had the opportunity of seeing our brother officers at the Regimental Mess or at other battery messes, and most evenings we entertained them, or they us. It is Sidney Beck's recollections which best capture the atmosphere of St André.

Originally we were told that we would spend four days at the Rest Area, but in the end we had eight days of well earned change from battle conditions, from July 20th to July 28th. I say 'change' rather than rest as we were soon to learn that resting and maintenance were impossible at one and the same time.

We had an unfortunate start, as our first day was completely miserable in pouring rain. We did make an attempt at cleaning and maintenance but the CO on his first visit quickly showed us that our attempts were not Yeoman Standards. The only man who earned his favour was a man who was getting wet cleaning his vehicle. To clean your vehicles you want water, and what better supply can you have than good honest-to-goodness rainwater? That was the dictum, so out of our bivvies we came, and set to to remove the mud of eight weeks battle. It was a hard lesson to learn but it was one we never forgot. When next we were to have a 'Rest' period, the mud and grime of battle came off very quickly. Inspections, cleaning and maintenance occupied most of our time in the first three days, and it was not until the last few days that we were able to see the countryside and visit Bayeux and the neighbourhood.

One piece of very useful work was done, and that was the conversion of our ammunition half-tracks into GPOs trucks. The REME Light Aid Detachment (LAD) worked overtime cutting back doors and welding gadgets inside, and undoubtedly the efficiency of the regiment was greatly increased by this changeover. It was in fact quite a hard time for all fitters and we were to see the value of their work later in the great dash to Antwerp!

During the course of one of his inspections, the CO observed a camouflage net lying in a corner of B Troop's orchard. 'Huh! what's this doing lying about?' he snorted, and poked it with his cane. 'Quack! Quack!' replied the camouflage net. Peering closer, he snorted again 'Huh! what's the meaning of this? Ducks? Loot I suppose! Well, I'll look into this, but I don't want to see them again, see!' So the fate of Donald the Duck and his companions was sealed. Very regretfully Tydeman wrung their necks and one evening prepared a sumptuous spread for certain friends of Donald's. He died in a good cause and it was the best meal we had had since leaving England.

One memory of the camp which stands out in my mind was the memorial service to our fallen which we held on the Sunday morning. Our casualties, especially in officers, had been high. In action we had been too preoccupied to remember them, but there in the quiet Normandy orchards, we suddenly realized they were no longer with us. It was altogether right and proper that we should remember them, and we were grateful to the Corps Commander Royal Artillery (CCRA) for adding his dignity to the service.

One could not help being struck by the incongruity of the setting, in the grounds of a French Château, until recently a German HQ where the Nazi officers had slept with their French mistresses. British soldiers stood in a hollow square. L/Sgt. Bracey, so familiar at a typewriter, had an air of solemnity as he played the piano, brought by the Padre in a lorry and manhandled by the RSM into position. There was a jarring note when the over zealous BSM of another battery addressed his men by saying 'For Christ's sake get into line!' Yet somehow, with all this incongruity, we did manage to create a tiny British Church under the open sky, and for a brief while paid our respect to the dead and the mystery of life.

Our chief recreation lay in trips to Bayeux for ENSA shows and to sample the Normandy wares (and women?). If memory serves me right, the films showing were 'Wintertime' with Sonja Henje and 'Going My Way' with Bing Crosby. Although we had seen both films in those far off days in Romsey, we did not much mind seeing them once again. There was the usual ENSA Concert Party at the Bayeux Theatre, with plenty of jokes about the sea-sick soldiers and how the comedian found his way to Normandy by following the train of vomit bags in the Channel!! For most of us it was our first visit to a Continental Theatre and we were interested in the little private boxes on ground level and the crude latrine arrangements.

There was the Cathedral to see, the replica of the tapestry, and that quaint carved wooden pulpit. On the Sunday afternoon there was a football match between a British Services team and the Bayeux Sporting Club. It was a lovely sunny afternoon and many of the local inhabitants turned out in their Sunday best to watch the game. Just over two months previously, German soldiers had played here, but they never played any French teams and the people did not come to watch.

We were surprised by the excellent football the French played, their goalkeeper giving a very fine display. I cannot remember the result, but I fancy the French won by the odd goal. But I do remember that once a rabbit dashed across the field and the players and spectators, as one man, forgot the game. In his headlong dash, the rabbit left the pitch littered with the bodies of players who had made vain dives to catch him. The crowd jumped to their feet and cheered like mad before the frightened creature made a headlong dive into the crowd near the goal posts. An Irish Guardsman caught him and in a trice the rabbit was dead and being tucked away in a Battle Dress blouse. It took some time to get the game restarted.

One other feature of Bayeux was the bath, where upwards of fifty soldiers had hot showers all in one large room together, and where the attendant shouted 'Time' after every seven minutes or so, to permit another fifty to bathe. However, our bathing facilities improved, and at the end of our stay in the rest area we had the pleasure of using for the first time a Mobile Laundry and Bath Unit. Admittedly, it was a bit draughty in the marquee but it was a great boon to get a complete change of laundry and receive new shirts and towels in exchange for the worn ones we handed in.

No description of our rest area would be complete without a passing reference to the sports side. With our limited resources we did play a few games of soccer and, by a little 'Press-gang methods', we persuaded certain people that they could play hockey. The pitch was covered with mole-hills and ant-hills but even this and Meyer's inexperience in goal does not quite explain why 342nd Battery beat us by 14 goals to nil!

Last, but not least, was the pleasant invitation from the Devons, an infantry battalion of 50th Division, who were resting in the orchards just behind us, to visit their concert. Somehow or other they had contrived to make a stage with curtains and screens. From somewhere, and by means only the infantry knew, they had acquired a piano. Bdr. Jarvis fitted up a Tannoy system. The Devons Company Commander was an amazingly forceful person who got us singing community songs and rattled off sketches very quickly. Those who were there will never forget the sketch of the dying soldier lying in a shell hole pitifully crying for water. In a nearby shell hole lies another wounded soldier, who does the Sidney act and throws over his water bottle with its last few precious drops. Does the dying soldier drink the water? Of course not, he's British. He whips off his gaiters, out with his brush and cake of blanco, and blancoes!

Yes, we appreciated those jokes at the end of our rest camp. But when all was said and done we were not sorry when we heard that we were to go back into action and begin work again. We were to relieve the 90th Field Regiment who were up by La Belle Epine. La Belle Epine! Heavens! We were there on July 7th and it is now July 28th! Three weeks, and our front line had not moved forward. Things must have been very difficult. Were the Germans going to succeed after all and prevent us from breaking out? Very soon we were to learn that at that very moment the breakout was just beginning, and we would soon be far beyond La Belle Epine.

I will now follow with some 'verses' written in St André by 'BLOM', the *nom de plume* of two of 342nd Battery, Messrs Blakeby and Bottom. If you can stomach the poetry, these will give you another flavour!

The 342 in Action

You've heard about our fighting men
who invaded Scotland's shores, [Our pre-invasion exercise in Bute]
here is another ode about them
now they are really in the wars.

After frantic preparations
at Romsey's C14
they have entered into battle
which before they had never seen.

T'was on the sixth of flaming June
the day we know as D,
that they sailed across the Channel
to the shores of Normandy.

The wind blew strong, the waves rose high
and despite the heaving seas,
the gunners kept on firing
from those gallant LCTs.

At zero hour plus sixty
the SPs stormed the land,
and took up their position
by some shell holes in the sand.

The infantry advanced with speed
and pushed the Hun right back,
and the SPs lumbered forward
to support this great attack.

Hour by hour we gained more ground
each counter-attack was quelled,
and after three days fighting
the bridgehead was formed and held.

The going at the OP's tough
we're sure that you'll admit,
and there are some who cannot take it
and eventually they quit.

At the OP Ted will take a turn [Not Ted Hall!]
a slit-trench is his pet,
he ducks from mortars, shells and bombs
and Russell checking net. [Wireless operator? tuning in]

There's some worthy Scotsmen in our midst
young Gordon Smith is one,
with knocking knees and shaking sten
he captured sixteen Hun.

There is a sergeant in HQ
of whom we're very fond,
he hasn't seen much action yet
but then he's no dumb blonde.

After thirty days hard fighting
there came storming down the ramps,
a band of fearless heroes
who'd been guarding Larkill's Camps.

[A reference to the rear party left in England with our reserve stores under command of Captain Norman who before the war ran a laundry]

They knew no fear these gallant men
and led by Mr. Woo,
they sallied forth to battle
and the rear-guard was our Q.

They had to get the cargo through
to our B.K. Captain Hanko,
it wasn't ammo, food or kit
but bags and bags of blanco.

[Battery Captain of 342nd Battery Claude Hankins]

After days and days of sweat and toil
and giving of our best,
it was with joy we heard the news
we are going for a rest.

It didn't take us very long
to get our kit packed up,
and on arrival there we found
that we'd been sold a pup.

The rest turned out to be a farce
bullshine appeared once more,
and the BSM was king again
laying down the law.

We had to blanco straight away
and make up kits as well,
and what with bags of maintenance
we worked like Little Nell.

When we had a Church parade
the men were smart and snappy,
excepting one, you know his name,
his tunic was bomb-happy.

We used to cook the food ourselves
and did quite well you see,
the rations seem much shorter now
they must be on Q three. [i.e. rations provided from the Battery Quartermaster's truck Q.3]

But in spite of all our troubles
we really mustn't cry,
for anything is better
than to be a P.B.I. [Poor Bloody Infantry]

Our rest at St André gave us all time for reflection, and it now gives me a chance to describe various aspects of our short war, and to answer some of the questions which I am often asked. The commonest of these must be:

'Were you frightened?'

Fear, I believe, affects everyone at some time, but each individual is affected differently. For myself, I was rarely frightened in battle, and if I was, it never lasted for long. My fear was always of the unknown, and occurred particularly when I was alone. The fear which grows so that it is uncontrollable by the individual is not only devastatingly traumatic to him, but is contagious to those around him.

Medically, I suppose this kind of fear is a form of deep shock. Certainly the patient loses all control of his actions. He goes deathly pale and sweats profusely. 'Shell shock', as it was described in World War I, or 'Bomb Happy' in my War, seems unpredictable, and manifests itself very suddenly. I have recalled one incident at Tilly on 10 June. George Fanshawe recalls one occasion when the CO of the brigade we were supporting, who was a veteran of Africa and a very brave man, broke down and simply refused to come out of a deep slit trench for a day and a half.

I remember when one OP officer was affected and evacuated, and I was given the task of taking his bren carrier, with its crew of three, back to the rear area. It was all quite peaceful, but at every bend in the road the driver would stop, and he and the crew would refuse to go on unless I reassured them it was safe. I even had to walk round the corners first. I had to take over as driver and constantly reassure them that it was safe and I knew it was safe. The whole crew were quite incapable of reacting normally.

'Did you hate the Germans?'

Again, a personal question. Some of the bravest men I met in Normandy certainly did hate them intensely and personally. I never did, but I never had to stick a bayonet in a German; a gunner's war is generally more remote. I remember once when I was with a troop of tanks, a German truck came down the road beside us, we opened fire and the truck blew up. I advanced on foot to find several German soldiers dead, and lying in the road. As I stood over one he twitched and moaned. I remember drawing my revolver thinking I ought to finish him off – rather like putting a dog out of its misery – and then suddenly realizing that he was a young man of my age and that instead of shooting him I ought to help him, which we then did.

No one who fought in Normandy had anything but admiration for the fighting ability of the German soldiers regardless of whether or not they hated them. In my view, as professional soldiers, they were superior to any but the very best troops in the Allied Forces.

'Were you depressed and did you think you might be beaten?'

Reading people's diaries tends to give the impression that one was living on a perpetual 'high'. As far as D-Day and the advance to Antwerp was concerned, this was true. During the carnage in the bocage from 11 June to the end of July I was never really depressed, except at the killing and the mud, but one did become apathetic and disinclined to be adventurous. One became wary and careful. I remember one period in July when we were manning an OP west of Caumont. Things were quiet and we were comfortable alongside an American OP. I knew, as a Major, I ought to be out visiting the infantry in the front line first thing each morning, but somehow it was easier and probably safer to lie low and do very little. It was very easy to withdraw from the war.

In Normandy, no one I met had any doubt that we would win the battle. We never believed that the Germans would hold us, and breaking out was only a matter of time.

'What did you eat?'

Another vital question. In the early days in Normandy and while we were mobile, our rations consisted of the '14 Man Pack'; This was a box about two feet by nine inches, which contained a complete diet for fourteen men for a day or seven men for two days and there were six different menus. They were really superb; mostly tinned or dried food, but of excellent variety. Army biscuits about 2½″ square and ½″ thick, though some were smaller, tinned stews, steak and kidney puddings, corned beef, spam, tinned bacon, Ambrosia rice pudding, cheese, marmalade and strawberry jam remain in my memory, as well as boiled sweets, chocolate bars and of course tins of cigarettes and latrine paper.

My favourites were corned beef with strawberry jam on an army biscuit, bacon and marmalade on a biscuit, or creamed Ambrosia rice with dollops of jam. Garton Ash remembers the steak and kidney puddings and currant duff.

On a tank we 'brewed up' (made tea) on a primus stove, or merely a tin of sand with petrol in it. We always had tea, never coffee, unless we were with the Americans, when great swaps went on and we got instant coffee from them. In Normandy of course there was plenty of butter, cheese and often eggs to buy or liberate. At the gun end, once things settled down, each troop had a cookhouse and normal army cooking was done.

'What about toilets?'

This varied. On the gun positions, or where we were in a settled position, proper latrines were always dug. These consisted of a deep narrow trench, over which one either squatted or usually sat on a pole – flat and as smooth as possible! Hygiene was rigorous, the rules were clear: never dig a latrine within thirty feet of a stream, well or river; never uphill of a water supply; always fill in afterwards and always mark the site so that the next occupiers know what to avoid.

When we were mobile, we carried entrenching tools, and each person dug his own hole and squatted. I always preferred a backrest, and would find a convenient tree, dig my hole, and then squat with a nice backrest, light my pipe and enjoy the summer morning air.

In a tank during a battle, having a pee was a problem, because no container was leak proof while the tank was bucking over obstacles. We held our water and then prayed to be let out. I remember one terrible case where the Tank Commander had to stop to relieve himself, so they pulled up in a quiet spot and out he got. As he was spending his penny a few yards off, a German gun got his tank, which blew up, killing all his crew and leaving him as the only survivor (three lives for a penny).

'What was the relationship like between Officers and Men?'

Traditionally in all armies, disciplinary requirements make a distinction between officers and 'other ranks'. At the same time, although a Sergeant-Major is 'an other rank', the difference between him and a Gunner is vast. During this campaign, officers did eat or mess separately; we did have camp beds in rest areas, and we did each have a 'batman'; but at war, particularly in a tank, the difference between ranks did not exist. We slept together, ate together, peed together and fought and died together. Any extra comfort the officer had was fully earned. He was always last to sleep, as he had to attend midnight order groups. He was invariably more likely to be killed or wounded, and he took decisions for the rest of the men.

THE NORMANDY CAMPAIGN IN RETROSPECT

By 27 July when we left St André the Normandy campaign had been decided. The British attack 'Goodwood' east of Caen on 18–20 July had ground to a halt in mud, 88mms and Tigers but prepared the ground for the US attack in the west. This attack, 'Cobra', carried out by General Bradley's 1st Army started on 24 July and by 27 July was breaking through. So this is an appropriate moment to analyse Montgomery's Normandy campaign.

Although the success of Montgomery's tactics in Normandy are now generally recognized, accounts by some writers and displays in the French museums tend to concentrate on the US, and naturally the French, contributions. I am in no way wishing to belittle the role played by the US 1st Army under Omar Bradley; they had to do the hard task of clearing and advancing in difficult country against determined German infantry and succeeded brilliantly. The US 3rd Army, however, under General Patton (which included the French Division), who figured so prominently in the later advance across France, had little fighting to do in Normandy. In summer 1944 they reaped the benefit of the fighting done by the British 2nd Army, the Canadians and the US 1st Army.

Geography, our command of the air, and the German dispositions dictated Montgomery's strategy, which was to keep the German armour around Caen on the east away from the US 1st Army, so that Bradley could take Cherbourg and then break out.

Geography

Our air forces and the French Resistance effectively cut all bridges across the Seine between the sea and Paris, and across the Loire between the sea and Orleans. Thus all German troops coming to Normandy had to detour through the gap of sixty miles between Paris and Orleans or cross the rivers by ferry. And of course, the nearest part of the Normandy front to this 'gap' was the Caen area, in the British sector.

Deception

It was an extraordinary achievement of the Allies' deception plan that the Germans regarded the Pas de Calais area as our main objective and Normandy, even after we had landed, as a diversion. The Allied deception plan succeeded to the extent that right through June and even July, they still kept forces north of the Seine.

Air Control

The Allied air control over Normandy was vital to the protection of our troops during and after the landing, and of course, played a major part on the actual battlefield all through the campaign.

Resistance

The French Resistance also played an equally vital task. All German reinforcements lost tanks, vehicles and time to Resistance attacks. The 2nd SS Panzer Division, as we have recorded, arrived in Normandy in late June, and some part of it was thrown into the 'Epsom' battle on 29 and 30 June. This division was stationed in south-west France at Montauban in Gascony, and started north to Normandy just after D-Day. It took them six days to cover the first 90 miles! Then they had to make diversions and a journey of 400 miles took them over three weeks, with constant battles against the Maquis. They shot 100 hostages near Brive, 600 near Limoges and another 50 near Périgeux. I can find no record of German casualties in men, tanks or vehicles, but they must have been considerable to merit such savage reprisals.

German Panzer Divisions in Normandy

Figures 16–18 and the following information compiled from Eric Lefevre's *Panzers in Normandy – Then and Now* show the success of Montgomery's strategy and they vividly illustrate the difference between the armoured forces facing the British and those relatively few facing the US armies. Of course, armour does not tell the full story, but the Panzer divisions with their tanks and their Panzer Grenadier infantry were elite fighting forces and their infantry and anti-tank gunners were usually much superior to the ordinary German infantry division. Furthermore, a great preponderance of the German 155mm and 8mm guns were opposite Caen.

Figure 16 shows the Panzer attacks against the Allies from D-Day until mid June. You will see that they were all against the British and Canadians. Figure 17 shows the relative forces facing the British and US forces at the time of 'Epsom' at the end of June. Figure 18 shows the same at the end of July. The following statistics give German Panzer division strengths in June and July against the British and US sectors with dates and areas of their first battles.

Against British Sector in June

21st Panzer Division	6 June Caen
98 Mark IVs	
43 75mm Assault Guns	
68 obsolete tanks	
12th SS Panzer (Hitler Jugend)	7 June west of Caen
91 Mark IVs	
48 Panthers	
10 88mm Assault Guns	
Panzer Lehr	9 June Tilly-sur-Seulles
100 Mark IVs	
90 Panthers	
14 Tigers	
31 Assault Guns (some 88mm)	
2nd Panzer	15 June Tracy Bocage
94 Mark IVs	
67 Panthers	
41 Assault Guns	
2nd SS Panzer (Das Reich)	29 June Epsom (part)
44 Mark IVs	
25 Panthers	
44 Assault Guns	
1st SS Panzer (Liebstandarte Adolf Hitler)	30 June Epsom
42 Mark IVS	
38 Panthers	
44 Assault Guns	
9th SS Panzer (Hohenstaufen)	29 June Epsom
41 Mark IVs	
30 Panthers	
38 Assault Guns	
10th SS Panzer (Frundsberg)	29 June Epsom
32 Mark IVs	
7 Panthers	
34 Assault Guns	

plus the following heavy brigade:

Schwer SS Panzer Ab 101	13 June Villers Bocage
37 Tigers	
3 Assault Guns	

It will be seen how formidable Panzer Lehr was: twice as powerful as, for example, 2nd Panzer or 21st Panzer and three times the power of 9th or 10th SS Panzer. SS Panzer Ab 101 was a superb heavy strike force attached to 1st SS Panzer Corps (1st and 12th SS Panzer Divisions).

Against the US Sector in June

17th SS Panzer Grenadiers (Götz von Erlichingen) 37 Assault Guns	6 June Carentan
Panzer Ersatz. Training Unit 15 old French tanks Some Assault Guns	6 June Ste-Mère-Église
Panzer Ab. Training unit 22 old French and Mk III tanks Some Assault Guns	9 June Contentin peninsula

During June, therefore, the following armoured vehicles were engaged in the two sectors:

	British and Canadian	*US*
Tigers	51	0
Panthers	282	0
Mark IVs	520	0
Assault Guns	266	37
Obsolete Tanks	68	37

These figures on the British and Canadian front are based on the known strength of Panzer divisions used (but 50% only of the 2nd SS Panzer) plus SS Panzer Ab 101's Tigers.

July

By 1 July the German Panzers had been reduced to the following figures, including replacements, so actual losses were higher. Note that 2nd SS Panzer was only half strength in the beginning and received sufficient new tanks to increase its strength even after its losses. No figures are given for 9th and 10th SS Panzers but their losses at 'Epsom' were heavy.

21st Panzer	Mark IVs	from	98 to 61
12th SS Panzer	Mark IVs		91 to 32
	Panthers		48 to 24
Panzer Lehr	Mark IVs		100 to 36
	Panthers		90 to 32
	Tigers		14 to 0

2nd Panzer	Mark IVs	94 to 85
	Panthers	67 to 21
2nd SS Panzer	Mark IVs	44 to 50
	Panthers	25 to 26
1st SS Panzer	Mark IVs	42 to 30
	Panthers	38 to 25
Schwer SS Panzer Ab 101		37 to 11

During July the following forces moved to the US sector:

Panzer Lehr	30 Mark IVs and 30 Panthers	7 July
2nd SS Panzer	50 Mark IVs and 20 Panthers	9 July
2nd Panzer	32 Mark IVs and 6 Panthers	29 July

The following arrived in the British sector:

Schwer Pz Ab 503	45 Tigers	7 July	Caen
Schwer Pz Ab 102	28 Tigers	9 July	Caen
Schwer Pz Ab 654	25 Jäger Panther Assault Guns	29 July	Aunay

So until the very end of July, the approximate position for the month was:

	British and Canadians	*US*
Tigers	84	0
Panthers	107	50
Mark IVs	281	80

It is no surprise at all, faced with these facts, to realize that a breakthrough at Caen was always highly unlikely, but that a breakthrough in the centre or west was always possible, and it was achieved in the west. It is important also to stress Montgomery's strategy of constant attacks, which was intended not only to keep the Panzers on the eastern sector, but also to prevent them being withdrawn from the line to refit and concentrate so that they could form a formidable Panzer attacking force, which could have been used as a battering ram against any part of the Allied Front. There were just not enough German infantry divisions to replace the Panzer forces in the front line to contain our continual attacks.

The success of Montgomery's tactics are shown so clearly by the fact that when 'Cobra' struck at the end of July it was opposed by only the remnants of Panzer Lehr with about sixty tanks, and the remainder of 2nd Panzer and 2nd SS Panzer Divisions, and they could be overwhelmed. When the Germans finally used their armour against the US sector at Mortain on 6 August, it was too late, and they were destroyed.

8
Breakthrough

The US Army's breakout at the end of July 1944. The regiment's advance south and south-east with 43rd Division of 30 Corps. The capture of Mount Pinçon in Operation 'Bluecoat'. The advance through the retreating German forces to Condé-sur-Noireau and Flers.

On 28 July we were back in the line, still waiting for the US breakout. However, the next day the news was good; by 1 August the US troops had broken through, and were spilling out of Normandy through Avranches and Pontaubault (Figure 19). General Bradley had taken his time, and rightly so, as the US forces had had to fight all the way in difficult country against tough German opposition. They could never have done it had they been faced with the German armour and guns that faced the British and Canadians. But the plan worked and it was worth every week of waiting.

By 30 July we knew that the 'front' was breaking up. There was a new feeling in the air; the bonds were broken. We left 50th Division after nearly two months of fighting alongside them, and joined 43rd Division.

On 31 July we were to take part in the advance south-eastward from Caumont, to capture Mont Pinçon and go on to Condé-sur-Noireau. This advance, called 'Bluecoat', was to be supported also by our old friends of the 8th Armoured Brigade (Map 19). On 31 July the guns were in action south-east of Caumont. Instead of advancing, however, we were held up south of Caumont while priority on the roads was given to the 7th Armoured Division on our left flank for their attacks on Villers Bocage and Aunay-sur-Odon. We sent OPs to help their attacks, and watched while our bombers pounded the two small towns. The 7th Armoured Division proceeded slowly, and it was not until 3 August that we could move. The delay was frustrating, especially since everyone on our right was moving forward. However, on 3 August we moved to Jurques, and by 7 August we had taken Mont Pinçon. Then we moved due south to Condé-sur-Noireau and arrived there on 14 August.

On 15 August we left 43rd Division, and joined the 11th Armoured Division at Flers on 17 August. We then moved east round the bottom of the Falaise Gap to spend the night of 18 August at Ecouché.

We travelled from Caumont to Mont Pinçon, about twenty miles, in four days, and from there to Condé-sur-Noireau, which was about fifteen miles away, in seven days. From Flers to Ecouché was thirty miles, and the journey took a day and a half. 'Motoring' or 'swanning', rather than fighting, had started. It was rather like driving a car; first you are held up in a traffic jam, then you are crawling in second gear, then all of a sudden the road is clear and you are in top gear and away.

While we were held, the Americans were away. On 31 July Avranches and Pontaubault were taken, and the breakout had started. From 1 August onwards Patton's 3rd Army was spilling out south, west and south-eastward over Brittany and Normandy, with no German opposition. It was like the spring coming in the Arctic Sea; one week everything is frozen solid, then the ice begins to crack and you can move again, slowly at first in case you hit an iceberg, and then as 'leads' of water open up, you follow them and suddenly you are in the open sea and away. Patton's 3rd Army, who had not yet done any fighting, were launched direct into the 'open sea'. We, like the US 1st Army, with whom we had made the breakout possible, still had a fortnight's hard fighting to come, battling through the 'ice floes' of German tanks. On the left of the bridgehead the opposition was still solid, and the Canadians and Poles south of Caen had a bloody three weeks of battling against the main German resistance ('Totalaize', Figure 19).

Montgomery's battle of Normandy, though not yet over, had been won convincingly, exactly as planned and exactly as we had expected. The Germans tried to shut the door with a Panzer counter-attack at Mortain on 7 August, but it was too late. The US 1st Army repulsed them with massive air support, particularly the RAF Typhoons with their rockets, which virtually wiped out an entire Panzer division caught in the open. By 9 August the Germans were in full retreat. By 13 August the Poles and Canadians had fought forward to Falaise with great determination and many casualties. Patton had advanced swiftly from the south against little opposition, to reach Argentan on 13 August.

The German armies from Normandy were trapped in the Falaise pocket and shelled and bombed relentlessly as they fled eastward between Falaise and Argentan. On 20 August the Falaise Gap was closed, and the Germans left in the pocket were either killed or surrendered. The battle for Normandy was over, and the race to Germany itself had started.

OPERATION 'BLUECOAT'

Our part in this last chapter of Normandy was Operation 'Bluecoat' (Figure 20). The country through which we were to advance south-east of Caumont was some of the most attractive in Normandy; rolling hills with open fields of pasture and many small woods and apple orchards. It was apple and dairy country, lush in the summer weather; it had now stopped raining. As we moved south-east, the hills became more wooded, and were higher with steep river valleys. The area of Mont Pinçon and the hilly country to its east is known as the Suisse Normande, because of its lovely wooded hills and ravines. Beyond this to the south and east it is flatter and more open.

On 2 August I was with the leading column of armoured cars and tanks when we halted just outside a little village called Jurques (Plate 35). Jurques was on a south-facing ridge, with a main road running north–south through it down to the valley to the south, across a river and up a wooded hill. German tanks, from a wood on the other side of the river to the south about 1500 yards away, had knocked out three of our tanks as they tried to cross the main road at Jurques. I was called forward and, moving carefully and using my glasses, I could see a flash or two of sun glinting at the edge of the wood. I called 'Battery target', and soon our shells were falling, the Germans withdrew and our advance continued.

Such determined German resistance, with guns and tanks, was to be repeated time and time again for the next ten days with tank casualties on our side. On 1 August Stephen Perry reported that eleven Churchill tanks had been 'brewed up' by a Tiger in ten minutes flat (actually an 88mm Jäger Panther assault gun of Schwer Pz Ab 654).

On 3 August the guns moved up east of Jurques. Stephen Perry is with his troop of guns:

August 3rd. We move off and at 0800 hours arrive in our new gun area half a mile west of Jurques. But what a gun position! We are on a forward slope overlooked by a long ridge 2000 yards in front, but the Commander Royal Artillery (CRA) of 43rd Division has ordered us in here despite our CO's attempts to dissuade him, so here we have got to stay.

At 1130 the inevitable happens and we are heavily shelled by 105mm guns, but luckily there are no casualties because we have a sunken lane behind the guns which provides good cover. At 1200 the 105s come over again and we remain safe and sound in our sunken lane; but here is something coming over quicker than a 105, probably an 88, perhaps it is a Tiger. I take a dekko through my glasses and there is the flash, and the tank, sitting just below the skyline. What a target for him, 24 SPs all lined up on a forward slope within easy range. Well, we will have a go at him. I grab the first three chaps I can see and jump onto E subsection's SP. As we get up, Sgt. Fielding gets hit by a high explosive shell (HE), but the rest of us are all right. Tulloch jumps into the driving seat and I direct him onto the tank and lay the gun for the first round. Just after it is fired there is a hell of a bang and G Sub's SP is covered in dust and smoke – it has had a direct hit. It will be us next if we do not get a move on. We bracket him with 4 rounds, but he has spotted us, because

PLATE 35. *Jurques. The main street looking north towards crossroads where wreckage of tanks can just be seen. German guns were firing up the street from the other side of the valley behind where this picture was taken, 2 August 1944.*

an armour piercing (AP) shot digs into the ground four yards in front. Then starts a ding-dong battle, round for round. We are getting them off as fast as we can and back comes the reply at about the same rate. Why he hasn't hit us heaven knows! I am becoming deaf and my ears hurt like hell every time a round goes off.

With the eleventh round a cloud of smoke comes up from the Tiger. Gosh, this is exciting, we have hit it. Keep going! AP expended, oh blast! Well, fire HE but the first round is short and we raise the elevation and get half a dozen rounds before he waddles off pouring forth smoke from his turret. Well that is that, he is damaged but not dead. However, it's as well we tickled him up or he might have got all our guns. As it is he has written off one SP, killed Cox and wounded Sgt. Fielding and Sgt. Smith, who we patch up with field dressings and pack off to the Regimental Aid Post (RAP).

I go up to RHQ ten minutes later with one of the 88 AP shot for the Regiment's Information Officer. I persuade the Adjutant to let me move the Troop behind the crest, where we feel a bit more comfortable. We check up and find we got off 22 rounds at the Tiger, with the result that I am deaf as a post and remain so for four or five days. It was a really exciting party and the thrill of hitting him and seeing him 'brew' is one I will not forget in a hurry. At 2300 we move off back at an OP.

August 5th. We are on the move most of the night, stopping and starting, owing to reports of enemy on our new position. However, we get into action at first light, only to find that a further move is expected within an hour. So, up sticks and off we go again. Into action again and a spot of breakfast. I go off for a recce in the tank and find a German Mk IV Special in an orchard; the crew have obviously just gone off, and in a hurry, because the escape hatches underneath are open, the gun loaded and the wireless still netted. We decide to drive it in and Lathwell, my tank driver, eventually gets it started. Dandy drives the Sherman in front and I sit on the turret of the Mk IV brandishing a vast tablecloth on the end of a stick, while Lathwell drives. We drive into the gun position in triumph with our prize. Meyer is highly delighted with the black uniform of the SS, complete with Iron Cross, which we find on board with a Nazi flag. He reckons his Iron Cross will earn him many a free round when he gets back to England. We lunch sumptuously off chicken, two between five of us, and move off to join 13th/18th Hussars in a laager, where we eventually find them at 2300. Wireless watch all night.

August 6th. Up at 0430 for orders with the CO and off to join B Squadron, 4th/7th Dragoon Guards. The Squadron Leader is Stephen Jenkins, whom we last saw at Verrières, just after he had had his third tank shot from under him. He is in grand form and gives us the 'gen' for the battle, which is to take us to Condé-sur-Noireau, about 15 miles – luckily for us the battle is cancelled and we remain in harbour all day.

Sidney Beck picks up the story with the guns of 'B' Troop, following the shoot-out on 4 August at Jurques described by Stephen Perry above.

August 4th. An unpleasant night follows an uncomfortable day. We are worried by intermittent Boche shelling. We fire a complicated harrassing fire target on the Boche escape road all night. 2 guns firing HE, 2 guns firing smoke and 2 guns firing airburst. B Troop has only 2 guns in action (H sub in workshops, G sub knocked out by the tank yesterday). Gunner Cox, who was killed on G sub, is given a simple burial in the 43rd Division cemetery. We hear that the Boche are retreating fast, and that we are to join an armoured thrust that night. We move at 2100 hrs in the gathering darkness and mist. Roads are very congested in Jurques and we wait patiently in the ruins, in the bizarre glow of burning buildings. Eventually we get clear of Jurques and head south towards Montamy. At approximately 2300 hrs we halt in the village of Le Mesnil Azouf. The newly liberated French people cluster round our vehicles and offer wine, but disperse quickly when an infantry carrier catches fire.

August 5th. The advance seems to be held up temporarily and we are ordered into action immediately. In the eerie darkness we journey down sunken lanes, where the stench of decaying flesh is very strong. We are in action by 0200 hrs and immediately fire two targets to assist our OPs. Just before dawn we are ordered forward to the original position allocated to us, at Les Moeux a few miles west of Mont Pinçon. We retrace our route along the sunken lanes and watch our tracks crushing the many carcasses of dead horses lying in the lanes. Our new position is occupied before first light, and when dawn finally comes we find that both troops are so close together that the GPOs seriously consider forming a 7-gun troop using one Command Post. The idea, however, does not find favour! When we are settled in we are able to examine our area. The Battery Command Post is in a farm where the barns have been attacked with enemy small arms ammunition. In the grounds of the farm there are two dead German soldiers, killed last night, according to the dazed French farmer. The area seems to have had a heavy mortar barrage and several animals are lying dead and wounded. L/Bdr. Sharp performs very humane work with his sten by despatching cows and a farm horse out of their misery. Some excitement is caused when we hear over the Regimental net that 'B' Troop OP has captured a German tank intact! Sure enough, Capt. Perry and L/Bdr. Lathwell arrive at the Command Post, driving a German Mk IV. Except for a punctured radiator it is intact and everyone swarms over it for souvenirs. In the end Capt. Perry chalks 'Mined' all over it to prevent it being damaged, as Army HQ has been given its location. A knocked out German motor cycle combination in the lane near the Command Post provides another source of souvenirs. We fire a few Regimental targets, but the attack up the west slopes of Mont Pinçon does not begin until tomorrow. Towards evening 'A' troop are ordered forward to a very advanced position within a thousand yards of the front and overlooked by the enemy. They are to fire a smoke screen to support the attack on Mont Pinçon.

August 6th. Bank Holiday in England but no holiday for 'A' troop today. They are right among the Forward Defence Lines (FDLs) and have an uncomfortable time owing to shells and mortars. The smoke rounds prepared for them are never sent up as sniper patrols are ambushing transport. 'A' troop are ordered to stay put becase movement would bring down heavier fire and probably disclose the plan of attack. The infantry attack up the west slopes of Mont Pinçon begins badly, the infantry meeting heavier resistance than expected. We fire several Victor targets on enemy concentrations, but by sheer determination the infantry press on, and by nightfall have gained the most dominating feature of the Normandy battlefield – Mont Pinçon – the key to victory.

The story of the capture of Mont Pinçon on the initiative of a troop leader of 13th/18th Hussars has been told elsewhere, but is worth repeating. Garton Ash takes up the story, having been supporting 13th/18th Hussars advancing on Mont Pinçon from the north-west for the previous two days.

After a slow approach to Mont Pinçon against considerable opposition on August 4th and 5th, the leading troop of the squadron I was supporting reached a road on the west of the main escarpment early on August 6th and the leading Troop Commander found a very narrow track leading upwards through woods towards the summit. This appeared to be undefended and he received permission to explore up the track as far as possible. He took two troops totalling seven tanks and, driving very carefully because of the danger of falling off the side of the track (one tank did fall), they eventually emerged on the top of the mountain without any opposition on

PLATE 36. *Ondefontaine. Sherman tanks advancing through a typical lane towards Ondefontaine. Note the front 'slicer' on front of tank to cut through hedges (a marvellous US Army invention).*

the way. I was immediately asked to try to join them and Driver Bullen, in whose tank I was then operating, well remembers driving very gingerly up to the summit.

When we arrived there was much mist and the tanks of the 13th/18th Hussars were spread out on the summit. There were many Germans around but they surrendered much more quickly than expected, and as the mist cleared we could see the magnificent view southwards giving command of the country through which the advance would have to continue.

A few shells landed near us, one close enough to spatter the tank with mud and earth and Driver Bullen well remembers the alacrity with which he obeyed my command to 'reverse 50 yards'.

Both the week we spent fighting to Mont Pinçon and the week that followed were passed in a repetitive way: an advance of a mile or so, then German resistance; a few of our tanks 'brewed up'; a halt; a small battle; and then on again.

The words 'brewed up' do not convey the horror of a tank on fire with crew trapped inside. If one of our tanks was hit, the crew might get out if they were quick and unwounded before she caught fire. Of course, not every tank hit did catch fire, but many Shermans did so – too many for us. But those in a tank which was hit were often wounded by flying steel, and unable to escape. At Jurques, once we had silenced the German tanks, I helped with the grisly task of helping out the wounded, but in the burnt out or 'brewed up' tanks there were no wounded, just the smell and charred remains of the crew.

Another major hazard in this advance was the enemy mines and booby traps. The Germans had mined many roadside verges and all the obvious pull-ins, so whenever we stopped, we stayed on the road surface. Many of the farms and orchards were booby trapped, and many abandoned German lorries. I remember one evening we bivouacked in a farm near Ondefontaine, between Jurques and Mont Pinçon. We carefully checked the orchard and the farm buildings, and then one of my signallers said he was going to the loo. I shouted at him just in time and of course, when we checked the loo seat, that had been booby trapped.

I remember another trap which we recognized – just a wire strung out at head height between two apple trees, attached to a hand grenade in the branches. But sometimes all was not as it seemed; George Fanshawe remembers one German lorry parked by the roadside, marked all over 'Beware Mines' and 'Achtung Minen' with skull and crossbones to boot! He got the engineers to help clear it, only to find no mines at all, but a lorry load of French wine carefully being preserved for Divisional Headquarters! RHQ mess took it over!

Another problem was the result of our own bombing. Our Airforce had flattened towns like Villers Bocage and Aunay-sur-Odon so completely that they were just heaps of rubble, with huge craters and no existing roads. They were impassable, and had to be bypassed through fields and lanes – again, often mined.

As we moved south from Mont Pinçon, Stephen Perry takes up the story again.

August 9th. At 0730 we move off to join the 13/18 Hussars for an attack on the high ground south of Mont Pinçon. We hook into the tank column as they move up the road and eventually tee in behind the Sqn. Leader. All is quiet until we show ourselves over the crest of Mont Pinçon and then guns of all calibres open up on us. One shell lands about 20 yards away and the blast knocks me down into the turret, to the discomfort of the crew. A moment later another bang behind, and the Sqn. Leader's tank is brewing up. However he jumps out with his crew and they manage to put it out, despite HE bursting all round them. It is not very funny at the time, but we laugh afterwards when we hear that it is one of his troop leaders who has hit him: the troop leader's tank is stooging along behind him when it is hit by HE; the shock of the explosion causes his 75, which is by luck loaded only with HE, to go off and the Sqn. Leader catches it on the back of the turret; his wireless is burnt out, but otherwise no damage done. I climb into the Sqn. Leader's turret, expecting every moment to be my last, as we are on a forward slope, and obviously a perfect target for enemy gunners. However, I get the dope for the battle, frequencies etc., and disappear into the turret just in time to miss the next round of enemy fire. It looks as though it's going to be a rough battle. We are off again, down the hill to Plessis Grimault, where the squadron knock out a Royal Tiger, the first to be seen in Normandy. The village is fairly successfully beaten up and 50 prisoners are on their way back to the barbed wire, but the squadron has lost three out of its fourteen tanks by now, one bogged down and two hit by AP. However, we push on towards St Pierre.

As we emerge through a wood there is a colossal explosion 30 yards in front of us, and the Sherman goes for six on a mine, the tank is blown back bodily three yards, four bogies and the o/s track have just disappeared, but the crew hop out shaken but otherwise unharmed. We find a good OP on the high ground, although three or four German 150mm guns are coming unpleasantly close with their shelling and have already taken the aerial away and two or three jagged holes have appeared in the ration box. We bash down the hill in search of a better OP but unluckily we can see less from there; as we are returning two more of the already depleted squadron get knocked out, but a 17-pounder Sherman gets the Panther which is causing all the trouble; and we remain where we are on our objective for the rest of the day. At last light we are relieved by anti-tank guns and withdraw to a forward rally near Plessis Grimault. We have not been out of the tank all day except for a short break of ten minutes for a cup of char, so that a quick cup of tea and tinned steak and kidney pud go down well, even though we do lose half an hour's precious sleep while it's hotting up. It's been quite a rough day, and the Squadron which started this morning with 14 tanks is now only 6 strong. By 0130 shells are falling thick and fast in the area, a house 300 yards away is brewing up furiously and the ammunition inside popping off intermittently. However, we eventually get our hole dug, refuel with petrol, and bed down for a few hours' sleep.

August 10th. 13th/18th Hussars lick their wounds in harbour and we with them. By the evening six new tanks have arrived complete with crews, and we are all victualled up and ready for tomorrow's battle, scheduled to start at 0300.

August 12th. The battle is on today and we set off at first light with the 13th/18th. Our objective is high ground to the south-east of St Pierre. The battle goes well and we capture the high ground after beating up about a company of German infantry and three anti-tank guns, one of which pops an AP shot through Peter Cherry's tank, killing the signaller and wounding Peter in the chest; luckily it does not 'brew up' and the remainder of the crew get out all right. [Peter Cherry was a Captain and Troop Commander, taking over in Normandy after our casualties there.] We have a brush with a Panther, which ends up with a cloud of black smoke pouring from its turret. An 88 takes a few pot shots at us when we are on the objective, but they are all over our heads and no damage is done. At last light we are relieved by the anti-tank guns and the squadron withdraws.

The Germans were still fighting back, as Sidney Beck also records:

August 9th. There is little firing in the morning but the enemy are still shelling the forward slopes on Mont Pinçon. Recce parties go forward and the Battery moves at 1500 hrs to the area of Le Plessis Grimault [Plate 37]. Our dust attracts some shells, but we arrive without casualties. However, we are not long left immune. We have not been in position more than an hour when the area is shelled for about 20 minutes by the Boche 155mm shells. 'A' Troop and the Battery Command Post are most unfortunate. 'A' troop has 3 casualties. HQ has 4: BSM Markham, TSM Wilson, Gnr. Jefferson and Gnr. Offord are seriously wounded and evacuated to England. Sgt. Bullock, Gnr. Chapman and Pte. Gibbs are slightly wounded and evacuated, to return some weeks later. We dig ourselves in deeper and the Battery Command Post evacuate its farm and orchard and moves to a deep ditch in a hedge behind 'B' Troop.

August 10th. We are still a bit shaky after yesterday's casualties. We curse all tanks and any vehicles which cause dust, as we are not far from the main axis of advance. There are many shells falling near the main road in front of us, but fortunately, no more come our way. Our targets are mainly counter-battery and the CO spends much time in finding the guns that shelled us yesterday. After several shell-reports we manage to obtain the services of the Air OP. At last we get the exact location of the German guns and we fire scale 10 rapid from the Regiment. We are not troubled any more by their guns in that position.

Suddenly, after fighting all the way to Condé-sur-Noireau, and reaching it on 14 August, it was all over. German resistance collapsed as they escaped eastward. On 17 August we moved to Flers, but even then John Morgan-Smith, the regiment's second in command, was blown up in his jeep by a mine and lost a leg. We reached Ecouché on 18 August, having passed through the German Army, and we were now with the Americans and the Free French divisions of the US 3rd Army. Flers was badly damaged but was *en fête* as we passed through it (Plate 38).

To the north and east of us, the holocaust of the Falaise pocket was nearing its end. We, like the Americans, were out in the open, ready to 'swan' too. We transferred from 43rd Division and joined the 11th Armoured Division for our advance across France, but it was not easy to move, as the congestion on the roads was terrible. There were British, Free French and US troops, all wanting priority, and we had to reach the Seine and then somehow cross it, with all the bridges blown.

THE BREAKOUT AND THE FALAISE GAP IN RETROSPECT

Once the US 3rd Army was launched out into the open into the undefended areas south of the German forces facing us in Normandy, we expected that the Germans would retreat, but quite the reverse happened. We have related

PLATE 37. *SP guns in action on forward slopes of Mont Pinçon on 9 August. Note gun crews stripped and dust as described by Sidney Beck.*

the arrival of new heavy 88mm assault guns, Jäger Panthers, at Aunay-sur-Odon on 29 July, and it was typical that new forces were thrown against us and the Canadians.

The German Mortain counter-offensive of August 6th against the US breakout was made by four Panzer divisions and was repulsed; it was too late and too little. Four Panzer divisions sounds a lot, but the actual number of German tanks overall was around 250, about the equivalent of Panzer Lehr on 6 June. The German failure to retreat laid them open to encirclement which finally happened at Falaise on 19 August.

I have described that when we fought through to Flers, arriving on 17 August, we met the US 3rd Army there, which included the French Armoured Division. They had been there for a week sitting on their backsides and not advancing north. Had those US and French forces moved against the rear of the German troops fighting us and the Canadians and Poles, then there can be no doubt that the Falaise Gap might have been closed much earlier, trapping virtually the whole German army.

Why did they stop? Apparently, so we are told, on Bradley's orders. He feared that Patton's 3rd Army might not cope with a German counter-attack, and also that there could be a clash between his 1st Army and the 3rd, or

PLATE 38. *Sherman tank advancing through the devastated centre of Flers, 17 August.*

between Patton and the Canadians. It might have become a real muddle. However, had the chance been taken, liaison between Patton's forces and the Canadians and British could have been arranged, and the effect of, say, two divisions attacking from the south would surely have been worth a risk. To us it always seemed a timid and stupid decision. The way the US and French forces sat there for a week without lifting a finger to help the British, Canadians and Poles dying ten miles north of them has always rankled with me, and no doubt the Canadians and Poles.

However, by 19 August the Falaise pocket was closed without the help of Patton, and all the Allied armies were advancing across France.

9
Pursuit to Antwerp

The advance from the Falaise Gap to the Seine with 30 Corps. The crossing of the Seine at Vernon on 29 August. The night advance of 90 miles from the Seine to Amiens and the crossing of the Somme on 30/31 August with the 11th Armoured Division. The pursuit through Lens and across the old battlefields of World War I. The problems and exhilaration of liberating the French and the Belgians. The advance to, and liberation of, Brussels and Antwerp on 3 and 4 September.

By 20 August the battle for Normandy was over. We were outside Argentan on the south side of the Falaise Gap, but taking no part in the liquidation of the German armies to the north of us.

On 18 August we had met up with the Free French Armoured Division of General Le Clerc at Ecouché. They had a distinguished record in the desert, and had landed in France as part of General Patton's US 3rd Army. With them they had swung south with little fighting, and then north to enter Ecouché from the south with no opposition. They and Patton's other divisions had reached Ecouché and Argentan on 13 August and had remained there, we have seen. However, we and the Free French occupied Ecouché together. They had billeted themselves around the town, and particularly with the locals in the caves nearby, which were occupied as safe houses in a war. Ecouché had been badly damaged by bombing.

On the morning of the 19th, we all moved off together towards the Seine, with the French bound for Paris. I say the French, but all the troops I met turned out to be ex-Spanish Republican soldiers who had fought against Franco in the 1930s. They were a tough, swarthy lot and swarmed out of the caves and houses pulling up their trousers, as their vehicles moved off to liberate Paris. We gave them priority, and they entered Paris in triumph on 23 August, four days later.

Sidney Beck recalls his memories of our advance through the remnants of the German 7th Army, with the US and Free French troops milling across our line of advance.

August 18th. In action, just east of Flers, but not for long. Advance parties go off almost as soon as we are in action, but the whole column comes to a halt for about four hours. The Americans have advanced so that they have cut our centre line. The

British 11th Armoured Division are held up by a couple of American MPs who claim they have to keep the road open for US troops! The matter takes a little sorting out, but by 1500 hours the 11th Armoured Division resumes its advance along the centre line, the US troops having come too far north. There is tremendous congestion on the road, so swift is the advance, and it takes a considerable time for the regiment to pass up the column on this long march. On either side of the roads we see knocked out German tanks and vehicles, the remnants of the proud 7th Army, knocked out by our Typhoons and our shelling. We are catching up on the enemy, and buildings are still burning where the Hun tried to make a stand. It is almost midnight before the guns reach the new area south-west of Ecouché. The advance parties are only kept awake by studying the stars while they patiently wait five hours for the guns (and food) to arrive. It is almost 2 am before anyone gets a meal and many cannot face the prospect of meat and veg at 2 am, and go to sleep instead! Except the unlucky night duty men, who have to fire some harrassing rounds until daybreak.

August 19th. We do not move again until midday, which gives us a little time to recover from yesterday's very tiring march. This time we move onto the southern outskirts of the town of Ecouché itself. The town has been badly battered by shells and bombs, and we have some difficulty in negotiating the piles of rubble. The two gun positions are in exposed fields outside the town, with the Battery Command Post in a small quarry about 40 feet below ground level. Between this quarry and the town is a much larger quarry, which becomes the hiding place for the whole of the regiment's wagon lines. We are very interested to find that the town itself is occupied by a Brigade of the Free French Armoured Division. They have been in occupation of the town for almost a week and have suffered some casualties, when the town was bombed by Allied aircraft. They are very well established in the town, being on very good terms with the local people. We understand why they are called the 'Free French'! In the evening, two of the French soldiers approach B Troop Command Post and ask us to warn our sentries not to disturb them in the bushes! The sentries' comment is 'just give us the chance'! However, rain, the first for nearly a fortnight, put a damper on their feelings and rejoicing. I blush to record that, owing to an error in the Troop Command Post, B Troop fire 60 degrees off line on a harrassing fire target!

August 20th. We suddenly get orders to move in the morning. The Battery Command Post Officer (CPO) decides to take his tank on the advance party and dashes off in fine style, determined not to be late. Alas, he forgets to unfasten the canvas covering the Battery Command Post and drags it after him out of the quarry! We move due north out of the Ecouché [Plate 39] into some open ground, fringed with orchards. We just have time for a meal, then we move on again. The Colonel gave the order 'Move independently', and there is a grand sight as six columns of guns charge across country [Plate 40], all converging on one narrow road, the road to Argentan. Our gun area is in the open fields, about three miles west of Argentan, whose ruined skyline we can just see over the rising ground. Away to the north are wooded hills, where we watch our Typhoons diving and circling, columns of smoke rising. There is no firing to be done and it seems quite peaceful in the open fields, until drenching rain drives us into our bivvies.

PLATE 39. *Sgt. Stackwood's SP of 342nd Battery moving out of Ecouché on morning of 20 August. In background Sgt. Reg Munt on motorcycle guiding battery through the ruined town.*

August 21st. It is still raining heavily in the early morning as we pack up and prepare to move on again. We are ready to move by 0845 hours, but it is 0945 hours before we are on the road, owing to traffic congestion. Just as the last vehicle in the regiment reaches the road, the head of the column in Argentan is halted at the Brigade Start Point. We wait for nearly three hours in the pouring rain, surveying the ruins of what was once a beautiful old-world town. GI Joes pick their way over the rubble and the inevitable jeeps dash around, splashing us with water coloured brick red from the pitted road. At midday we move on again, only to be pushed off the road a few miles further on, while more tanks go through. We finally occupy a position to the west of Exres, but our targets are well out of range and we quickly move on again. We get a terrific reception from the villagers at Exres before finding our final position for the night, west of Croissilles. The Command Post and wagon lines are well established at a large farm and the hospitable farmer and his wife, to say nothing of their charming daughters, distribute as much cider and Calvados as

PLATE 40. *Going across country! An SP of 86th Field Regiment advancing towards the Seine August 1944. The SP is possibly C Sub of 342nd Battery.*

we can drink. There are many refugees from Croissilles living in this farm, all very pleased to see us. Eggs and butter are a welcome addition to our compo rations.

August 22nd. The advance continues, this time without any rain. We move first to a position north-east of the village of Le Merberaut. It is in large open pasture land, the grounds of a modern château which was formerly a Nazi SS HQ. 'A' Troop and the Battery Command Post are in the area of one of the farms belonging to the château. The chase goes on and we have our fastest move of the campaign. The route is changed while we are on the move, and we catch up with the advance parties. We are held up only once, when some snipers in the woods cause some trouble and the local French Maquis warn us of mines. At last, after a week of moving down lanes, we come onto the main road to L'Aigle and make rapid progress. We receive a grand welcome from the town of Aube-sur-Rile before going into action, just south of it, facing towards L'Aigle. The CPO finds another hospitable farmer and his wife. This farmer turns out to be a very active member of the French Maquis.

August 23rd. We are ordered out of action. No one is quite clear what is happening, but later we learn that the whole of the 11th Armoured Division is being rested for maintenance and replenishment. There is talk of a dash to the Seine. We settle down to the routine of maintenance that we learnt at St André, our first rest area, and prepare to make ourselves comfortable. There is great rejoicing when we hear that Paris has been freed by her own citizens and the French Armoured Division. A great day for France and freedom everywhere, and our good farmer the Maquis kills the fatted calf in our honour. He is so pleased and proud to have us that he keeps inviting his friends to come and be introduced. We learn that he has been supplied with arms by parachute. He also tells how some of the Maquis in the neighbourhood have been shot by the retreating Germans.

On 18th August Stephen Perry was promoted to take over the command of 462nd Battery. Major Eric Scammell, its previous commander, took over as the regiment's second in command, as Major John Morgan-Smith had been wounded by a mine in the advance to Flers some days earlier. Stephen Perry's diary ceases at this date. He was acting in these few days as a liaison officer with the 11th Armoured Division, whom we had joined on 17 August.

The plan now was an exciting one. 30 Corps, consisting of the 11th Armoured Division, the Guards Armoured Division, 43rd Division, 50th Division and our other old D-Day companions, 8th Armoured Brigade, was to lead the British advance across the Seine and up into Belgium, Holland and the Rhine. Major-General Brian Horrocks had taken over as 30 Corps Commander just before we had captured Mont Pinçon, two weeks earlier. General Horrocks, or 'Jorrocks', had been one of Montgomery's outstanding generals in Africa. He had been badly wounded in Tunis a year earlier, and had made a remarkable recovery.

The first step was to move up to the Seine, secure a bridgehead across the river and build bridges capable of taking tanks across. This task was given to the 43rd Division, who started their assault across the Seine on 23 August at Vernon, between Rouen and Paris. As described by Sidney Beck above, we were ordered into a maintenance area at L'Aigle on that day until we could cross the Seine.

Sidney Beck's diary for 25 August describes a typical late August day at L'Aigle:

August 25th. We remain in this quiet backwater while the tide of war still surges on. Paris has fallen and a new army from the Mediterranean is advancing swiftly up the Rhône valley driving towards the Belfort Gap and the Swiss frontier. Everywhere in central France the Maquis are rising and disarming the disorganised enemy. To the north of us, the Canadians advancing along the coast are approaching the mouth of the Seine and Le Havre. In the meantime, we rest, clean and repair our vehicles. We receive two new SPs in replacement of two that have given good service. It is not all work, and some of us are lucky enough to get into L'Aigle where wine is freely distributed. The local French hid these stores of wine in the river and today, feeling quite certain that the enemy will never return, they haul the casks and bottles out and rejoice in traditional style. The town has suffered quite badly through shell fire, and the Church has many scars. Some of us in the afternoon take time off to have a swim in the river Rile which flows through Aube. We approach the river through the local electricity works badly damaged by shell fire and sabotage. A mined 88mm gun on the roadside is another reminder that there is such a thing as war, but we quickly forget that in our enjoyment of the sun and water. Someone finds an old rowing boat built for four, but somehow or other about 20 Herts Yeomanry get in with much pushing and shoving, with the result that many unexpected duckings take place!

43rd Division made a very efficient assault across the Seine and by 28 August the bridge was complete and our tanks could cross. The first across were the 8th Armoured Brigade! Some OP parties also crossed on the 28th, but the main body of our guns crossed at dawn on 29 August (Plate 41).

The weather had now turned fine and the roads were covered in dust. Claude Hankins, my Battery Captain, had a miraculous escape as we approached Vernon. He was riding a motorcycle in the column of tanks, and in the dust he hit a rut, came off right in front of a following Sherman whose driver, blinded by dust, never saw him. Claude managed to roll under the centre of the tank which passed over him, catching one foot only. He hopped clear before the next tank arrived, and when I saw him he was cheerfully lying by the road, missing his big toe, smoking a cigarette and grinning all over his sunburnt and dust-covered face.

I crossed with 342nd Battery's guns in the very dull early morning of 29 August. We went over on a long pontoon bridge spanning the river, which was about 200 yards wide at this point. The crossing was uneventful, and once on the east bank I was ordered forward about five miles up the road towards Gisors to take up an OP on the north side of this road, in case the bridgehead was attacked by Germans moving from the Rouen/Dieppe area. The guns went into action behind us. We stayed patrolling this northern flank while the main column moved forward (see Figure 21).

Sidney Beck describes his approach to the Seine from L'Aigle:

August 28th. Last evening we were placed under a moment's notice to move. There is something big in the wind! Our Recce parties leave at 0830. The Regiment once more lines up ready to move, but owing to road congestion, we do not leave until 1700 hrs. This is to be the start of a great adventure, but we do not realise then how great an adventure it is going to be. This, the first of our long moves, is a 10 hour, non-stop journey which takes us nearly 90 miles to the village of La Chappelle on the west bank of the river Seine near Vernon. It is very, very dusty on the roads

PLATE 41. *A Sherman tank crossing the Class 40 bridge at Vernon on Seine on 28 August 1944. The demolished bridge to the right.*

after the long columns of tanks have passed through, and many of us suffer from eye-strain and swollen lids. As we arrive at our harbour area in the undergrowth on the outskirts of the village, searchlights sweep the sky to the north over Le Havre and to the south towards Paris.

August 29th. Bleary-eyed, we wake before dawn and make a hasty breakfast. In the early morning light we journey into Vernon and, after a short wait, rumble across the famous pontoon bridge alongside the iron bridge destroyed by our bombers. The steep bank on the east side has a commanding view of the crossing, and if the Germans were at all organised, they could make the crossing very sticky. The approaches and exits from the bridge were shelled early on, but we cross without incident and roar up the steep winding road. High banks, wooded and overgrown, flank the road, ideal for ambushes; and a burnt-out recce car shows where one ambush has succeeded. Further on, we pass a burnt-out Panther with the blackened, twisted bodies of the crew lying awkwardly on the turret and hull. At the top of the hill, with the Seine behind us, we roar into action on some open ground, now muddy from the steady rain. Behind us, our wagon lines park in the area of a burning farm and haystack. We do not remain long here. At 1100 hrs the CO orders 'Move independently', and again we charge across flat open fields to our new RV. On the way we pass Captain Perry and RB waiting in a lane with the reserve squadron of the 15th/19th Hussars. Ahead of them we have a fine view of the other squadrons in extended order, advancing cautiously across open country seeking the enemy. At 1430 hrs comes another quick cross-country move. The going is becoming sticky. The wheeled vehicles are frequently in difficulties and the motorcyclists have a tiring time. We are now at the village of Cantiers, but remain for an hour before another quick advance to Samaches-en-Vexin. Here we roar into action alongside a large and prosperous French Château, whose occupants bar and shutter their windows in case we fire. We just have time to eat a hastily prepared meal before making another dash forward. We pass through the town of Etrepagny, whose inhabitants give us a great welcome. Flags and bunting already decorate the houses, although the leading tanks have only just passed through. Our gun area for the night is north of the town, in a small hollow. Behind us a large explosion in the town causes a huge fire, but we are too tired to worry what caused it. Despite the tiring day and the miserable rain, everyone is elated with the advance and the hearty welcome everywhere.

August 30th. The advance continues at dawn in the pouring rain. Again we move independently, but 'B' Troop are a little too independent. The 'George' Truck, followed by three carriers, takes the wrong turning and heads south instead of north. Approaching a village, they spy a tank with its gun pointing up the road. Fortunately, it turns out to be a Sherman which has just liberated the village. We have a hasty conference with the Tank Commander who tells us that the last thing seen going up the road we have come down was a German horse-drawn battery! The half-track and carriers hastily turn round and return the way they came, but not before the happy populace ply us with wine and beer and thrust eggs into our eager hands. The battery in the meantime has occupied an open position north of Sancourt. We are not called upon to fire and very soon make another dash forward. In the late afternoon there are rumours of harbour parties, and we actually set off to our new area. The roads become very congested and the Regiment is ordered off the road to allow more tanks of the 11th Armoured Division to move up. Here we wait an hour or so, cheered by the sight of long columns of prisoners marching back down the column. Then comes a surprise. At 2000 hrs we are told that we are moving immediately to Amiens, more than 70 miles away! It gets dark early because of the heavy rain and no lights are allowed, except tail lights. Stealthily we journey through the night, passing through sleeping villages whose inhabitants peer anxiously at us from behind curtained windows. It is a great strain on our drivers and operators to keep awake, but they do and we arrive safely. Later we learn that in this night march we have passed clean through six enemy divisions.

This night march to Amiens was one of the great feats of 30 Corps. Having crossed the Seine, the next major barrier to our progress was obviously the Somme running from St Quentin through Amiens to just north-west of Abbeville. The river runs in a considerable gorge in places. Once across the Somme, we could move to the high ground towards Arras and Cambrai and the battlefields of World War I.

The early seizure of Amiens and the Somme bridges was therefore vital. I was just settling down with my tank crew to cook supper, when the orders came through to proceed to meet the Colonel. He briefed us on our route through the night with 11th Armoured Division, to Amiens, which we were to seize by dawn.

That night's drive will always live in the memory of those who took part in it. The weather was terrible, dark and wet drenching rain. The Division advanced on a number of roads with vehicles nose to tail, reading our map as we went, and keeping the drivers awake. Halts were frequent, and one I remember very clearly. Just before midnight, the whole column halted on the outskirts of a small French town. The column was bypassing the centre of the town, which lay two hundred yards to our right. A lot of noise was coming from the town square, so I set off on foot to investigate with one of my troop commanders, Roy Marshall. Roy had joined 342nd Battery in Normandy to replace Geoffrey Street. He was an exceptionally able officer, having won both the Military Medal and the Military Cross, a rare distinction, and was older and more experienced than I was, although I was his Major.

Roy and I soon reached the town square, which was full of lights and people. In the centre were four or five girls, all weeping and being held by a group of French men, having their hair cut off and heads shaven amid acclaim from an ugly-looking crowd. It was a pathetic sight in the pouring rain, and I was wondering what to do, when Roy went into action. Drawing his revolver, he advanced and in passable French ordered them to stop and release the girls. This they refused to do and an ugly scene looked likely. At that moment one of our bombardiers, carrying a sten-gun, arrived to tell us that the column was about to move again. His arrival, armed, tipped the balance. Reluctantly the girls were released, and they made off. We then shook hands with some of the French, and I persuaded Roy that our main priority was to advance on Amiens! Similar scenes must have been going on all over France (Plate 42). This performance at midnight in the pouring rain was a macabre and nasty affair, and in great contrast to the scenes of rejoicing we were now witnessing every day.

We moved on relentlessly with no German opposition, and as dawn broke, we were about two miles outside Amiens on a long, tree-lined road with open fields on either side, and a wood about 400 yards away to our left. Our tanks and vehicles were halted nose to tail as a grey dawn broke. It had at last stopped raining. However, I realized as the dawn light seeped across the sodden fields, how vulnerable we were, and found a tank squadron commander who thought as I did. He deployed several of his tanks off the road to take up firing positions. They had hardly done so when out of the wood to our left appeared German troops and a couple of tanks, all carrying white flags of surrender.

We moved shortly afterwards down into Amiens, through the town centre, and across the intact bridges. Amiens early that morning looked wet and

PLATE 42. *French Maquis about to shave a woman collaborateuse, September 1944. Note hair of earlier shavings on ground.*

bedraggled with a number of German soldiers standing in groups, some still in pyjamas. The local population were still unsure what had happened and certainly only a few French were on the streets to cheer us.

Once we were clear of the town, we took up an OP position off the road to Arras and had our breakfast. We had covered over eighty miles that night and had never seen a German until we reached Amiens. Although we manned our observation post, I could make no contact at first with our guns, but did so later that morning. They were not that far behind, as Sidney Beck recalls:

August 31st. Dawn finds us on the outskirts of Amiens and we are immediately ordered into action just off the main axis. As we dash out to our gun platforms, the tanks and mobile Bofors guns engage some enemy MT and SP guns in the valley to the left of us. Ammunition explodes intermittently as the enemy vehicles 'brew up'. We hear over the air that our leading tanks have entered Amiens. We have two more moves before lunch time, finishing up at the village of Dury about two miles from Amiens. Here our leading tanks have used their flame-throwers to sort out the enemy, and the Command Post staff turn fire-fighters to quell the blaze at the farm they have chosen as our HQ. We manage a hot meal, the sun comes out and, while waiting to move on, some of us journey up the main road to peer over the hill at Amiens. We have a clear view of the Cathedral towers and the spire. Away to the right on the horizon is the famous Vimy Ridge and through glasses we can just discern the striking white monument to the fallen of that other war. In the late afternoon we pack up and have our triumphal entry into Amiens. The people are almost hysterical with joy, and give us a marvellous reception. Everywhere Union Jacks, Tricolors and Old Glories; and everyone tries to shake hands with a Tommy. All too swiftly we are out of the city and into action north of it. As we go into action the leading tanks are only a thousand yards ahead, and are being engaged by enemy guns. The tanks consolidate for the night and we spend that night as the most forward artillery of the spearhead supporting the 3rd RTR and the 23rd Hussars. We turn in for a well earned rest, glowing with the knowledge that we have made history, for history would surely remember that audacious advance from the Seine to Amiens right through the enemy defences (and the capture of the German Commander in his pyjamas!).

It is interesting to note that the Hertfordshire Yeomanry must have been the only regiment in the British Army that had the distinction of being part of the D-Day landings and among the first troops across the Somme, and in a few days' time being the first into Antwerp.

I remember little of the rest of 31 August except that that evening I was sent by George Fanshawe up a road leading north towards Calais and Boulogne. It will be recalled that all through Normandy, Hitler had expected an Allied attack on the Pas de Calais coast and that area still contained large numbers of German troops who were now faced with being cut off and surrounded by our advance. We were warned that they might stage an attack on us from the north. My task was to record targets on this road, and other OPs were doing the same on all roads leading north. Should a counter-attack develop, we would be able to call down fire on these roads on targets which we had registered. This meant that I had to fire ranging rounds on the road so that the exact range and direction of each target was recorded in advance.

I arrived with my tank and a jeep to register the first target. Impossible! The whole road and the villages and towns along it were *en fête*. We had great difficulty in even driving through the crowds. After a mile or so it dawned on us that we were the first Allied troops they had seen. Once we were in sight of our first target we stopped, and were immediately overwhelmed with wild French girls and boys. We dismounted, only to be embraced and kissed and hugged. Eventually some sort of order was restored with the arrival of the Mayor of the town armed with champagne. We toasted ourselves, Churchill, de Gaulle and a few others and then in my poor French, with the help of a young lady who spoke English, I explained that my task was to fire on the road and register it as a target and would he, the Mayor, please clear everyone out of the way.

'Mais pourquoi?'

'Because the Germans may come down the road tonight.'

'Impossible! Les Boches sont finis.' Signs of throat cutting all round.

'Many German tanks to the North.'

'Mais vous êtes ici.' 'Boom' 'boom' signs of us shooting the Germans.

More wine, more toasts, and I was getting nowhere at all except more tipsy. My drivers and signallers were by then enwrapped by large French ladies and small boys, and the situation was getting rapidly out of hand. How should I explain to a Mayor and 500 French people who were drunk with exhilaration, that I wanted to shell their villages? They had waited four agonizing years, and in the past few days rumours of our advance had come through and then, joy of joys, we arrived as their liberators. The first Allied troops they had seen. Now those liberators wanted to fire upon them!

The situation was saved by the arrival of a serious-looking Frenchman, who turned out to be the local Maquis leader. I explained the military situation to him. I said that the German armies were to the north, and if they came south our guns would fire on the road. I selected my three targets on the road between the villages, and he agreed to keep the French away from those targets. We agreed to establish our OP that night with him, so all that now needed to be done was for me to register the targets. We agreed that to fire on the road at the moment was impossible. This road ran away north in a straight line, as far as we could see. It was covered with French people dancing. To its west were open fields rising to a tree-covered ridge.

I suggested that I would register on this ridge, and having done that I would alter the range and direction and so record the targets on the road itself. I suggested that he go off in my jeep with my driver to make sure there were no French on the ridge. Whilst this was in hand, I got through personally to my guns and warned the GPOs of what I was going to do, telling them to make quite sure that the guns fire straight.

After half an hour all was ready, except that now I wondered if I could see straight let alone fire straight. All the locals were now warned, and as I gave the order to fire a hush descended. Thank God, the shell landed in an open field 300 yards away, to a great deal of cheering. All was well: four more rounds and I had registered on one of the local barns. Consternation further up the road where the revellers obviously had not been appraised of the situation. They scattered very quickly as the shells exploded in the fields to their west.

Now the evening was drawing on, my targets were recorded, and the OP established with the Maquis, so I made my farewells and returned to the guns. Here they were in action, but only just, as they too were overwhelmed with the local population. There were girls and boys all over the guns and even helping to carry ammunition.

My officers had called an Orders Meeting just before my arrival and we laid down very strict orders. No civilians were to be allowed on the gun position, and every gun would be manned by at least four men at all times. Fraternization, in other words, was to be strictly controlled. Each sergeant was to control drinking and the girls. We enrolled a team to rope off the guns and to explain things to the locals. Then I was off to Regimental HQ for the orders for the next day.

Our objective with the 11th Armoured Division was to advance as fast as possible, pushing on regardless of opposition on a centre line, which was a central axis of advance around Arras, through Lens, south of Lille, through Tournai to the outskirts of Brussels, then north pass Antwerp and on to Breda across the lower Rhine, and eventually to Hilversum on the Zuider Zee (Figure 22).

The first target was Antwerp. The Guards Armoured Division would be on our right aiming at Brussels and then on to the Rhine. 50th Division and 8th Armoured Brigade would follow up, and in particular protect our left flank from German attacks from the Pas de Calais and from Lille. My own particular task in this advance was on the left flank, with a screen of armoured cars to protecting the main column against any German advance from the north until 50th Division and the 8th Armoured Brigade could get forward.

The next day, 1 September, we were off again. There were no Germans, but scenes of liberation all the way. Every stop in a town meant a speech and a mobbing. Once we saw Germans advancing across fields and I called for a troop target, but my guns were ten miles in front of me and had to come into action backwards. By the time they were ready, we had used the tank machine-gun, and about a hundred Germans surrendered.

Prisoners were a problem; all we could do was to disarm them, put their weapons on the jeep or the tank, and tell them to walk south. Soon we had no room for weapons, so we dumped them with the French in the next town or village.

That evening we camped in the ruins of a monastery in the little village of Mont St Eloi a few miles north-west of Arras on the road leading to Calais. The village was on a small hill dominating the road. We established an OP on the north side of the church covering the road to the north to give us warning of any German approach. With the other tanks we positioned ourselves on the slope to the south of the village covering the road with our guns.

As we ate supper, we were surrounded by dogs and French children. One of us threw a piece of meat to the dogs. This was fatal, as not only did a dogfight ensue, but the children and adults turned on us for feeding the dogs when they were starving. It was a lesson quickly learned, so what rations we had spare were given out and never again did we eat in sight of a crowd.

That evening our OP gave warning of a convoy of German vehicles approaching from the north. We allowed them through the village and down the road to the south; soon a dozen of our tanks opened fire and the German lorries and half-tracks were shot up and bodies and wounded collected. They never stood a chance.

Sidney Beck tells his version.

September 1st. Another day of general advance all along the line. We leave our bridgehead position just north of Amiens and advance swiftly across country keeping to the main axis as much as possible. We are heading in the general direction of Arras, and with the memory of our welcome in Amiens still vivid, we look forward with anticipation to the liberation of that town too. We pass through a village containing dark-skinned men in a foreign uniform who wave cheerily at us. These are French Senegalese troops who the Germans had kept as prisoners of war and who have just been liberated. We journey through woods containing curious heavily camouflaged buildings which we suspect to be connected with V1 flying bombs. The thought that we are at last putting an end to the ordeal of Southern England and cutting off the V1 sites keeps us eager to push on swiftly. We are bypassing any resistance. Occasionally French men and women tell us excitedly that 200 Germans are hiding in some woods or other on our route, but we cannot stop to worry about them. We know the infantry following up will deal with them, our job is to push on. We are the advance guard! Push on we do. By nightfall we have travelled 45 miles and encamp at the village of Savy a few miles west and north of Arras. The Colonel congratulates the Regiment on the excellent advance. Although we travel across country all the way, with the main body travelling by road, yet we never lose ground, and all our guns are in action by midnight at the right place. Great celebrations in the village that night, we are the first British troops the villagers have seen. Our Fighter Bombers give us a scare when they dive on the village, but yellow smoke and strips convince them we are friendly.

September 2nd. Another great day of liberation. Again the Regiment moves off at 0700 hrs and continues the northward advance. Our route lies through the great industrial area, and we are given a truly magnificent reception from the great crowds of people lining the streets. The crowds are so great that progress can only be made at a crawling pace. In consequence, the more adventurous French boys and girls crowd into the tanks and we look more like a carnival procession than a fighting column. A great day for the Despatch Riders (DRs) whose pillions are very much in demand by all the fair Mademoiselles. Cries of 'Bon Santé', 'Good Luck', 'Good-bye', 'Vive le Tommy', 'Welcome', fill the air and we are pummelled, slapped, pushed and jostled and our hands wrung almost from us by the delirious people. Just as we enter Lens we are told a sad story of a woman who had not lived to rejoice. During last night a small patrol of British troops had entered Lens and were sheltered by this woman. Unfortunately they were discovered, but made their escape. The Germans had left Lens four hrs before we entered this morning, but before leaving they shot this brave woman. We are more eager than ever to push on. Capt. Benson is shown a magnificent OP, on the top of the railway station at Bethune, by the

Maquis. Here he sees about 200 of the enemy and some anti-tank guns less than 500 yards away, but alas, the guns are on the road and he is not allowed to use the Mediums. We are brought into action on the outskirts of Lens on some open ground in front of a huge factory. There is a rumour of a report on the Maquis radio that the Germans have asked for an Armistice. We are sceptical, especially when at 2300 hrs we have a stand-to. Tank alert is ordered and we turn our guns through 160 degrees to face the left rear. However, the report of the tanks also comes from the Maquis and we turn in at midnight without firing a shot.

September 3rd. The 5th Anniversary of Britain's entry into the war with Germany. And what an anniversary! The most tiring and exciting day of the war. Our advance to the Belgian frontier continues by leaps and bounds, as we go into action and out again in record time. Just before midday the column is held up while the Regiment is passing through the town of Avelin. Enemy guns and tanks hiding in woods on either side of the road ambush the column after the leading tanks have passed through. Suddenly a fusilade of shots rings out and the line of 3-tonners carrying ammunition and petrol burst into flames. Our BC, Major Corke, dashes down the column in his jeep to investigate the danger. As he is passing a blazing truck, the ammunition explodes. Major Corke is killed instantly; the driver, Gnr. Brown, is blown through the windscreen, and his hand is sheered off above the wrist by another piece of shrapnel.

Mardell, the signaller, has an amazing escape. His set is smashed to smithereens, yet he escapes with shock and minor injuries. Meanwhile in the town of Avelin itself the battery goes into action in the streets as tank alert is signalled. Sergeant Couzins is ordered forward with his SP gun to recce the position and establishes himself at the north entrance of the town. Turning the corner he sees in the valley to his right, less than 2000 yards away, an enemy 6-gun battery in action. 'E' Sub immediately engages No. 1 gun over open sights, and with their third round knocks out the enemy gun. They fire a few more rounds at the gun crews, who take fright and dash to shelter across the open fields. By this time the rest of the Regiment are in action south of the town of Avelin, Sergeant Couzins is pulled back to join the Troop. While this is going on the burning trucks close to the gun area are still cascading ammunition. Major Scammell of 462nd Battery takes an SP into the wood and shoots up the HQ of this enemy pocket hidden in a Château, capturing 4 officers and 87 ORs as prisoners. British and enemy wounded are lying on the roadside being tended by our ambulance men as we prepare to continue the advance.

After about two hours delay we advance, giving the burning vehicles a very wide berth. Just as well we do, because it means going below the skyline. No sooner do we set off than the German tanks on the opposite side of the road open up. They have kept quiet during our mopping up and no one suspects their presence. Vehicles that go too near the crest are fired on. The CO orders 342nd Battery into action below the crest and they put down a smoke screen while the remainder of the column dashes past. The whole exciting affair is a very creditable performance. Undoubtedly the skill and coolness displayed by everyone in the sudden emergency saves many lives and many vehicles in the column. Sergeant Couzins is mentioned in dispatches for his action of this day. We are now catching up with the enemy, and prisoners become an embarrassment. Some are wounded and we have to carry them all the way in our transport.

At 2 o'clock in the afternoon we cross the Belgian frontier. A great occasion, and the joy of people reaches new heights. Now we understand why we were called the British Liberation Army. We now know what it is to see people overjoyed. As we journey on through Courtrai and Tournai we have a confused picture of frantically waving men, women and children, all with eager arms outstretched to touch 'Tommy'. Gay blooms, vivid reds and yellows are tossed into our tanks, and fruit, tomatoes, biscuits, and bottles of beer are thrown up and skilfully caught. In Normandy it had been 'Cigarette pour papa' but here in Belgium the people are giving *us* cigarettes!!! Whenever a tank stops, the crowds surge forward swarming all over the tanks, and babies are held up to be kissed by 'Tommy'. On and on we race in a mad dash through Belgium. It is every man and vehicle for himself, no speed limits. Towards nightfall we begin to look anxiously at our petrol supplies and watch our overheating bogies. Antwerp tonight – can we make it??? That is the great question. Darkness falls and weary eyed we follow the red light of the tank in front. There is confusion in some towns where collaborators are being rooted out. Furniture is moved into the streets and set ablaze and the burning buildings give a bizarre look to our tanks racing through the streets. Patriots add to the confusion by firing their small arms into the air. It begins to rain and we finally receive orders to harbour for the night in a large open field just south of the town of Assche. Away to the south-east a great blaze lights the sky. It is the Palace of Justice at Brussels, which has been set on fire by the Germans before Brussels is liberated by the Guards Armoured Division. It is well after midnight before we are resting.

As I followed the guns through Billy Montigny, we halted in the main street opposite a photographer's shop, whose owner was photographing the chaotic scene. I asked him to photograph my tank and crew, which he did. I paid for the pictures, and gave him my home address in England, and lo and behold, three weeks later a set of photographs arrived (Plates 43–4).

On 3 September I was ordered to come forward, and by making a number of detours and by forceful driving, we overtook the column ahead of us. By the afternoon, we had caught up well and were rapidly approaching Brussels. Another small detour and we would be up with the leading tanks. We detoured to the south, and then rejoined the main road close to Brussels, only to find an empty road. We had overshot our left turn to Antwerp, and at five o'clock we were all by ourselves, liberating the outskirts of Brussels.

I still believe that we (my tank and I) were the first British troops in Brussels. However, we extricated ourselves, leaving Brussels to be liberated that evening by the Guards Armoured Division, who were coming up behind us on our right.

We retreated down the road to a little village with a crossroads just to the west of Brussels. Here our troops were due to make a left turn to the north, bypassing Brussels, and up to Antwerp, about thirty miles away. We arrived

PLATE 43. *'X' tank of 342nd Battery halted at Billy Montigny south of Lille on 2 September 1944. Major Kiln (author) on top with goggles, Bdr. Williams (signals) top right, Gnr. Hunter (OPAck) top left, photographer and shop owner E. Heller holding gun barrel. Driver Bullen on his right.*

PLATE 44. *'X' tank again showing E. Heller's shop in background.*

to find one of our SPs parked by the roadside, apparently broken down. We stopped to investigate and found the No. 1, a sergeant, in the local café on the crossroads. The breakdown appeared to be a 'tactical' one, and as his Commanding Officer I was just about to start laying down a bit of discipline. However, as I crossed the threshold of the café, Madame, a magnificent red-haired woman about twice my size, seized me in her arms, kissed me warmly and called me 'mon brave colonel' (a calculated flattery of promotion). I then had to dance and drink with her. My sergeant, looking not at all abashed, was sitting with a glass of wine and a girl on his knee, grinning at me. What the hell! It had been a long day, and a little liberating would do us no harm. So I made a rota of duty on the crossroads to direct all our vehicles away from Brussels and up to Antwerp, and settled back to enjoy Madame's hospitality.

It was now seven or eight o'clock, when in came our sergeant to say that the Colonel was approaching. He had the good sense to appraise Madame, who took in the situation in a flash and was at the door with her most attractive barmaid to welcome George Fanshawe while I hid in the darkest corner. George got the full treatment. 'Ah mon brave Général', a voluptuous embrace and a glass of champagne from the barmaid, and George too is captured.

Things sorted themselves out, and George said 'Bob, you seem to be settled here, so stay here all night and make sure all our vehicles turn to Antwerp. Get that gun of yours repaired and on the road, and report to me at dawn, or when the Military Police take over here.' Off he swept, with Madame blowing kisses.

Our vigil continued all night long. We supplied Madame with all our rations, she organized her cook, and we had a magnificent dinner with half the village. That night was memorable for two things. Firstly, on the first floor of the house opposite, a very drunken Belgian stood at the window; every time one of our vehicles approached, up went the window and he leant out and saluted them. He kept this up all night long. Secondly, at around ten o'clock we were joined by three Belgian resistance fighters from the Armée Blanc. They asked for our help, as some of their comrades were fighting the Germans a mile down the road. We left two sentries on the road to direct the traffic, and with the jeep proceeded off to the rescue with the resistance fighters.

We moved a mile, no Germans; another mile, no Germans. After an hour of this we reached a large farm which was apparently a headquarters of the White Army. Here the farmer welcomed us with open arms. The three resistance men had escaped, and they had captured six of the Germans and locked them in the cellar. Around midnight, in the midst of celebrations attended by all his friends and neighbours, one of his two daughters suddenly said 'Ah, où est Georges?' George was still apparently in the attic, and was then invited down to the party. He turned out to be a young RAF officer who had been comfortably hidden away in the attic for three weeks and carefully looked after by the girls. He looked well and dapper.

We embraced and I told him he was liberated, that we would take him back with us and that he would soon be home in England. He would have none of it. He told us to push off (rather more rudely). He did not want to be liberated, and with one arm around each daughter, said he was very happy where he was. We left him and returned to our café at the crossroads. At around three o'clock, the Military Police arrived, we caught two hours sleep and then proceeded to Antwerp to report at dawn to George Fanshawe.

10
Antwerp and Nijmegen

The occupation of Antwerp and the halt of our advance. Operation 'Market Garden'. the battle to cross the Rhine at Arnhem. The regiment's support of 15th/19th Hussars, the 44th Royal Tank Regiment and the US 82nd and 101st Airborne Divisions in securing the Arnhem corridor. Tributes paid to Colonel Fanshawe and the regiment. Arnhem in retrospect.

ANTWERP

The leading tanks of the 11th Armoured Division, with our OPs in support, crossed the last bridge south of Antwerp early on 4 September. The seizure of this bridge before it was destroyed owed much to the Belgian resistance, the White Army, who prevented it being blown up. I only had time to visit my battery in action a few miles south of Antwerp for a short time, when I was sent forward into the city to support its occupation that afternoon. For some reason we had been halted in Antwerp and were not ordered to continue the advance up into Holland as originally planned. We soon occupied the main city area, and at one time I had my OP in the cathedral right in the city centre. However, strong German resistance was being met in the industrial area across the Albert Canal in the northern part of the city (Figure 23).

Antwerp lay on the east side of the Schelde River, which was very wide and really an arm of the sea. There was one major tunnel under the Schelde which led from the city centre just north of the cathedral to the west bank. The west side of the estuary was occupied by the Germans and was then open ground. To the north of the city centre, the Albert Canal ran due east from the Schelde and then turned south-east once out of Antwerp. Beyond the Albert canal to the north and north-west lay the huge area of docks. To the east of the docks lay the railway station and a maze of roads, railways, waterways and factories: this was, in fact, the industrial heart of Antwerp. The Albert Canal itself was a pretty formidable obstacle.

Our attacks across the Albert Canal from 4 September were intended to capture the docks and then we were to force our way through the factory area and so continue our advance north-east to Breda. An advance round

Antwerp was not carried out for some reason. At first all went well. The 11th Armoured Division got two battalions of infantry of the 159th Infantry Brigade across the Albert Canal, and with the help again of the White Army, the docks were captured intact. However, the fighting in the railway sation and industrial area was bloody and no quick progress was made. Our guns stayed on the southern outskirts of Antwerp. Lieutenant Beck's diary covers the next few days.

September 4th. At dawn we are on the move again! We pass through Assche at the same time as our leading tanks enter Antwerp. 15th/19th Hussars, whom we are still supporting, are ordered to guard the western approaches to Antwerp, as it is thought that the Germans cut off at the coast might attempt to break through. We go into action near Lebbecke just south of Antwerp and all our brens and tanks are sighted facing west. Flat dykeland here, cultivated land split up into allotments. The Battery Command Post in a Flemish house whose greenhouses are stacked with tomatoes. Lt. Kalbrier goes back to last night's harbour area and brings back three Germans. They are scarched amidst a curious throng of soldiers and civilians, and we stare in amazement at the thousands of francs that are taken from their pockets. Between them they possess nearly 1,000,000 French francs! We are rather astonished to see the Belgians patting the Germans on the back and even shaking hands with them! Maybe it is plain curiosity, although there may be something in the prisoners' story that they are Greeks!

September 5th. We spend the night at Lebbecke before moving to the outskirts of the town of Willibroek. During the night a despatch rider from the Regiment has been shot by Germans making their way through our lines. Advance parties go off armed to the teeth, consisting of 341's half-track, three Officers and three assistants armed with Brens at the ready. The Regiment occupies an allotment area just west of the town. We are given a respite by being allowed to maintain ourselves at half strength and half the Battery has a drink and a song in the local inns and houses.

September 6th. Still in Willibroek. The Battery Command Post has a comfortable time established in a house which was once a *collaborateur*'s. Plenty of Nazi emblems and literature all over the house. The day is spent on maintenance and cleaning up. Some get baths at the local public baths. The hospitable people visit our bivvies and mend our clothes. The children are a great delight. Every soldier is a Pied Piper with a swarm of children running around him. They are clean and fresh in bright coloured clothing. They shake hands with everyone. In the morning they walk round the gun area presenting a lovely red tomato to everyone. The other half of the Battery who are due to visit the town are disappointed. Just as we don our 'Glad Rags' for the first time for a long time we are ordered to move. That night we enter Antwerp and we go into action on the southern edge with our guns trained across the heart of the city. We manage to accommodate ourselves in private houses, which were once the homes of the Nazis, and we spend a very comfortable night. There is a battle going on in the northern suburbs as our troops try to cross the Albert Canal. The enemy are firmly established in factory buildings.

September 7th. We are in action several times during the day, and the battle still continues north of Antwerp. Our firing breaks many house windows in the neighbourhood. However this does not stop us making friends with the local population and everyone soon organizes a place to get his feet under the table. We have come to the conclusion that we like the Belgians. The shops in the town are closed but most of the cafés are open. Nearly all the windows carry bills, printed in English, 'The Belgian people are grateful to their British and American liberators'. People are dancing and drinking, yet less than a mile away across the canal, one can hear the vicious rattle of machine-guns, and occasionally the quick, sudden rush and bang of an 88mm shell, and the whine and bang of our own shells going the other way. Through the streets a lorry races, from which men are throwing the first edition of the first free paper published in Antwerp since the liberation, a communist paper.

Our OP crews have a most curious time. To reach their OPs they drive through Antwerp in their Shermans, stop and do some shopping on the way, then drive up to a building, catch the lift to the roof and spend the rest of the day observing the enemy in the factory areas. A most odd experience watching a battle fought with desperation by men and tanks, while down in the streets below, men and women are going about their daily business, apparently unconcerned.

On the afternoon of 7 September I was withdrawn and returned to the gun end. Orders from the Colonel that night were dramatic. The whole of the 11th Armoured Division were to withdraw from Antwerp and proceed south-east to reinforce the Guards Armoured Division who had established a bridgehead and a bridge at Beeringen some thirty or so miles along the canal to the south-east. 50th Division also were to move south-east along the Albert Canal. Antwerp was to be evacuated until the 51st Highland Division arrived. This division was moving up the coast on our left and they were not expected to get to Antwerp until first light on 9 September although armoured cars might make it late on the 8th. The 86th Field Regiment were told to hold Antwerp for a day and a night until the 51st arrived.

That night the 11th Armoured Division, without us, moved completely out of Antwerp. George Fanshawe's orders were that 341st Battery and 462nd Battery were to guard the north of the city, that is the Docks and the Albert Canal. With 342nd Battery, I was given the task of guarding the tunnel under the Schelde on the west side of the city centre, and at all costs preventing the Germans on the other side coming through it. We were also to protect the east side of the town, particularly the crossing of the Albert Canal at Wijnegen, from which a main road led into Antwerp from the east. The regiment's guns were to remain in their position on the southern outskirts of the city, so that they could cover the whole city area and its approach from west, north and east. We were instructed to take any spare men, tanks and bren carriers forward with our OPs as required, to provide 'infantry' support.

We were to make as much noise and vehicle movement as possible, for example, we should fire at the smallest enemy movement, to persuade the

Germans that they had a division against them! In addition, we were to liaise with and arm the White Army and to use them to help us where possible.

When I returned to my battery's gun position that evening we had two conferences. Firstly, I called together all officers and NCOs. I congratulated them on their advance and all they had done. Then I explained that the fighting was now stiffening and set out the plan for next day. We then had a warning about discipline, as one gun had lost two of its team, who had presumably succumbed to local hospitality. I warned all the men that soon we would be in Germany, facing an unfriendly population. This was, as it turned out, somewhat optimistic!

At the close of this discussion the Battery Sergeant-Major said that he and some of 'the lads' had found that other regiments had been receiving parcels and 'goodies' from home, including nice knitted scarves and even wireless sets. He suggested that, as we were the Hertford Battery, it might be a good idea for me to write to the Mayor of Hertford and tell him of our D-Day, Normandy and Antwerp experiences, putting in a suggestion that the poor troops would love some parcels! Then and there we composed a letter which we censored. Weeks later I heard that the goods had arrived, and when I was in hospital, I was also sent a copy of the *Hertfordshire Mercury* with a front-page spread describing our exploits. There was a picture of the Mayor, Cyril Vance Packman, shown with my letter. Fifteen or so years later, when I became a Borough Councillor of Hertford, I was sponsored by Vance Packman, and my letter was quoted again.

Writing this letter was almost my last act as Battery Commander. Having finished it, our second conference was with my two Troop Commanders, Captains Garton Ash and Roy Marshall, and we made our plans for the morrow.

Garton Ash was to establish an OP before dawn in an office building overlooking the Schelde tunnel and to take with him a half-track and a bren-gun carrier with enough men to take up positions to fire down and through the tunnel should the Germans try and get through. Roy Marshall would deal with the east side of the town, and at dawn he and I would go there and find the best OP. Having established him, I would contact the White Army, liaise with them, and arm them as best we could. This being settled, we collected spare arms, detailed off our three parties and retired to sleep.

Before dawn, all three of us set off together to install Garton Ash first, so Roy Marshall and I would both know where to find him and his team. He had recced an OP the evening before, and we saw him and his tunnel-blocking teams installed. His instructions were simple; if any Germans approached the tunnel on the other side of the Schelde, he was to open up with our guns at once. He records:

The OP was in a tall office building with a small cupola on top, reached by a small circular staircase. As I climbed up the staircase (the lifts were not working) I heard other footsteps apparently coming down to meet me. Fortunately this was only a Belgian who greeted me warmly. There was a small platform outside the cupola with a perfect view across the river to a block of flats on the west bank close to the entrance to the tunnel. The main problem was communicating because the wireless in the carrier parked at the entrance to the building was masked by the surrounding buildings and there was considerable interference thought to come from the city's trams still running. We took the '18' set up to the OP but its range was not really good enough. During the day I was visited by George Fanshawe who arranged for the Royal Signals section to bring up a more powerful set and two large and heavy batteries. This made all the difference.

There was some movement by the block of flats and I fired a troop target at that, hitting the flats and gradually climbing up the side until one round skimmed the top of a small projection on the roof, which appeared to be in use as a German OP. The Germans all disappeared and a round of gunfire immediately to the north of the flats kept them out of the way.

After dark on September 9th we were told to evacuate the OP as 51st Division had arrived, but evacuating that OP was easier said than done and getting the wireless and the big batteries down the circular stairs in the dark was quite a problem. However, all succeeded and we loaded up the carrier and drove down the street on the east bank of the river, the carrier's tracks making a terrific noise on the cobbles, and hopefully that gave the impression that Antwerp was strongly occupied.

Roy Marshall and I left Garton Ash and crossed Antwerp. It was eerily deserted as dawn broke. The previous day it had been full of tanks and troops, and now there was only the sound of our tracks on the cobbles. Roy and I drove through the centre and out to the east side along the road to Wijnegen, looking for a suitable OP for him. We searched for some time and made a reconnaissance of all the approaches. We soon discovered the perfect solution. To the north of our road on open ground, between us and the Albert Canal, stood a massive football stadium. It commanded views of the Albert Canal crossings and the roads in from the east. Roy and I went there and installed him with an OP on the top rows of seats, 100 feet or so in the air. He could move all around the top and have a superb view. As we left, the Germans opened fire on me, but Roy was pretty safe.

We reached the road out of Antwerp, to be stopped by a group of Belgians who introduced themselves as the White Army, and one of their number as the commander. I asked them in particular about German movements, and they took us down to the Albert Canal so that we could see the German positions across it. We proceeded on foot, leaving my jeep some way from the canal. After that we withdrew to a small café close by the canal for a conference. Their main concern was the lack of arms and ammunition.

In the midst of our talk, suddenly a German patrol passed along the street outside. The four of us had one revolver, mine, so a quiet but hasty retreat was made out of the back door, into my jeep and away. We returned to the football stadium to meet Roy Marshall, brief him and arrange for him to keep in contact with the White Army. Two of them arranged to stay with Roy. I then agreed to go back into Antwerp to our gun position, and to bring forward, if possible, a tank or gun for support and as many spare arms and ammunition as I could. We arranged a rendezvous on the main road. I then returned to our guns and collected spare arms, wishing we had not dumped so many of the German arms we had captured in France.

In addition, I found David Benson, a Troop Commander of the 341st Battery, at the gun end without a job. David's Sherman tank had not been modified and had a real 75mm gun with ammunition. I got permission from Regimental Headquarters and he joined me. I took a jeep with arms for the White Army, and we proceeded back through Antwerp and out eastward to our rendezvous.

There was one Belgian at the rendezvous, who told us that the Germans were crossing the Albert Canal at Wijnegem a mile or so down the road, and that his comrades had gone down to attack them. We made our own way there with all haste. Wijnegem was then a small town, or large village, on the south side of the canal, with one main road running eastwards passing through it and crossing the canal by a bridge. This bridge was blown and half collapsed into the canal, but it was possible to walk over the remains of it quite easily.

On arriving at Wijnegem David and I were told that the Germans had a spandau strong point just across the canal, and that some of the Belgians were trapped under the bank of the canal. We were asked to rescue them. We went up the street, spotted the spandau position, and also saw that German soldiers were crossing the bridge about 300 yards from us. David brought up his tank. Lance Bombardier Beavis, the gunner, opened fire on the spandau with the 75mm gun. His first round bounced on the road, right in front of the tank. Recovering his aim, he scored a direct hit on the Germans and we used the tank's machine-gun on the Germans crossing the bridge. Very satisfactorily they all ended up in the canal, and the Belgians scrambled out from their trap.

We were quite content so far. We distributed our arms and then I decided to leave David, the tank and the jeep to guard the bridge while I went round with the White Army to organize them as infantry to take up defensive positions to prevent any more German moves across the canal. If this had happened and the Germans had discovered how weak we were, they might well have pushed into Antwerp.

One of the younger resistance fighters spoke English, so communication was easy. We established one strong point at the crossroad, organized a barricade, and gave them a field of fire. We then set off down a small lane towards the canal to the north, to establish another post. Before we left, I consulted David, and we agreed that we should register the river crossing as a target for our guns. I gave out the target map reference and left David to order the fire and register the target.

Our party, consisting of myself and the four Belgians, set off down a lane, which led past allotments on one side and a row of cottages on our left. I was walking a few paces behind the Belgians when there was a loud bang behind me. I collapsed, somewhat surprised, into the mud of the lane and found I simply could not stand up. My next recollection is being picked up, carried into one of the cottages and being laid out on the kitchen table, with the housewife cutting my trousers with a large pair of scissors.

I remember having a pain in my right arm, but no pain at all in my legs, just numbness and faintness. A bottle of brandy was shoved into my mouth, and soon two of my soldiers came up with a stretcher and carried me through the village street to a local school which was being used as a Casualty Centre run by nuns. Later that evening they rolled out a horse-drawn ambulance, and two civilian casualties and I were sent off into Antwerp. As I left, two armoured cars from 51st Division arrived and I remember handing over Wijnegem to them before I lost consciousness.

From Antwerp I was moved later that night to a big hospital in Brussels, which was still run by German and Belgian staff. I gather I was too ill to be moved for three days, but on 12 September I was flown back to Lyneham in Wiltshire, and then taken by hospital train through the night to Birmingham. I had been wounded badly in both legs, and had a smaller wound in the right arm, from a mortar or shell. It is curious that when I was badly and suddenly wounded, I felt little pain at the time – that came later. My thoughts were of surprise and annoyance.

Had I been hit by a German mortar? This was quite possible, as we were visible at times from across the canal. Or was it one of my own 25-pounder ranging rounds? Our guns were in position way back to the south of Antwerp, and the distance to our target was very near their maximum range, so the fall of shells may well have been variable. Had I actually shot myself? I think the answer to this is yes! I still have the shell fragment from my right leg, so a metallurgist could probably tell me the answer, but that would achieve little. War is many things, but above all it is a great lottery with people's lives. I was lucky; I had gas gangrene badly, lost a leg and just survived because penicillin was available, and the surgical and medical care at Queen Elizabeth's Hospital at Edgbaston, outside Birmingham, was superb.

In January 1945 I was discharged from Queen Elizabeth's and transferred to Queen Mary's Hospital, Roehampton. There I was examined by a consultant surgeon who brusquely told me that my stump was too long and that he would re-amputate the next morning. I walked out, ordered a taxi and went home. I only returned weeks later for the fitting of my artificial limb.

OPERATION 'MARKET GARDEN'

On 9 September the regiment left Antwerp and proceeded south-eastward through Malines to Beeringen where the Guards Armoured Division had made a bridgehead over the Albert Canal. They crossed the canal over a Bailey Bridge and went into action to form an anti-tank defence of this bridgehead. On 15 September they joined the Guards Armoured Division on the Escaut Canal, in preparation for the major offensive about to be launched to capture bridges across five important canals and rivers: the Wilhelmina canal north of Eindhoven at Zon, the Willems canal at Veghel, the Maas at Grave, the Waal at Nijmegen, and lastly the lower Rhine at Arnhem (Figure 24). This operation, called 'Market Garden', better known as the Arnhem Battle, failed at Arnhem and has been told by better pens than mine.

In essence it was an advance by 30 Corps up a single road (The Club Route) combined with drops by three airborne divisions on the bridges up that route. The advance was led by the Guards Armoured Division. Our part in it was to provide artillery support to armoured regiments from 11th Armoured Division who followed the Guards advance and to join up with the American airborne divisions and provide them with support to keep the route open. For this purpose each battery was allocated to support a tank regiment; 341st Battery were to support 15th/19th Hussars and join up with 101st Airborne Division at Zon, 342nd Battery supporting 44th Royal Tank Regiment would then pass through to support 101st Airborne Division further north at Veghel, whilst 462nd Battery would subsequently go through to Grave to link with the US 82nd Airborne. As will be seen, the regiment played an important part in providing the artillery support for the US Airborne Divisions, thus enabling them to hold all four bridges and to reopen the road whenever it was breached, and to beat off German attempts to ruin the whole operation.

While this was happening I was semi-conscious with a temperature over 106 °F at times so I must leave Garton Ash with Sidney Beck to finish this chapter. The preparations and first part of 'Market Garden' mainly involved the guns of 341st Battery. Sidney Beck tells their story and the advance of 341st Battery to Zon and St Oedenrode.

On September 15th the guns move up to the Escaut canal through Beeringen. There is a considerable amount of artillery already in position along the banks of the Escaut canal. Our position is less than 500 yards from the canal and we can see clearly the woods on the far bank. Our forward troops have a small bridgehead on the opposite bank and are slowly mopping up the woods on either side of the road leading north from the bridge. The guns and Command Posts are in the back gardens of houses in the village of Lommel. The civilians are still going about their daily lives unconcerned with the preparations for battle going on around them. We bake some bread in the wall-oven of one farmhouse. We have an amusing time trying to explain to the farmer that we want to bake bread. And it takes him a long time explain to us we do not need bread tins, the bread is baked on a hot iron pan.

The next day, September 15th, is a fine sunny day and is spent in preparation for the fire-plan. The details of the next operation are explained. The map of Holland is shown to us and the route to the Zuyder Zee pointed out. We learn of the big Airborne Invasion to start tomorrow. The British 1st Airborne Division are to be dropped at Arnhem; the American 82nd at Nijmegen and Grave; the 101st US Airborne Division to be dropped north of Eindhoven at Zon to guard the road to Grave. As soon as the airborne invasion starts, the Guards Armoured Division will break out of their bridgehead over the Escaut canal. Advancing along the only main road, they are to race at all speed to Arnhem, and if possible push on to the Zuyder Zee. Advancing as they will be through enemy territory on a single road, our supply lines will be particularly vulnerable. Speed is essential to the whole operation, and they cannot succeed if the supplies are cut. To defend the route, three armoured regiments of 11th Armoured Division, each with a Battery of the Regiment attached, are to form strong points along the route. Working in conjunction with the American troops, we are to keep the supply route open at all costs. 341st Battery are to link up with the US paratroops at Zon and St Oedenrode, and we will defend the bridges there. 342nd Battery will pass through and help defend the bridges at Veghel. 462nd Battery will pass through them and go to Grave. So for the first time since Normandy, we will really operate as independent Batteries. It looks an awfully long way to the Zuyder Zee; it is over a hundred miles, and there seem too many SS troops *en route*, but the thoughts of the Airborne Invasion and the daring scale of the plan make us confident it will succeed. We turn from studying the map to prepare for the barrage, the 'milk-round', which will be fired before the break-out from the bridgehead. As we discuss the plans for tomorrow's attack, optimism runs high, and many of us begin making plans for spending Xmas at home.

The next day, September 17th, is another fine bright day. Zero hour is about 1300 hrs. It cannot be fixed until the Corps Commander General Horrocks actually sees the Airborne Troops coming over. The morning is passed watching squadrons of bombers and fighters passing to and fro high overhead. Then come thrills. Lightning fighters and dive-bombers make daring low-level attacks on enemy gun positions just across the canal. As zero hour approaches, Typhoon rocket planes add their deadly attacks on the enemy. These pilots seem more daring than ever as they dive low into the AA fire. Then in the distance to the north-west we can dimly make out the long trail of gliders making their way to Zon and Grave and Arnhem. The 'Milk-Round' begins almost at once and a terrific concentration of shells pours into the enemy gun positions surrounding the bridgehead. After this we fire a rolling barrage to saturate both sides of the main road, as the leading tanks edge their way forward towards the Dutch border. Immediately the barrage is over, our Battery ceases fire and moves over the canal by the Bailey Bridge. We go into action again about 1000 yards from the bridge, immediately in front of a Battery of Medium guns. In this open space just north of the canal are packed many hundreds of tanks and vehicles and guns. Shells from our own guns on the other side of the canal are whistling overhead as the 'Milk-Round' goes on and another barrage is fired. The leading tanks are meeting stiff opposition. The first nine are knocked out in the space of 200 yards!

We dig in. At dusk the bridgehead area is subjected to heavy enemy shelling for nearly 45 minutes, and although many shells fall close, no one in the Battery is injured, although one man is evacuated with shell-shock. During the night the enemy stage a counter-attack on the bridge, attacking the factory area to the east of Lommel. After some sharp fighting they are beaten off but the Guards have not succeeded in breaking out.

September 18th is another long day of firing as our tanks make further efforts to break out. Road blocks south of Eindhoven are causing great difficulty, but with the great co-operation of the Typhoon rocket-firing planes, enemy resistance is gradually worn down. In addition the whole advance is held up because the bridge at Zon was blown up before the US paratroopers reached it. Evening, however, finds the Battery still in action just 1000 yards from the Escaut canal bridge and quite close to the main road. Remembering last night's shelling, we begin to dig even deeper. A German sniper opens up from the flank and bullets whistle uncomfortably close. It is getting dark and he is difficult to locate. Soon, however, we have worse worries than snipers, the Luftwaffe arrive. Several Ju 88s dive-bomb the bridgehead area. Many HE bombs and AP bombs rain down bursting like crackers down the line of guns, amongst the concentrated vehicles, down each side of the road and around the bridge approaches. We spend a most uncomfortable half hour shivering in our slit trenches, watching the scores of tracer shells weaving patterns in the sky. One AP bomb falls on the end of a slit trench where several men are sheltering.

The trench collapses. Two men only are slightly injured. One AP bomb bursts on the back of a Bren carrier setting it on fire. When things become quieter, we survey the damage. Apart from minor splinter damage, three of our 3-tonners are riddled with AP splinters and are immovable. A medium gun just behind us is knocked out by a direct hit and the AA gun guarding the bridge is also a casualty. There are many small fires burning all around the area but considering the concentration of troops and material, our casualties are remarkably light. It has been a very trying time for all concerned. It is our first experience of deliberate air attack on our own position and it is not pleasant. Already we are revising our opinions about being home for Xmas.

Lt. Harry Dovey, CPO of 342nd Battery, is killed by a bomb as he crosses the bridge over the canal.

However, today the Guards move north, a Bailey Bridge at Zon being completed, and we receive orders to move with the 15th/19th Hussars. We line up on the main road waiting to cross the Dutch border. Then we move up into Eindhoven and receive a very colourful reception from the inhabitants. All the girls and women are wearing orange; orange dresses, orange shirts, orange sashes and orange ribbons in their hair. Flags gaily waving and everyone very happy at the liberation. The people, whenever we stop for a few minutes, always want to know where the Prince of Orange is, have we brought him with us? They seem to expect us to produce him out of the back of our vehicle! A few miles north of Eindhoven we get into action on the north-west side of Zon, a village important for its canal bridge on the main supply route. Our gun position is on the edge of a large open space which is an astonishing sight when we arrive. Great Horsa gliders are strewn haphazardly all over the fields at various angles; some with their noses in the woods bordering the fields, some crashed with their tails jutting awkwardly into the air, others with their noses gaping high in the air where they have been opened to unload jeeps and equipment. In the woods we meet the American glider pilots living in holes and bivvies made of crashed gliders. Living on their pack rations, they are very glad to see us and our guns. In the late afternoon six Panthers start shelling Zon and the bridge from the south-east, setting fire to the American Hospital. The US Divisional Commander comes to the Command Post, and our OPs man the Church tower, directing our guns onto the tanks. An enemy tank puts an AP shot through the Church steeple, but does not dislodge our OP officer, Lt. Craston. With our artillery support and the threat of an attack by the 15th/19th Hussars tanks, the Panthers withdraw. Later a few enemy planes raid the area, dropping AP and HE bombs around the bridge and down the main street of Zon. Our water-cart is a casualty. When the enemy tanks begin shelling the bridge, the water-cart is drawing water from the canal and receives a direct hit. The driver and his companion manage to escape and crawl back to the gun position. During the night there is intermittent sniping from the surrounding woods, but it passes off quietly.

The enemy tanks return to the attack in the morning. The 15th/19th Hussars put in an attack supported by our gunfire. We get two, and the 15th/19th get four. Total bag for the morning, six Panther tanks, and another dangerous threat to the supply lines is removed. At midday the American ground forces begin to raise clouds of red smoke. Very soon another great sky train of gliders arrives overhead. One train goes on towards Nijmegen but the other circles overhead. The Dakotas wheel round, cast off their gliders and make for home. We see one or two gliders hit by Flak and crash into the trees a few miles from the gun position. The enemy AA fire is generally quite heavy. About half an hour later we have the astonishing sight of watching parachutists landing from Dakotas. As the flight of about 50 Dakotas roars towards us, the sky suddenly fills with great green mushrooms and we can plainly see the men swinging underneath. They land about a mile from the guns. In the evening we have another scare of tanks approaching Zon and stand-to for several hours.

The next day, September 21st, the American glider pilots, with whom we are now firm friends, begin to pack up to make their way back down the route. Their instructions are to get back to England as soon as possible. One of them, a Lt. Sheppard, offers to telephone our relatives when he arrives back in England, and we eagerly give him our phone numbers. He promises to spend his first Sunday in England sitting in the telephone box, phoning all the numbers we have given him. [He did – the following Sunday.]

That afternoon more gliders and supplies are dropped by parachute. The sky is more cloudy and, taking advantage of the extra cover, enemy fighters attack the returning Dakotas directly overhead. Three of the transporters are shot down in flames in as many minutes, and it is an awe-inspiring sight to see them crash behind the trees. 'B' Troop spend the day searching the woods, picking up the surplus equipment left by the Americans: tommy guns, blankets, parachutes, harness, torches and many items of food and cigarettes etc., are added to each man's store.

Stephen Perry's full diary had finished, but his brief notes tell part of the story of the advance of 341st Battery with the 15th/19th Hussars. On 18 September he broke out of the Escaut Canal bridgehead with the leading tanks of the 15th/19th Hussars as the airborne forces passed overhead on the way to Grave, Nijmegen and Arnhem. He engaged a number of targets and was bombed that evening. On 19 September he moved through Eindhoven with the Hussars and joined the 101st US Airborne Division who had landed north of Eindhoven to seize the bridges over the Wilhelmina Canal at Zon, the river Dommel at St Oedenrode and the Willems Canal at Veghel. He recalls shooting up many German targets at Zon on the 19th.

The capture and holding of Zon completed the first stage of our advance, the next stage was to push ahead to Veghel. After passing through Zon, Garton Ash joined up with the 101st US Airborne Division and now describes his move with 342nd Battery to Veghel. Major Neville Whitmee had now taken command of that battery, Robert Kiln having been wounded.

By September 21st the 15th/19th Hussars had reached St Oedenrode but had not been able to make contact with the Americans trying to hold Veghel. The advance to Veghel was the job of 44th Royal Tank Regiment and 342nd Battery so we passed through the 15th/19th Hussars and 341st Battery.

Everything seemed very quiet to the north of St Oedenrode and Neville Whitmee told me to drive ahead and see if I could contact the Americans. The road was empty and fairly exposed and we seemed to be the only vehicle on it. It was the loneliest drive I have ever done, but late in the afternoon we contacted the Americans south of Veghel in a heavily wooded area. The Regimental Commander, Colonel Johnson, explained the situation to me, with his troops in contact with the enemy to the west in a heavily wooded area. It was impossible to get the tank through there and in any case by then was almost dark, and he was unable to spare any guide. I ascertained as accurately as possible where the leading American units were, selected a likely target area where the enemy might concentrate round a crossroads with some buildings, and gave a map reference battery target. We were rewarded with a fine pyrotechnic display, having clearly hit German tanks or other vehicles and brewed up a considerable amount of ammunition. Colonel Johnson was delighted and told me it had boosted their morale considerably as it was the first real artillery support they had had since landing.

The next day we moved forward with 44th Royal Tank Regiment into Veghel and for the next two days were fighting on all sides of the town to try and keep the road open.

On September 23rd the 44th Royal Tank Regiment pushed on north-eastwards towards Uden but there was much enemy shellfire on the outskirts of Veghel and quite a battle to move forward. Further airborne supplies were going overhead through heavy flak and one Dakota was shot down nearby, some of the crew baling out at the last minute in the hope that their fall would be broken by the trees and hedges, but they were too far away for us to find out whether they survived. As we moved forward I found Stephen Perry in his carrier, having been hit in the leg, and as I was able to continue support for the attack northwards, he decided he would have to retire. I was conscious that this left me as the last of the original Troop Commanders who landed on D-Day still in action.

Stephen Perry was evacuated to Deist and then to Brussels where he was operated on and flown back to England by Dakota on 27 September.

This battle at Veghel was intense and was to continue for several days as repeated German attacks tried to sever 30 Corps' communications. The 86th played a major part in this and 341st Battery were called forward to join 342nd Battery there. Sidney Beck relates his experience of the battles at Veghel on 22–3 September.

Having secured Zon, there is trouble further up the main axis where the enemy has cut the main road at Veghel, so on September 22nd we are ordered forward and hurriedly pack up. The road is congested with traffic and there is a long stream of transport belonging to the British 1st Airborne Division. Traffic is at a standstill in St Oedenrode, but we find our way through and take up a position just east of the main road and south of Veghel. Our OPs find the Americans in Veghel hard pressed, as the Germans are astride the road leading north from the town. A fire plan is quickly laid on, and under cover of this the Americans succeed in driving the enemy back some distance from the road. In the afternoon some shells from a German 88mm gun land on 'B' Troop's gun position, wounding Sgt. Hazeley, 'H' Sub No. 1, in the back of the neck. He is evacuated to St Oedenrode which is itself subjected to intermittent shelling. Overhead there is much aerial activity as great armadas of gliders and Dakotas pass to and from the Arnhem area. We see many gliders caught by enemy AA fire, but it is cheering to see them landing behind us at Zon. We feel rather unprotected in this position. The area to our right flank has not been cleared. There are no Allied troops there and our local defence has to be strong and alert all night.

The next morning, September 23rd, was a very, very exciting morning for our OPs, and hard work for the gun end and command post staff. The enemy, intent on preventing supplies reaching Arnhem, make repeated attempts to capture the road from Veghel. Supporting their attacks with 88mm guns, they keep the Americans and our tank regiments hard pressed all the morning. Our OPs, under constant shellfire, do great work in bringing down fire from our guns on to enemy concentrations. Many attacks are broken up before they get moving. Others are stopped

PLATE 45. *Club Route. A lorry blown up by German counter-attack near Veghel, 23 September 1944.*

by our shellfire just when the Americans are in a dangerous situation. The gun end is kept constantly on the alert, answering many calls for fire. The Battery Command Post is now a miniature Royal Artillery Headquarters. A battery of 25-pounders, a battery of mediums and a battery of 3.7 Heavy Anti-Aircraft (HAA) guns have been surveyed on to our grid. Telephones are laid to them and all orders for fire are passed on, so that the OPs have quite a useful concentration of artillery to call on. The HAA guns put down airburst concentrations over the enemy, which prove particularly effective. By tea time the excitement dies down, the enemy withdraws defeated, and the route is saved, for a time anyway. Our OPs have had a very difficult time. Captain Perry MC, our acting BC, is wounded in the legs by shell splinters, but insists on carrying on. He is later evacuated, and once more we are without a Battery Commander. Captain Benson again takes over command of the Battery. Convoys again start moving up the main axis, and we sleep a little more soundly at night when we learn that our infantry recce has reached the canal bank to our east and has found the area clear of the enemy. We are also heartened by the sight of many more sky trains of planes carrying supplies to the front. On their way back some Stirlings give us a thrill by skimming the trees over our gun positions. We cannot help noticing the absence of gliders, or wondering why it is necessary to keep sending so many supplies by air. We have had little news from the front.

Garton Ash concludes the story at Veghel.

The night of September 23rd was spent with one Squadron of 44th Royal Tank Regiment in the main street of the town where the road from the south makes a sharp right-hand turn into a wide street, to the left of which there is a stretch of water, part of the Willems Canal. My tank was parked on the western side of the main street, clear enough from the high kerbstone to enable us to sleep between that and the tracks to obtain some protection. I drew the short straw for wireless watch between 2 and 4 a.m., sharing this with the Squadron.

Early the next morning we heard that the battery had had a very uncomfortable night with German armoured vehicles harbouring only a field or so away from them to the south of Veghel, and that they had to move through to the north. Before they arrived a German tank or SP opened fire up the main street from the other side of the water, brewing up a petrol tanker on the opposite of the main street. Moving the battery through the street was obviously going to need some luck and I met each vehicle and gun in turn before they turned into the main street, explaining the position and telling them to go to the western side and drive flat out round the bend higher up the street. All of them got through safely.

342nd Battery remained in the area of Veghel and Uden for several days trying to keep the road open or to reopen it when it was cut by Germans. The supply columns suffered severely at times and it was a sad sight to see hundreds of yards of burnt out 3-tonners on the verges where a column had been caught by a German attack [Plate 45].

462nd Battery had remained in the Escaut bridgehead waiting to move forward. They were ordered up to Arnhem on 22 September and made their way up the route, arriving south of Arnhem to support 82nd US Airborne on 24 September.

Sidney Beck relates the advance of 341st Battery from Veghel and the end of the Arnhem battle.

We have cleared Veghel and repulsed the German counter-attacks, so on September 24th, a warm and sunny Sunday, the road is open and everything is on the move again. We pack up and journey through shell-torn Veghel, passing the wreckage of carriers and vehicles knocked out in yesterday's severe fighting. A German light tank near the road is still smouldering. There are dead German soldiers sprawling in the ditches by the roadside.

We have quite a long journey up the famous 'Club' route through Uden! We cross the Maas at Grave by the magnificent steel bridge, marvelling at the manner in which it has been captured intact. On either side of the river we see gliders sprawled in the open fields. After crossing a large partly damaged canal bridge, we turn south along the canal and go into action due west of a large wooded hill in the woods of Grossbeek south of Nijmegen. But now we are fairly comfortable and in good spirits. We have our first glimpse of Germany (the Reichswald forest can be seen from the

PLATE 46. *A drawing by Bryan de Grineau for the* Illustrated London News *of the 86th SPs in action near Overloon in the Nijmegen Salient.*

road near Grave), and we are anticipating crossing the border soon. Our gun position is near some Dutch farms and we make full use of the amenities, which include electricity! We anxiously listen to the news bulletins. We know enough about the situation to realise the undercurrent of anxiety in the news, and our eyes turn north to Arnhem only ten miles away, where the rumble of guns continues all day and night. There is a sense of relief when the evening news announces that our patrols have crossed the Dutch Rhine near Arnhem, but we know that these patrols should have been across days ago if the plan is to succeed.

During September 25th we remain with ten miles of Arnhem. There is great aerial activity with many exciting views of dog fights between our fighters and German sneak raiders. We see a few planes shot down over Arnhem and Nijmegen. The canal bridge behind us is the object of an attempted bombing raid by enemy fighter planes. We suspect the enemy are using jet planes as there are peculiar whistles in the air that we have not heard before. The bombs which fall harmlessly in the fields behind us seem to have dropped out of the blue, as no planes are visible.

We hear that the main supply route was cut again yesterday after we left Veghel. The enemy put in a determined counter-attack and actually overran the gun position we vacated yesterday morning! Our brother battery, 342nd Battery, who has remained in action at Veghel have a very difficult time in the counter-attack, one

Sergeant being killed by a direct hit on his gun by an 88mm shell. News is still vague and disturbing. Our thoughts are still with the boys at Arnhem. That night we stand outside our bivvies in the dark and watch the almost continuous flash of gunfire. To the north the skyline, as far as we can see, is illuminated by the brilliant yellow flashes of cordite. The continuous dull roar of the guns throbs in the air and at times the ground trembles with the intensity of the barrage. It goes on for hours, seemingly without a pause, and we stand silent and fascinated, wondering . . . There is something angry in the air, as though great dragons are at bay, roaring and spitting defiance. Is it the last assault crossing, the crown of the operation, or, and none dared to voice these thoughts, is it withdrawal, a desperate rearguard action? Sometime after midnight there is a sudden hush and the horizon darkens and quietens. We turn in, puzzled but hopeful.

The next morning we are woken early. Bad news travels fast. It is a withdrawal. The news seeps through that our patrols have been withdrawn across the Lower Rhine and our gallant paratroopers brought back. The details are vague and the full import of the news does not sink in at once.

On 29 September the following letter from Lt.-General Horrocks was received and read out to the regiment's guns over the tannoy system:

For some weeks now, 30 Corps has been privileged to lead the advance of the Second Army. Our recent operation, which started last Sunday week, was one of the most daring that has ever been attempted in modern war.

In conjunction with the Airborne Corps, we were asked to penetrate deep into enemy territory, along one road and to force a passage over three of the most formidable rivers in Europe.

We have burst through the enemy's defences and have secured a passage over two of these rivers. We now stand poised between the second and third river, ready to advance again as soon as our larders have been re-stocked.

I should like to congratulate all ranks on this magnificent achievement, and I have received the following letter from the Commander-in-Chief, Field Marshal Montgomery: 'Your Corps has done splendidly and I congratulate you, and every officer and man in the Corps. Please tell them all how well I think they have done.'

I want all ranks to realise that the German is putting up a stubborn resistance as we approach his frontier. He is, however, very stretched, and provided we can maintain the offensive as we have done in the past, he is bound to crack in time.

Very soon I hope we shall be advancing into Germany, and carrying the war onto German soil.

Well done 30 Corps.

(sgd) B. G. Horrocks.
Lieut. General

Main HQ 30 Corps
26 Sept. 44

Commander 30 Corps.

The regiment's part in support of the US 101st Airborne Division was again an outstanding success and was recognized, not only by a visit to the regiment by General Horrocks on 30 September to congratulate them, but by the following two letters. The first was written to George Fanshawe by General Dempsey, Commander of the British 2nd Army, enclosing the second from General Maxwell Taylor, Commander of the US 101st Airborne Division.

October 9th

Headquarters
Second Army

Dear George,
I have had the enclosed from Commander 101 Airborne Div. I hope you realise what you and your Regiment did in this action. You played a large part in saving a most important bridge on the only road we then had to Airborne Corps and 30 Corps. Its loss would have made things more difficult.

You have also impressed an American Division with your skill and fighting qualities, and forged a hand between The Hertfordshire Yeomanry and 101 Airborne Division, which I am sure will continue.

Please accept, and pass on to all ranks, my thanks and congratulations.

(sgd) Dempsey

The second letter, from General Maxwell Taylor to General Dempsey, was dated 3 October 1944:

SUBJECT: Commendation of Lt. Col. G. D. Fanshawe, OBE, RA,
Thru: Commanding General, 30th Corps.

1. It gives me great pleasure to commend to you Lt. Col. G. D. FANSHAWE, OBE, RA, and the 86th (Herts. Yeomanry) Fd. Regt., RA, which he commands, for the timely and invaluable assistance they rendered this division in the repulse of enemy attacks on the town of VECHEL (4837), Holland, on 22 and 23 September, 1944.

2. At noon on 22 September, VECHEL was defended by the 2d Battalion, 501st Parachute Infantry, only. The normal supporting artillery was absent because of a poor drop caused by bad weather. At this time, the enemy launched repeated attacks by infantry and tanks, well supported by artillery, and cut the road between VECHEL and UDEN. Lt. Col. FANSHAWE, who was in the vicinity at the time, offered the support of his regiment. He immediately occupied positions and sent out observers who brought such a volume of effective fire on the enemy thrusts that none reached the bridges or the town.

3. Lt. Col. FANSHAWE coordinated defensive fires until the arrival of reinforcements permitted a counterattack. He assisted the counterattack materially with supporting fires. His enthusiasm and professional skill were an inspiration to those

associated with him and were in keeping with the finest traditions of the military service.

MAXWELL D. TAYLOR,
Major General, U.S.A. Commanding

The regiment's support of the 82nd US Airborne Division at Grave and Nijmegen from 24 September also received recognition from its Commander, General James Gavin, in a letter dated 17 October to General Horrocks, passed on with a brief covering letter to 30 Corps' artillery commander (CCRA).

Subject: *Letter of Commendation*
CCRA

Main HQ 30 Corps
18th Oct. 44

The attached letter from the Commander 82 US Airborne Division is passed to you for information.

I am delighted that Lieut-Colonel FANSHAWE has done so well; it is largely due to him that the present friendly relationship exists between the Americans and ourselves.

(sgd) BG Horrocks
Lieut-General,
Commander 30 Corps

SUBJECT: Letter of Commendation

APO 469 – In the Field
17 October 1944

TO: Commanding General, XXX Corps

1. Lieutenant Colonel GEORGE FANSHAWE, O.B.E., Commanding Officer, 86th Field Regiment, Royal Artillery, was detailed to the Division Artillery, 82nd Airborne Division on 24 September, 1944, as representative of the C.C.R.A., XXX CORPS. He remained in this capacity until 12 October 1944. Throughout this period, the regrouping of British units within the area has resulted in a constantly changing organization of artillery units available to give fire support. Lieutenant Colonel FANSHAWE has kept fully abreast of this rapidly changing situation at all times, and through his constant presence and close attention has insured timely and effective modifications of communications and liaison groups, both with Division Artillery Headquarters and with the lower units of this Division, toward a better mutual understanding of the technical functioning of the other units by each army. Through his efforts, Lieutenant Colonel FANSHAWE has contributed greatly to the most effective fire support that has played so large a part in the successful accomplishment of the missions of this Division.

2. I would like to express my commendation and appreciation of the exceptionally fine job that Lieutenant Colonel FANSHAWE has done in successfully working out

the complicated co-ordination of the employment of the British Artillery units in support of this Division.

JAMES M. GAVIN,
Brigadier General, U.S. Army, Commanding

These letters, though they may not be unique, certainly provide a suitable finish to our story of four months of war with a quite outstanding regiment, the 86th Field Regiment Hertfordshire Yeomanry and its Commander, George Fanshawe.

ANTWERP AND 'MARKET GARDEN'

By 3 and 4 September we were in Brussels and Antwerp. Patton was outside Metz, and Bradley on our right. Eisenhower had taken over command of all the field armies, and there we all stopped. No one reached the Rhine, let alone crossed it. Patton, not surprisingly, ran out of petrol. I have never understood why our advance did not continue. We had still enough petrol. There was no shortage of food or ammunition. Our objective was the Zuider Zee in Holland, but we were stopped in Antwerp for four days with only forty miles to go to the Maas to cut off all the retreating Germans on the coast to the north of us.

Eisenhower favoured a broad front approach, and gave priority to us seizing Antwerp. Montgomery wanted a narrow thrust across the Rhine into Holland, and to isolate the Ruhr, but both, in my view, overestimated the supply problem. Only petrol was short; why were our air forces not used to ferry petrol? We had captured masses of airfields. Why did Eisenhower not use his airborne forces then? Had he done so and not halted us all, Patton, Bradley and ourselves, or at least some of us, would have been in Germany by the end of September, either on a broad or narrow front.

Eisenhower was not a field general, and the tragedy was that he assumed command just when decisions in the field were wanted. If only Montgomery had stayed in operational command, or Bradley had taken over, they would not have halted everyone just at the moment when the momentum should have been carried on at all costs. I am convinced that, had we bypassed Antwerp, we would have been on the Maas in Holland within two days, that is by 6/7 September. As it was, we stayed on orders in Antwerp from the 4th to the 9th and the chance was lost.

Montgomery's uncharacteristic gamble at Arnhem can only be viewed as a desperate and rash effort to achieve what had been thrown away two weeks earlier. I have always felt that Montgomery acted out of frustration, and that

PLATE 47. *Nijmegen Bridge. British tanks crossing after its capture.*

is not a good basis for any big decision, so of course that gamble failed, but only just, and the costly winter of 1944/5 had to be endured. The fruits of Montgomery's Normandy victory were to a great extent squandered by the hesitation at the beginning of September. Without this delay we could have been in Berlin by Christmas and long before the Russians. With regard to Arnhem itself, Garton Ash supports my views in his retrospect on the causes of its failure.

ARNHEM IN RETROSPECT
by J. Garton Ash

With hindsight it seems very likely that the battle for Arnhem was lost two weeks before 'Market Garden' was launched on 17 September. At the time Antwerp and Brussels were captured, the German situation in southern Holland appears to have been chaotic with little really effective in the way of organized resistance, but during the following two weeks the Germans, with usual efficiency, mounted a substantial defence and were able to bring various elements of their 15th Army from the Pas de Calais area into southern Holland to fill the considerable gap in their defences. Our advance was halted close to Antwerp, although there were actions close up to the Meuse–Escaut Canal and to obtain a bridgehead over that, but it was apparently decided that for administrative reasons, particularly the very long supply lines from Normandy, insufficient petrol and other supplies were available to maintain the momentum of 30 Corps' advance. This was not, however, as it appeared to us on the ground. Letters home early in September all indicated our feelings that we were ready, and indeed anxious, to press on as fast as possible, and there was certainly enough petrol readily available for an advance of fifteen or twenty miles. If this had been directed immediately north of Antwerp to clear the north bank of the Schelde estuary, it is very probable that we could have cut off the escape route of large numbers of the German 15th Army from the Pas de Calais, whereas they were allowed to escape across the estuary to Walcheren and so to reach the one road back across the causeway into southern Holland. Thus they were in a position to interrupt the drive to Arnhem sufficiently to cause delays which in the end were fatal for 1st Airborne Division at Arnhem.

In spite of this, 'Market Garden' was not the failure which it has often been painted, but was instrumental in preparing the ground for the successful operations in February and March 1945 which brought about the end of the war. Four major water obstacles were overcome by a combination of the very successful drops by 82nd and 101st US Airborne Divisions, and the drive of 30 Corps to link up with them and reach a position very near Arnhem.

101st US Airborne Division was successful in capturing or enabling Club Route, the name given to the axis of the advance, to cross the Wilhelmina and Zuid Willems Vaart canals, the first at Zon and the second just south of Veghel. 82nd US Airborne Division captured the bridge at Grave over the River Maas and subsequently with the Guards Armoured Division the bridges over the river Waal at Nijmegen (Plate 47). These successes not only enabled Club Route to extend very nearly to Arnhem, but also provided a basis from which the rest of southern Holland could be cleared in the following months. They also provided the base from which the attacks were launched in February to clear the whole area between the Waal and the Maas up to the west bank of the Rhine, and in particular without the bridgehead north of Nijmegen the attack at the northern end of the Siegfried line would have been more difficult.

11
Postscript

The regiment's moves and battles after Arnhem until the end of the war. Personal post-war biographies of persons mentioned in this book.

Our story has ended, but the Hertfordshire Yeomanry continued fighting with 30 Corps until VE-Day on 8 May 1945 and then remained in Germany as part of the British occupying forces until disbanded in April 1946.

After Arnhem the regiment moved up to Grossbeek with OPs on the Grossbeek ridge looking eastwards into Germany, supporting the US 82nd Airborne Division and working with the US 319th Artillery Battalion. On 9 October they moved into Nijmegen and three days later back to Grave for a well-earned rest. While in the pub one night Garton Ash met Ronnie Lofthouse, the Company Commander of 'D' Company 6th Green Howards, with whom he had landed on D-Day, and whom he had not seen since the early days of Normandy. He was on his way back to England to take up a training job and told him that of the original Company who landed, only himself and his batman were still active.

On 16 November, George Loveday, wounded on D-Day, returned to the regiment and resumed command of the 341st Battery. He led the battery into Germany on that day.

From 18 November the 86th took a prominent part in the battles round Geilenkirchen. The following extract of a letter home describes typical conditions:

What was once a sown field is now a sea of mud. The tracks are deep channels of water where the tanks have bitten deep in the mud. Behind each gun you can see a wet shiny strip of canvas slanting above the slippery mud. Some of the luckier gun crews have a fire in their bivouac, a stove looted from a German house in Grotendrath and you may see a piece of piping smoking from one end of the canvas. The canvas is by no means waterproof, the wind has torn it in several places and the men have placed tins and mugs under the holes to catch the rain. The floor may be lined with wet straw, but that does not prevent the ground from becoming slippery as the boots tread in the mud. The 'bivvies' are draughty, low and dark. You cannot stand up so you lie on your bed, but your boots are muddy and you are cold, so you take off your boots and crawl into your bed in wet clothes. It is too dark to read so you think

PLATE 48. *Guns of 341st Battery in action at Menslage, north-west Germany, in full view of enemy across field to right, 9 April 1945.*

you will go to sleep or perhaps think, or possibly compose a letter, but you never get any further in your thoughts, every few seconds one or other of the Regiment's guns will fire shattering all your thoughts. You start again and the gun nearest you fires, shaking the earth and the bivvies, causing a lump of wet mud to roll onto your face. You compose yourself again, pulling the blankets tighter over your head, yet you cannot shut out that thud! thud! thud! of the hammering of the guns. Despite all this, not one of us would change places with the PBI whose life these days must be absolutely hell.

Garton Ash's letter home written at the end of November after Geilenkirchen is worth quoting, as he speaks for every artillery observer:

We've been pretty busy lately, the gun position was the worst ever but mostly I have been out as an OP first in one village and then in another trying in this flat country to find good view points.

I know when we used to go on holiday we always looked round lots of churches but one thing in the future, never to ask me to look at a church tower. They have an unfortunate way of being knocked down violently and frequently.

On 20 December they moved with 11th Armoured Division to take up positions on the Meuse near Namur as part of counter to the German Ardennes offensive (Figure 25). Christmas dinner was postponed until 28 December. By 2 January 1945 the regiment went over to the offensive with the 6th Airborne Division and 11th Armoured Division to throw back the

Germans from the Ardennes. From 8 February the regiment took part with 15th Scottish Division in the very hard fighting of the Reichswald Forest battles around Cleve and then Goch. By 10 March this battle had cleared the west bank of the Rhine, and they moved opposite Rees with the 51st Highland and 15th Scottish Division for the assault across the Rhine. On 27 March the regiment crossed the Rhine at Rees.

On 29 March they moved out of the bridgehead with the Guards Armoured Division to advance to Bremen (Figure 26). George Fanshawe left the regiment to become Commander Royal Artillery of 3rd Division, and Lt.-Colonel Symonds became Commanding Officer on 2 April. From then until 22 April, the regiment fought its way to the outskirts of Bremen, where they joined 3rd Division for the assault on Bremen, captured on 25 April. On 27 April there was more hard fighting with 51st Highland Division towards Bremerhaven and Cuxhaven and the Elbe, but by 5 May it was all over.

In August 1945 the regiment's SP guns were handed over to the Royal Ordnance Corps in preparation for a posting to the Far East, later cancelled. In April 1946 the regiment disbanded.

Readers may wish to know what happened to the main personalities in this book after the war was over.

George Fanshawe

I quote from his obituary in *The Times* of 1 March 1991:

Major-General George Fanshawe, CB, DSO, OBE, who commanded 86 Field Regiment (The Herts Yeomanry) RA, during the Normandy campaign, died on February 20 aged 89. He was born on September 27, 1901.

As a regular artillery officer, George Fanshawe always looked back with affection on his long association with the territorial regiment, the Herts Yeomanry, which shaped so much of his career. Over the years he was its adjutant, commanding officer and, finally, honorary colonel. In an unpublished memoir he wrote some years later he described the sense of surprise that went through the regiment in the summer of 1943 when it learned, rather by the way, that it was to become one of the first in the British army to acquire self-propelled guns. Fanshawe's first inkling of this news was a message from the station master at Warminster, near which the regiment was stationed, that a delivery of 24 tanks had just arrived by rail and was awaiting a recipient. Somewhat puzzled, Fanshawe sent a subaltern who knew something about tanks to investigate. When the truth – that the 'tanks' were in fact self-propelled guns – emerged, he was, as a gunner, naturally delighted.

Fanshawe commanded the regiment during the strenuous period of training as it learned how to handle its new equipment. It eventually changed its original 105mm self-propelled guns for Sexton vehicles mounting 25 pounders, and it was equipped with these for the D-Day assault. During the final exercise before the invasion an officious staff officer saw fit to observe to Fanshawe that the high command were 'expecting 90 per cent casualties on D-Day', a remark the Herts Yeomanry's CO thought particularly crass as a way of encouraging troops on the eve of such a momentous, not to say hazardous, undertaking. On the day itself Fanshawe waded the 300 yards ashore in waist deep water, his landing craft having stuck on a sandbank. Once on the beach he soon joined up with his unit which proceeded to gain all its objectives by dark, and did so with remarkably light casualties.

But after the breakout from the beach-head the situation changed dramatically. The *bocage* country, with its hedgerows and copses, provided the Germans with excellent defensive opportunities and the gunners, like the infantry, could often see only as far as the next hedge. Like many other units the Herts Yeomanry took heavy losses, particularly among its officers and NCOs. Fanshawe's second-in-command was blown up on a mine and lost a leg, an incident in which Fanshawe himself narrowly escaped injury. On another occasion he was hit by mortar splinters but was, again, lucky not to sustain a serious wound.

Fanshawe was awarded the DSO in December 1944 for his leadership of his regiment in these fierce Normandy battles and he continued in command throughout the campaign in France. In March 1945 he was promoted to command the artillery of the 3rd Infantry Division at the time of the Rhine crossings and continued to serve as the division penetrated deep into the heart of Germany.

Educated at Tonbridge, George Fanshawe was commissioned in the Royal Field Artillery in 1922 and served at home and in Turkey before being sent to India in 1928. He returned to the United Kingdom in 1935 and was adjutant of the Herts Yeomanry until the outbreak of war. After a period as brigade major, 54 Division, he returned to the regiment in 1941 and commanded it from 1942.

Among his appointments after the war was that of chief instructor at the School of Artillery and from 1952 to 1955 he commanded the 1st Anti-Aircraft Group. After retirement he farmed for 25 years in Wiltshire where he also played a part in public life as a county councillor and as high sheriff. He leaves his widow, Betty, and a son and a daughter.

John Morgan-Smith

Badly wounded in August 1944, he had a lot of pain and difficulty with his artificial legs. He entered the Church, and became a Vicar at Windsor until his death.

George Loveday

Wounded on the night of D-Day, he returned to the regiment in November 1944. The story of his return is worth telling. As a result of his wounds, he developed jaundice and was to be posted to a unit in England, but he was determined to return to the Hertfordshire Yeomanry. He went absent without leave from Woolwich Hospital. George Fanshawe was told and was ordered to put him under arrest if he turned up. However, Mrs Betty Fanshawe and Mrs Sylvia Loveday took a hand in things, as Mrs Fanshawe relates:

We had a great family friend, a Gunner General, Ambrose Pratt, whom we had known since we were both children, so I rang him at Larkhill at about 9 pm. I was answered by his ADC, John Sharpe, who said that the General had gone to bed as he had an early start in the morning. I said 'Well could you wake him as I want to speak to him *badly*.' John was horrified and said he couldn't possibly and that he was a very busy man. I said 'Tell him to ring me at 7 am or however early he likes', not realizing how important Ambrose was.

However, Ambrose did ring. I told him about my husband's letter. He told me that it was very difficult for soldiers to get back to France as they all wanted to go, and once having been, it was almost impossible to get back, but he said that he would do what he could.

To my great content, he rang me about three weeks later to say that George Loveday was recovered and (quite amazingly) off to France the next day. Sylvia Loveday also rang me. When he arrived to embark and have the usual medical check, it was found that he had jaundice! So he was not allowed to go. Can you imagine his rage? He recovered in a couple of weeks, but his chances of returning to France were nil.

However, I had an American friend who owned a small aeroplane somewhere in Gloucester and persuaded him to fly George back to the Regiment. Sylvia Loveday and I were constantly in touch and we both knew that he had gone and had arrived.

Two things happened pretty quickly; one, Sylvia and I were rung up by the War Office and asked if we knew where he was. We both denied any knowledge and were warned how serious it was not to give full information; and two, my husband had a message to say that if George Loveday arrived with the Regiment he was to be put under immediate arrest. However he returned to the Regiment and in the end all was forgotten!'

After the war George Loveday returned to the Stock Exchange and had a distinguished career there, and had the honour of being its Chairman.

Stephen Perry
He recovered fully from his wounds. After the war he finished his legal training and became a solicitor at Poole in Dorset. He and his wife were keen sailors and lived on the edge of Poole Harbour at Parkstone.

Sidney Beck
Continued as 'B' Troop GPO throughout the campaign. In May 1945 he became Acting Troop Commander and was a War Substantive Captain on demobilization. He returned to his old Department, Customs and Excise, as Higher Executive Officer. Later, as a Chief Executive Officer he was seconded first to the Treasury and then the Civil Service Department. In the

six years prior to his retirement in 1975 he served as a Principal in the Office of the Parliamentary Commissioner for Administration under the first two Ombudsmen, Sir Edmund Compton and Sir Alan Marre. He and his wife moved to Ilkley in 1976. His wife died in 1982. They had four children, the elder son born while he was at OCTU and the second, the elder daughter, born in January 1945 while he was in Holland preparing for the Reichswald Forest battle. He now has five grandsons, and shares a home in Ilkley with a widow, Marian Palmer.

Garton Ash
Remained with the regiment after VE-Day and was promoted to command 342nd Battery in preparation for going to the Far East, but this was cancelled through the sudden collapse of Japan. After winding up the regiment on demobilization he returned to qualify as a Chartered Accountant, joining his father's firm in 1949. He retired after forty years in practice during which he became the recognized leading expert on finance, accountancy and taxation for independent education.

Claude Hankins
Recovered, he joined British Rail and became manager of its Welsh Region, living in South Wales.

Roy Marshall
Stayed on as a regular soldier and rose through the ranks to finish a most distinguished career as a General.

Robert Kiln
After the War he rejoined Lloyd's of London. He formed his own company, R. J. Kiln & Co. Ltd, which is now a leading Agency in Lloyd's. He served on the Committee of Lloyd's for nine years, was one of the founders of the London Reinsurance Market, and is author of two successful books on reinsurance. He is also a distinguished archaeologist, was elected a Fellow of the Society of Antiquaries, is a member of the Institute of Field Archaeologists and an Honorary Doctor of Letters of Sheffield University. As a result of his wounds, his left leg was amputated at Queen Elizabeth's Hospital, Birmingham, but his disability has not prevented him from becoming a proficient skier. He lives in Hertford, is married with six children, three stepchildren and twenty grand and step grandchildren.

Appendix

BRITISH TANKS AND GUNS

Tanks

Britain had conceived the idea of two types of tanks: a fast, more lightly armoured 'cruiser' tank, and a slow, more heavily armoured 'infantry' tank. In 1944 the Churchill was the version of the latter used in Normandy and it was mainly used as a flame-throwing tank – the 'Crocodile'. The Churchill also had a 6-pounder gun. The British cruiser tank used in Normandy was the Cromwell with a 75mm gun.

The Cromwell was used by the British 7th Armoured Division, but most of the British and US armour consisted of American Sherman tanks armed with American 75mm guns. These were adequate, reliable, mobile and all-purpose tanks, high off the ground, which presented an easier target than one would have wished and which were very liable to burn if hit. The 75mm gun was ineffective against the German heavier tanks. About one in three Shermans were armed with the British 17-pounder anti-tank gun and were called 'Fireflies'.

Anti-tank Guns

Before I describe guns, the reader should be aware that the size of a gun is described, very confusingly, in two ways: firstly by the weight of the shell it fires, a 6-pounder or 17-pounder anti-tank gun or a 25-pounder field gun, secondly by its calibre, thus the 75mm gun or 14″ naval gun.

The performance of a gun depends on its weight of shell and its velocity. A high velocity gun has greater penetration and a longer range. Its accuracy depends on the skill of its gunners and the quality of its sights and instruments.

British anti-tank guns had developed from the 2-pounder in 1940, through the 6-pounder used on the Churchill tank, to the much more effective 17-pounder, which was a very great improvement. It had a calibre of 76mm, the same as the US 75mm gun mounted on most Sherman tanks, but the 17-pounder had a much higher muzzle velocity, and was thus a far superior gun. These 17-pounder anti-tank guns were sometimes also self-propelled, mounted on a tank chassis with a traverse that could give them all round fire. The 17-pounder gun, while not the equal of the German higher calibre 88mm with its superb telescopic sight, was the Allies' most formidable anti-tank gun and the only one able to cope with German tanks at a range above a few hundred yards.

Field and Medium Artillery

The British field gun was the 25-pounder gun howitzer, with a muzzle velocity of 1600 feet per second for AP shot. It is described later in this appendix. Each division usually contained three artillery regiments, each of twenty-four guns. A division also included one regiment of medium guns, usually firing a much heavier shell of 65 pounds weight.

Naval Firepower

Not only on D-Day, but for days afterwards, there were Allied destroyers, cruisers and battleships offshore, which had 9″, 12″ and 14″ guns at our command. The Navy had observation officers ashore or in spotter aircraft, but in addition we as artillery observers could on occasion call on them for support. The effect of massed 9″, let alone 14″, shells is absolutely devastating even on Tiger tanks, and provided we were not more than ten to fifteen miles from the sea, the Navy were a massive protection from German counter-attacks.

GERMAN MORTARS, GUNS AND TANKS

Mortars

The Germans used mortars much more effectively than we did. These were of great variety, from one throwing a 25-pound bomb up to one with a 250-pound bomb, and their range varied between 4000 and 7000 yards. Often these mortars were mobile, so spotting them was difficult. Some of their heavier mortars were mounted on a drum with nine barrels which could thus fire extremely quickly. These 'Nebelwerfers' were a devastating weapon in Normandy, particularly as their bombs were fitted with a siren which whistled alarmingly through the air, earning them the nickname 'Moaning Minnies'.

Guns

German field and medium guns were no match for us but the gun which we all came to respect most was the '88'. The '88' was a formidable high-velocity anti-aircraft gun firing a 20-pound shell. It was converted into an anti-tank gun which outgunned even our 17-pounders and far outgunned our 6-pounders or our 75mms. It was not only the gun which was so superior, but its optical, telescopic and range-finding devices, which enabled it to fire accurately up to 3000 yards, outdistancing anything we had by hundreds of yards. It simply knocked out any Sherman it hit.

Tanks

The German Mark IV tank had been used by them for several years. It was approximately the same length as the Sherman, but lower in profile and lighter in weight and armed with a higher velocity 75mm gun. Overall it was a better tank than the Sherman. In 1944 the Mark IV tank was being replaced by the Mark V tank, the 'Panther'. These were armed with a superior 75mm gun. In addition, the Mark VI tank, the 'Tiger', was used against the British in Normandy. There were three versions of this tank, the latest being the 'King Tiger', or 'Royal Tiger'. All Tigers were massive, heavily armoured and equipped with the 88mm high-velocity gun.

Panthers and Tigers in particular were far superior to our tanks, with the one exception of the 'Fireflies'.

Comparisons

Here are some comparative statistics for the Sherman tank with the 75mm US gun and the 'Firefly' against the three German tanks:

	Sherman	*Firefly*	*Mk IV*	*Panther*	*Tiger*
Tons weight	32	32	25	45	57
Armour	75mm	75mm	80mm	80mm	100mm
Front gun	75mm	76mm	75mm	75mm	88mm
Muzzle velocity (ft/sec.)	2000	2900	2400	2600	3400

In addition to tanks, German Panzer divisions used 'Jäger Panzer' assault guns. These were usually 75mm or 88mm guns mounted on a well-armoured tank chassis. They had a low profile with no turret and were as effective as their tanks in a defensive role.

The US 75mm shell could not penetrate the Tiger's front armour at all. It could only penetrate the Panther's at under 200 yards and Mk IV's at around 300 yards. The German 88mm gun could penetrate a Sherman at any range up to 4000 yards and the 75mm gun at any range up to at least 1000 yards. We gained, of course, in quantity, but quantity is little use if one Panther or Tiger can knock out ten Shermans at 1000 yards without being damaged. We used to have an evaluation as follows:

1 Tiger = 10 Shermans or 2 Fireflies
1 Panther = 5 Shermans or 1 Firefly
1 Mk IV = 2 Shermans

FIELD ARTILLERY

Our basic field gun was the 25-pounder, with a range of 13,000 yards. It was usually wheeled and was towed behind an ungainly but extremely effective tin box with four-wheel drive and a winch, called a 'quad'. The gun was good and accurate. It could fire ordinary high-explosive (HE) shells with an instantaneous fuse, or if the fuse cap was left on when it was fired, it became a delayed action fuse, which had greater penetration. The armour-piercing shot (AP) was a slug of solid steel, with no explosive, and the guns also carried smoke shells. The Hertfordshire Yeomanry's 25-pounders were self-propelled (SPs), which means they were not towed but mounted on a tank chassis. The turret and top of the tank was stripped off to form a flat platform on which the gun was mounted and fired. The crew manned the gun from this platform, being boxed in by thin steel sheeting to a height of about three feet. This provided some protection from small arms fire and shrapnel, but not much.

Being mounted on a tank chassis meant that the guns were more mobile and could go wherever tanks could go. They were quicker into action and were, of course, ideal for a beach landing, as the SP gun on its chassis could be waterproofed and could negotiate quite a depth of water, sand and shingle.

The 25-pounder gun was also an effective anti-tank gun, using its armour-piercing shot at a range of up to 1000 yards, but of course it was highly vulnerable to tank attack, having little armour above the chassis.

Each gun had a team of six gunners under its No. 1, who was a Sergeant. The No. 1 was in command of his gun and its crew, and on occasions he would act and fire independently. This happened when he could see the enemy over open sights; for example, where German tanks had broken through our defences. Normally the No. 1 fired on the orders of his Gun Position Officer (GPO), orders being relayed by voice and megaphone or by tannoy and acknowledged by hand or tannoy. Four guns made up a Troop, commanded by a Captain supported by two Subalterns. The senior subaltern was the Gun Position Officer (GPO) and the junior the Troop Leader (TL). The senior non-commissioned officer in a Troop was the Troop Sergeant-Major (TSM). The senior Subaltern (GPO) was in command of the gun position. The Captain or Troop Commander was forward with the infantry or tanks whom we were supporting, in other words, up at the 'sharp end'. In addition the troop had a signal vehicle, often a bren carrier, whose main job was to lay telephone lines to the Troop Commander's observation post (OP), its own command vehicles, its own local defence of bren-guns and rifles, and ammunition and supply vehicles.

Two Troops made up a Battery of eight guns commanded by a Major. The Battery Commander (BC) was, like his two Troop Commanders, normally forward with the tanks or infantry at the 'sharp end'. His second in command was the senior Captain or Battery Captain (BK). He was in charge of the gun end. His role was to organize administration, supplies, all logistics, food, lodging, to reconnoitre any moves and to command the whole gun end. The Battery Captain was supported by the Battery Sergeant-Major (BSM) and on the supply side by the Battery Quartermaster-Sergeant (BQMS).

The Battery Command Post was the technical gun control centre for the battery and was under the control of the senior subaltern in the battery, the Command Post Officer (CPO). He was assisted by a junior subaltern (ACPO).

The Battery Signal Sergeant had responsibility for all telephone lines to OPs, between Troops and Battery Headquarters (BHQ), to other Troops, and to Regimental Headquarters (RHQ), and of course for the Battery's wireless network, which usually consisted of '18' and '38' sets.

The Battery could operate as a unit, often being attached to a battalion of infantry or a regiment of tanks as in 'Market Garden'. Its three OPs, the Battery Commander and the two Troop Commanders, when in action, rarely saw their guns, only their shells! Each OP officer had a tank or bren carrier with a driver, a signaller, and an Observation Post Assistant (OPAck), usually a Bombardier or Lance-Bombardier, who was trained to direct the fire of the guns if anything happened to his officer.

As there were three Batteries in each Regiment, there were normally nine observation posts forward, all linked together to the Colonel and to their guns by wireless.

HOW WE SHOT

So that you can follow my story I think you should understand the basic principles of gunnery in a field regiment such as ours, and how a shell from 12,000 yards away could hit a small unseen target, that is, unseen from the gun.

The organization of the British Artillery's fire power was superb. It enabled a huge concentration of guns to be brought to bear upon a target quickly, effectively and accurately and was one of the great advantages our armies had in Normandy over the Germans. We relied to a great extent on a wireless network for this.

Normally in a battle the OPs were forward with the tanks or infantry. It was their job to work out, with the infantry or tank commander, the most effective targets or use of artillery, and then to relay orders for that fire by wireless or telephone line, and on occasions by despatch rider.

In a set attack or defence, predetermined fire would be organized on certain known enemy positions, or a barrage of fire or a smokescreen produced by smoke shells could be used in front of our troops. This fire was produced by basic mathematics, and if the mathematics were good, would be surprisingly accurate. It was corrected, if possible, by the OPs observing the fire. In addition, as the battle progressed, fire would be switched by the OPs to new targets, either by observation or from the map.

In order to produce accurate fire, the guns took up firing positions, troop by troop, in suitable gun positions selected by either the Battery Captain or the Troop GPO. The gun position was fixed by the map grid reference and then more accurately surveyed in. The guns were then all aligned in parallel on a zero line, fixed in the general direction of the battle. Each gun knew its zero line and could revert back to it by use of known markers or gun aiming posts, which were fixed points which can be seen through the gun's instruments. This job of aligning the gun and 'laying' it correctly was the job of the gunlayer who was the gun's No. 3. He was responsible for the correct alignment of the gun and for making sure the gun was level, using levelling bubbles before firing. His job was vital to accurate fire. No. 2 closed the breach of the gun when it was loaded, and opened it to eject the spent charge cartridge case. Nos. 4, 5 and 6 loaded the gun and humped the ammunition.

The GPO with his Command Post Staff received firing orders from his OP, or where a battery was all firing on the same target from the Battery Command Post, and had to translate them into bearings and range for his guns. In doing so he had to take into account wind speed, air pressure, temperature and any other factors likely to affect the path of the shell. His orders to the guns were in a prescribed form, conveyed by voice or tannoy, and relayed if necessary by his junior subaltern and the Troop Sergeant-Major, who took up positions behind the guns themselves. Their job was to aid the guns, to make sure they had ammunition, to check by prismatic compass that the gun was pointing on the correct ordered bearing, and to check visually that the guns were elevated correctly. Each No. 1 acknowledged orders by hand acknowledgement. When his gun was ready to fire he raised his arm and kept it raised until the GPO gave the order to fire. The gun fired under the order of the No. 1.

As an example, we will take an unseen target at 10,000 yards. The map bearing is Zero + 25°. Correct by, say, 1° for wind. Order to guns Zero + 26°. The map range is 10,000 yards, with a high temperature of 30°, high pressure, and wind neutral. Shell will travel faster the high the temperature and the less the air resistance, so deduct 400 yards. Order to guns Range 9600 yards.

9600 yards range is set on gun and gun barrel elevated until spirit-level bubble is level. This means that the gun's elevation will now produce a trajectory to hit a target at 10,000 yards. The OP overlooking target corrects fire, e.g. 'more' or 'less' 1° or 'Add' or 'Drop' 400 yards until target is bracketed and then hit.

However accurate one's predictions were, shellfire often needed correcting by an observer, particularly when aiming at a small target. Observed shoots such as this were normally started by one gun ranging, with the observer correcting the fire until it hit the target. He then brought in other guns; for example, with a troop of four guns, one, usually the No. 1 or right-hand gun of the Troop, did the ranging, and once he was satisfied, the observation officer called for 'one round troop' fire or 'ten rounds troop' fire and all four guns responded.

All gunnery officers, particularly Troop and Battery Commanders, who were the observers, were trained in observed shoots, and we spent many hours and many days at artillery ranges up and down Britain before becoming proficient. The art required a good eye and sense of direction and very good map and ground reading.

THE HERTFORDSHIRE YEOMANRY

This regiment was a Territorial Army volunteer force drawn from Hertfordshire, with batteries or troops based on different centres in the County. In 1939/40 the Yeomanry had two field regiments, the 86th and 135th, and an anti-aircraft regiment, the 79th. Its field regiments, originally horsed, were the volunteer equivalent of the regular Royal Horse Artillery. The Yeomanry were outstanding in the 1930s and were winners of the King's Cup, the premier competition for Territorial artillery units. The 135th was lost at Singapore.

The 86th Field Regiment RA originally comprised two batteries of three troops, the 341st Battery from St Albans and the 342nd Battery from Hertford. In 1940 field regiments were reorganized into three batteries of two troops: the 86th then comprised 341st Battery, 342nd Battery and 462nd Battery, the latter formed by the third troop from each of the previous batteries. The personnel of the original 462nd Battery split off in 1942, and with a similar battery from the Essex Yeomanry, formed the Herts and Essex Yeomanry, who also fought in Normandy as the 192nd Field Regiment RA. 462nd Battery was then re-formed so that by 1943, the 86th again consisted of three batteries.

The 86th Field Regiment RA was the first, or almost the first, British regiment to be self-propelled and to become gunners on tanks. Not only were the regiment pioneers in having and using self-propelled artillery, but during 1943 and 1944 we pioneered the whole concept of artillery support in an opposed landing. We worked out and wrote the scenario for others, and with them put it into effect on D-Day.

In recognition of its unique position, all members of the regiment were given the privilege of wearing the black beret of the Royal Tank Regiment. We were the only Royal Artillery regiment to be so permitted. I still use my black beret with its Hart badge still in place in the garden.

For Normandy we became 2nd Army troops. For the landing we were attached to 30 Corps and specifically to the 50th Division, and remained so attached for most of June and July. After that the regiment was attached to whichever division of 30 Corps was in the forefront of the battle from Normandy into Germany. Therefore the regiment's history in 1944 was really a distillation of the whole operation of 30 Corps. The original commander of 30 Corps in Europe was Major-General Bucknall, but in July 1944 his place was taken by Major-General Brian Horrocks, and George Fanshawe recalls that we became known as 'Horrocks' Own'. The regiment wore the Crusader badge of the 2nd Army, a blue cross on a white shield, as shown in the Frontispiece. The regimental number shown on all its vehicles was 1147.

Officers on D-Day 1944 of the 86th Field Regiment (Hertfordshire Yeomanry) RA are listed below. All ranks are those held on 6 June 1944. Contributors to this book are given in italics.

Commanding Officer	*Lt.-Colonel G. D. Fanshawe, OBE, DSO.* Wounded 15 June, returned 30 June 1944
Second in Command	Major J. B. Morgan-Smith, DSO. Wounded evacuated 17 August 1944

Regimental Headquarters Staff

Adjutant	Capt. R. R. Thornton, Croix de Guerre
Assistant Adjutant	Lt. M. M. Wood. Killed January 1945
Survey Officer	Lt. D. M. Coultas. Killed March 1945
Medical Officer	Captain Haggerty
Signals Officer	Lt. J. Hindshaw
REME	Capt. S. Reevie
Quartermaster	Capt. W. Felsted, MBE
Information Officer	Lt. Prentis. Sunk 6 June, rejoined July 1944

341st St Albans Battery

Officer Commanding (BC)	Major G. A. Loveday. Mentioned in dispatches, wounded evacuated 7 June 1944, returned November 1944
Battery Captain (BK)	*Capt. R. J. Kiln*. Wounded evacuated 8 September 1944
'A' Troop Commander	Capt. E. W. C. Hall. Killed 14 June 1944
'B' Troop Commander	*Capt. S. D. Perry, MC*. Wounded evacuated 23 September 1944
Command Post Officer (CPO)	Lt. Dorey
Assistant Command Post Officer (ACPO)	Lt. C. B. Mackie. Killed 9 June 1944
'A' Troop Gun Position Officer (GPO)	Lt. J. A. Craston
'A' Troop Leader (TLA)	Lt. S. Kalbrier
'B' Troop Gun Position Officer (GPO)	*Lt. S. J. Beck*
'B' Troop Leader (TLB)	Lt. A. G. K. Borrell. Wounded 1 November 1944
Attached as FOO	Capt. G. D. Greig, MC of 124th Field Regt. RA

342nd Hertford Battery

Battery Commander	Major K. C. Swann, MC. Killed 19 June 1944
Battery Captain	Capt. C. Hankins. Wounded evacuated 27 August 1944
'C' Troop Commander	Capt. C. C. Street. Hospitalized evacuated 15 June 1944
'D' Troop Commander	*Capt. J. G. Ash, MC*. Hospitalized 11 March 1945, rejoined May 1945.
Command Post Officer	Lt. H. Dovey. Killed 17 September, 1944
Assistant Command Post Officer	Lt. J. Bartlett
'C' Troop Gun Position Officer	Lt. D. Mathers
'C' Troop Leader	Lt. E. Smallman
'D' Troop Gun Position Officer	Lt. W. Gear
'D' Troop Leader	Lt. A. Dorling
Attached as FOO	Lt. K. Clarke of 124th Field Regt. RA

462nd Battery

Battery Commander	Major E. C. Scammell, MC
Battery Captain	Capt. H. Norman. Wounded March 1945
'E' Troop Commander	Capt. R. D. Turnbull. Killed 13 June 1944
'F' Troop Commander	Capt. H. M. Pamphilon. Killed 8 July 1944
Command Post Officer	Lt. P. D. Deshon

Assistant Command Post Officer	Lt. B. Heaton. Sick September 1944
'E' Troop Gun Position Officer	Lt. G. Eisen
'E' Troop Leader	Lt. J. A. Carpenter. Wounded evacuated 30 June 1944
'F' Troop Gun Position Officer	Lt. Jamieson
'F' Troop Leader	Lt. I. Yarnell
Attached as FOO	Capt. Hawkins of 124th Field Regt. RA

Select Bibliography

The official History of the Second World War. *Victory in the West*, Vol. I, *The Battle of Normandy* and Vol. II, *The Defeat of Germany*. HMSO, London, 1962 and 1968.

Victory in Normandy by Major-General David Belchem. Chatto & Windus, London, 1981. General Belchem was head of Montgomery's Operations and Planning staff 1943–5. His book is well written and illustrated and he gives one of the best explanations of Normandy.

Corps Commander by Sir Brian Horrocks, Eversley Belfield and Major-General Essame. Sidgwick & Jackson, London, 1977. Sir Brian was the commander of 30 Corps during its advance from Normandy to Arnhem, Eversley Belfield was an air observation officer with the Canadians, and Essame was in 1944 a brigade commander in 43rd (Wessex) Division. The book is a curious muddle in a way as it tells two stories, but its great merit lies in this. It contrasts the advance of 30 Corps on the right of the British Army with the little-known but tough and heroic work done by the Canadians and the Poles on the left flank.

Panzers in Normandy – Then and Now by Eric Lefevre. After the Battle, London, 1983. This book is more technical but it is a mine of information about the German Panzer forces facing us in Normandy and very well illustrated.

Caen – The Brutal Battle and Breakout in Normandy by Henry Moule. David & Charles, Newton Abbot, 1976. This is a concise and very readable book.

Books two and three above, in contrast to many others, are written by soldiers who actually took part. They have authority and knowledge as well as telling a good story. On the Hertfordshire Yeomanry there are two further volumes.

Hertfordshire Yeomanry and Artillery Honours and Awards by J. D. Sainsbury. Hertfordshire Yeomanry Historical Trust, 1976.

Hertfordshire Yeomanry and Artillery Roll of Honour by J. D. Sainsbury. Hertfordshire Yeomanry Historical Trust, 1972.

Glossary

I have included approximate numbers for military formations but readers should realize that these varied very considerably in practice.

Adjutant
The Captain in charge of a regiment's headquarters and administration.

Anti-Aircraft Guns (Ack Ack Guns)
High-velocity guns specifically used against aircraft. The heavier guns such as the British 3.7″ were not normally part of a field division which carried lighter guns such as the Bofors for defence against low-flying aircraft. The German 88mm Ack Ack gun was converted to a highly successful anti-tank gun.

Anti-Personnel Mines
Small land mines laid often in minefields to prevent infantry attack. They were exploded by pressure of a foot.

Anti-Tank Guns
High-velocity guns either on wheels or mounted on a tank chassis for killing tanks. The 17-pounder British and the German 88mm guns were the best in Normandy.

Anti-Tank Mines
Land mines laid often in minefields against enemy tank attacks.

Armoured Brigade
A formation comprising three or four regiments of tanks, around 200 tanks in all, commanded by a Brigadier.

Armoured Division
A formation of one Armoured Brigade and one motorized infantry brigade, plus support troops.

Armoured Fighting Vehicle (AFV)
A tank or any armoured vehicle equipped with guns or an offensive weapon.

Armoured Vehicle Royal Engineers (AVREs)
Specialist tanks manned by Engineers, e.g. the Flail mine-clearing tank.

Army
Used with two meanings. Firstly, land forces as opposed to Navy. Secondly, a formation of several Corps, commanded by a full General.

Assistant Command Post Officer (ACPO)
A Subaltern, assistant to a Battery's Command Post Officer.

Barrage
A line or blanket of shells laid down in front of our advancing troops. A creeping barrage moved forward with the rate of advance.

Battalion
British infantry unit consisting of four rifle companies, plus one support company and HQ, about 800 men, commanded by a Lt.-Colonel.

Battery
An artillery unit commanded by a Major or equivalent. In 1944 a field battery Royal Artillery consisted of two troops of four 25-pounder guns. Eight guns in all and about 160 men.

Battery Captain (BK)
Second in command of a Battery. Responsible for administration, supplies and the guns.

Battery Command Post
The fire control unit for a battery of guns under the command of the Command Post Officer (CPO).

Battery Sergeant-Major (BSM)
Senior NCO of a battery.

Bofors
A light anti-aircraft gun used mainly against low-flying aircraft.

Bombardier
An artillery non-commissioned rank with two stripes equivalent to Corporal in the infantry. Lance-Bombardier with one stripe was the lowest rank above a Gunner. A Bombardier ranked below a Sergeant.

Bombards
A 100-pound 'bomb' fired from a tank chassis with a short range of 200 yards or so but a devastating explosion which could blow in a heavy pill box.

Bracketing
The method of hitting a target by having one shell fall beyond and the next shell short of the target and then halving the difference in range so that the target is bracketed and eventually hit.

Bren-gun
The standard light machine-gun of the British Army, originally Czechoslovakian (Bruno).

Bren-gun Carrier
A lightly-armoured tracked vehicle for four men. No fixed armament but carried bren-guns or mortars.

Brigade
Formation comprising three battalions of infantry or three regiments of tanks, plus support troops, commanded by a Brigadier. Three Brigades normally comprised a Division.

Brigadier or Brigadier-General
Commissioned officer between Colonel and Major-General. He commanded a Brigade of troops.

Calibre
The inside diameter of a gun barrel.

Captain
Officer ranking above Lieutenant and below Major, commanding a troop of artillery.

Carpet-laying Tanks
Modified tanks which could lay roly polys over soft ground.

Carrier
See Bren-gun Carrier.

Centaurs
90mm assault guns manned by Royal Marines.

Charge
Amount of explosive used to propel a shell.

Churchill Tank
A British heavily-armoured infantry support tank. Slow moving, Armed with 6-pounder gun. Often used as a flame-thrower tank, the 'Crocodile'.

Colonel or Lieutenant-Colonel
The rank of Colonel was used for staff posts or as an honorary title. Lt.-Colonel, usually referred to as 'Colonel', commanded an infantry battalion, gunner regiment or tank regiment. A Colonel ranks above Major and below Brigadier.

Command Post Officer (CPO)
Senior Lieutenant or Subaltern of a battery in charge of the battery's fire control.

Company of Infantry
About 140 men, commanded by a Major or Captain.

Corporal
Non-commissioned officer with two stripes in infantry, below Sergeant. Lance-Corporal with one stripe was the lowest rank of NCO.

Corps (pronounced Core)
Army formation comprising one or more Divisions, often three or four, commanded by a Lt.-General.

Crocodiles
Churchill heavy infantry tanks equipped with a flame-thrower. They could eject a flame 100 yards or more to envelop a pill box. The nastiest weapon we had. The memory of seeing Crocodiles in action and the resulting screams of soldiers being burnt alive remains with me now and always will. Very effective but I think an unacceptable aspect of war.

Cromwell Tank
A British cruiser tank. Fast but with light armour. Armed with a 75mm gun (sometimes a 6-pounder).

DD Tanks
See Duplex Drive Tank.

Defensive Fire (DF)
A concentration of artillery fire put down on likely enemy forming-up positions. Often done at night to hinder their supplies or reinforcements.

Division
The largest fixed unit in the Allied Army. Usually three Brigades of infantry, full strength up to 15,000 men. German Divisions similar but usually not exceeding 12,000 men.

Duplex Drive Tank
A tank fitted with raisable canvas sides which converted it into a 'boat' able to float. Powered with twin propellors.

DUKWs or Ducks
A small amphibious lorry which could swim to shore and drive on land. Not used in the assault but invaluable in ferrying men and equipment ashore later.

Fascines
Tanks carrying large bundles of sticks which were lowered into anti-tank ditches to fill them in. Another variation was to use a tank chassis with a flat top and drive that into a ditch to fill it up.

Fireflies
Sherman tanks fitted with the British 17-pounder gun.

Flails
Sherman tanks fitted with forward projecting arms with a revolving bar of iron chains which beat or flayed the ground in front of the tank to set off mines, thus clearing a path through minefields.

Forward Observation Officer (FOO)
An artillery OP officer forward with advance troops.

Funnies
Term given to the specialist tanks developed by 79th Armoured Division under General Percy Hobart. These included DD Tanks, Flails, Crocodiles, Fascines, Roly Poly Tanks, etc.

Gun End
Slang for area where the guns were positioned, i.e. behind and back from the 'sharp end'.

Gun Layer
See Layer.

Gun Position Officer (GPO)
The Subaltern in charge of a troop of guns when in action.

Honey
British light reconnaisance tank.

Howitzer
A field gun using a low charge and a high elevation so that the shell lobs over intervening hills or obstacles. Similar to a mortar but more accurate.

Infantry Tank
A heavily-armoured slow tank for infantry support, e.g. the Churchill.

Jäger Panzer
A German armoured self-propelled assault gun armed with a 75mm or an 88mm gun. Very formidable as a tank killer.

Landing Craft Assault (LCA)
A small flat-bottomed boat with a bow ramp for carrying about 20 infantry into a beach assault.

Landing Craft Guns Large (LCG (L))
A Landing Craft Tank (LCT) armed with two large 4.7″ guns for close range fire.

Landing Craft Headquarters (LCH)
Not a landing craft but a small ship used as command headquarters during an assault landing.

Landing Craft Infantry (LCI)
Larger than an LCA with two side landing ramps. There were three sizes, one carrying 100 men or a Company, the others a Battalion or half a Battalion.

Landing Craft Mechanized (LCM)
Like LCA but larger. Could carry a vehicle.

Landing Craft Tanks (LCT)
A craft with flat bottom and a bow ramp with an open deck, with room for 7 tanks or other vehicles. Bridge at rear.

Landing Craft Tanks Rockets (LCT (R))
An LCT which carried rows and rows of fixed rocket launchers instead of tanks.

Landing Ship Infantry (LSI)
Any ship usually 8–10,000 tons used as infantry transports. Had no ramps and infantry normally went over the side into LCAs.

Landing Ship Tanks (LST)
Ships with bow ramps used for transport of tanks and vehicles, like a car ferry. Could not normally beach up to the shore, unless water was deep. Normally vehicles were unloaded at sea on a raft or Rhino. A very tricky operation in a heavy sea.

Layer
The No. 3 on a gun responsible for 'laying' a gun.

Laying
Positioning a gun and its barrel in the right direction both laterally and horizontally.

Lee Enfield
The standard rifle used by the British Army. Calibre .303 inches. Range over 1000 yards.

Machine-guns
Any gun firing belts or drums of ammunition without manual loading. British light machine-gun was the bren gun; German the spandau.

Major
Commissioned officer between Captain and Colonel, usually commanded infantry Company or artillery Battery.

Major-General
Between Brigadier and Lieutenant-General. Commanded a Division of troops.

Mark IV
The standard 1943 German tank. Mobile and armed with 75mm gun. Replaced in 1944 with Mark V or Panther.

Mike Target
A target engaged at once by all the 24 guns of an artillery regiment.

Mortars
Usually smooth-bore missiles, fired from a simple tube, which lobbed over obstacles. Standard British mortars were 2″ and 3″ with limited range. German mortars were more sophisticated and varied greatly in size and range. Some had a range of 5000 yards or more. The German superiority was very marked in Normandy. Their multi-barrelled mobile mortars or Nebelwerfers were devastating.

Mulberry Harbour
Artificial harbours. The British one was at Arromanches, the US at Omaha (destroyed by storm 21 June 1944).

Nebelwerfers
The German multi-barrelled mortar firing large mortar bombs which whined through the air, known as 'Moaning Minnies'.

No. 1
The Sergeant or NCO in charge of a gun and its crew.

Observation Post (OP)
Used specifically as an artillery observation post with a view over the enemy. Usually manned by one officer, one assistant (OPAck), a signaller and a driver.

Panther Tank
German Mark V tank, heavily armoured and fitted with a high-velocity 75mm gun.

Panzers
German tank forces.

Panzerfaust
German anti-tank infantry weapon. Like our PIAT but superior.

Panzer Grenadiers
The infantry forces working with Panzer Divisions. Also used as separate Divisions equipped with anti-tank assault guns.

Petard
See Bombard.

PIAT
Projectile Infantry Anti-Tank. A hand-held tube resting on one's shoulder which fired an anti-tank bomb 100 yards or so. British equivalent of German Panzerfaust.

Platoon
Infantry unit approximately 30 men commanded by a Lieutenant or 2nd Lieutenant.

Priest
A self-propelled 105mm gun.

Quad
A four-wheel drive vehicle used for towing 25-pounder or similar guns.

RA, RB, RC, RD, RE, RF. A Troop Commander's vehicle.

Ram
A Canadian Sherman tank chassis used for SP guns.

Ranging
The correcting of shell-fire to hit a target done by observing and correcting the fall of the shells.

Rascines
See Fascines.

Regiment
Regiment of Field Artillery consisting of three Batteries of eight 25-pounder guns, about 650 men commanded by a Lt.-Colonel. Alternatively, a Regiment of tanks of three squadrons, about 60 tanks in all.

Regimental Sergeant-Major (RSM)
The senior non-commissioned officer and senior warrant officer of a Regiment.

Rhinos
A raft with two small engines towed across the Channel and used to unload tanks from an LST at sea. The Rhino then chugged heavily laden to the beach.

Roly Polys
Rolls of matting laid down to provide tracks on soft or wet sand, also used for the vehicles that laid them.

Round
A single shell or one shell from each gun, e.g. 'one round troop fire' is each of the four guns firing one shell together.

Run-in Shoot
The firing of SP field guns from their LCTs as they approached to land. Technique developed by 86th Field Regiment.

Section
Smallest infantry unit 6 or 8 men commanded by a corporal: or half an artillery troop, i.e. two guns.

Sexton
SP 25-pounder gun on a Ram chassis used by us on D-Day.

Self-propelled (SP)
Normally a gun mounted on a tank chassis and thus self-propelled and not towed.

Sharp End
Slang for the front-line or Observation Posts forward with tanks or infantry.

Sherman Tank
The standard tank of American design and manufacture used by Allied Forces in Normandy. It was very mobile, not heavily armoured and had a high profile. It caught fire easily. It was armed with a 75mm gun, but see Fireflies.

Spandau
German machine-gun with very fast rate of fire, 1200 rounds a minute. Over twice as fast as the bren and more reliable.

Squadron of Tanks
Consisting of five or six troops of three tanks, about 20 in all, commanded by a Major.

Sten-gun
A British short-range sub-machine-gun or machine pistol.

Subaltern
A Lieutenant or 2nd Lieutenant. The lowest commissioned officer ranks.

Subsection (Sub)
Half a section of artillery, i.e. one gun in a field regiment, named alphabetically in a Battery A–H.

Tiger Tanks
The most formidable German tank used in Normandy (Mark VI). Heavily armoured and armed with the 88mm gun with telescopic sights.

Troop
Unit of four field guns commanded by a Captain, or unit of three tanks.

Troop Leader (TL)
The junior Subaltern in a Troop who acted as assistant to the GPO. TLA, TLB, TLC, TLD, TLE, TLF designated the six Troop Leaders' vehicles.

Troop Sergeant-Major (TSM)
Senior NCO of a Troop.

Twenty-five Pounder
The standard British field gun in 1944. A Howitzer with a range of 13,000 yards. Accurate and reliable. Usually towed on wheels behind a quad but in armoured divisions it was mounted on a tank chassis (SP). Manually loaded with rate of fire with experienced gun crew up to six rounds a minute. Shells propelled by choice of three charges with a supercharge for armour-piercing shot (AP). Muzzle velocities: Charge 1 800 feet per second (fps), Charge 2 1100 fps, Charge 3 1300 fps, supercharge 1600 fps. Gun crew six. In Normandy we always used maximum charge.

Typhoon
A British fighter aircraft armed with rockets. Devastating against enemy tanks.

Uncle Target
A target engaged at once by Division artillery.

Victor Target
A target engaged at once by Corps artillery.

Warrant Officer
The senior grades of non-commissioned officers above the rank of Sergeant.

X Car or Tank
A battery commander's vehicle.

Z Car or Tank
A regimental commander's vehicle.

Zero Line
The line on which a gun is laid out. It is fixed by reference to known and recorded aiming points.

Figures

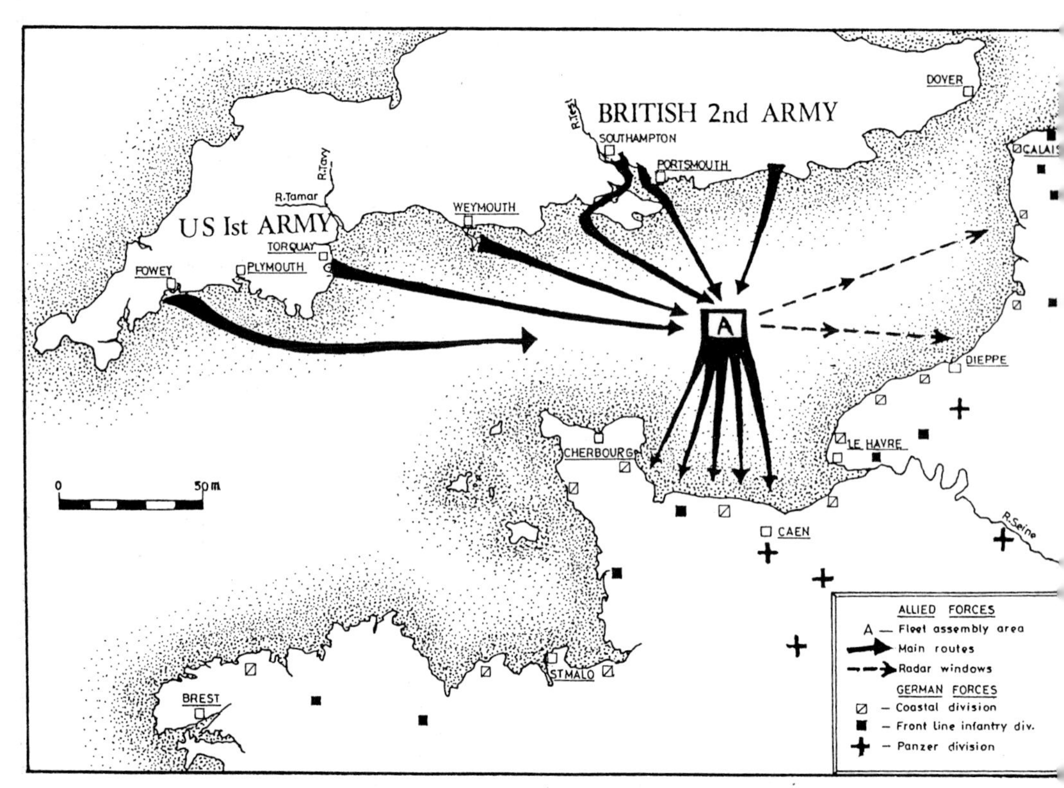

FIGURE 1. *Allied crossing routes on the night of 5/6 June 1944 and German divisions facing the invasion forces.*

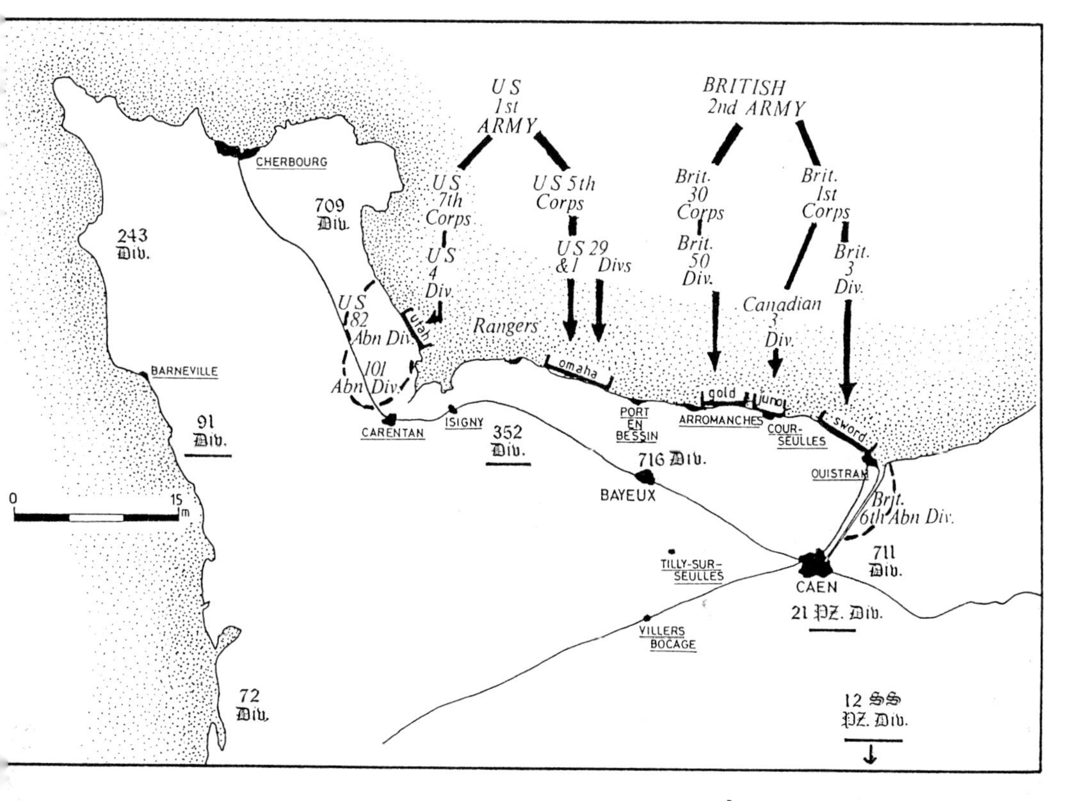

FIGURE 2. *Allied landings 6 June 1944 and position of German divisions, with front-line fully or semi-mobile divisions underlined.*

FIGURE 3. *50th Division's D-Day Phase III objective and final positions.*

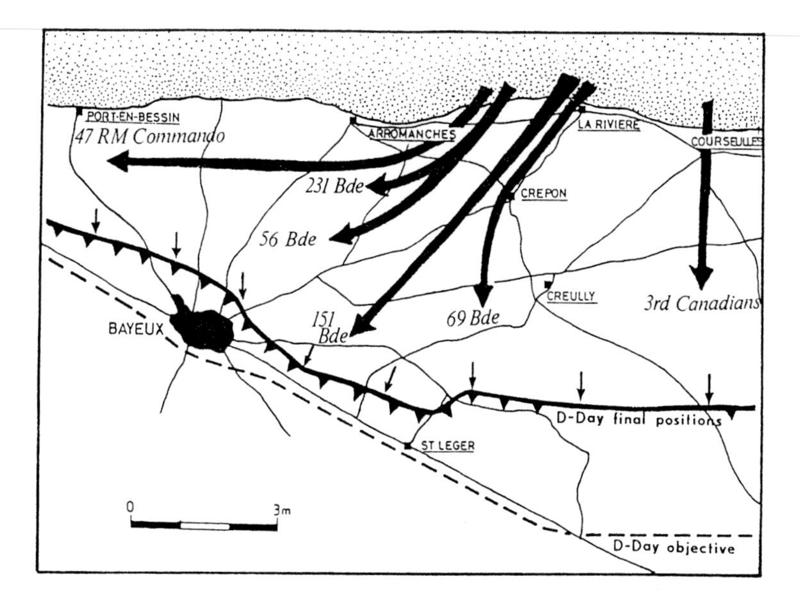

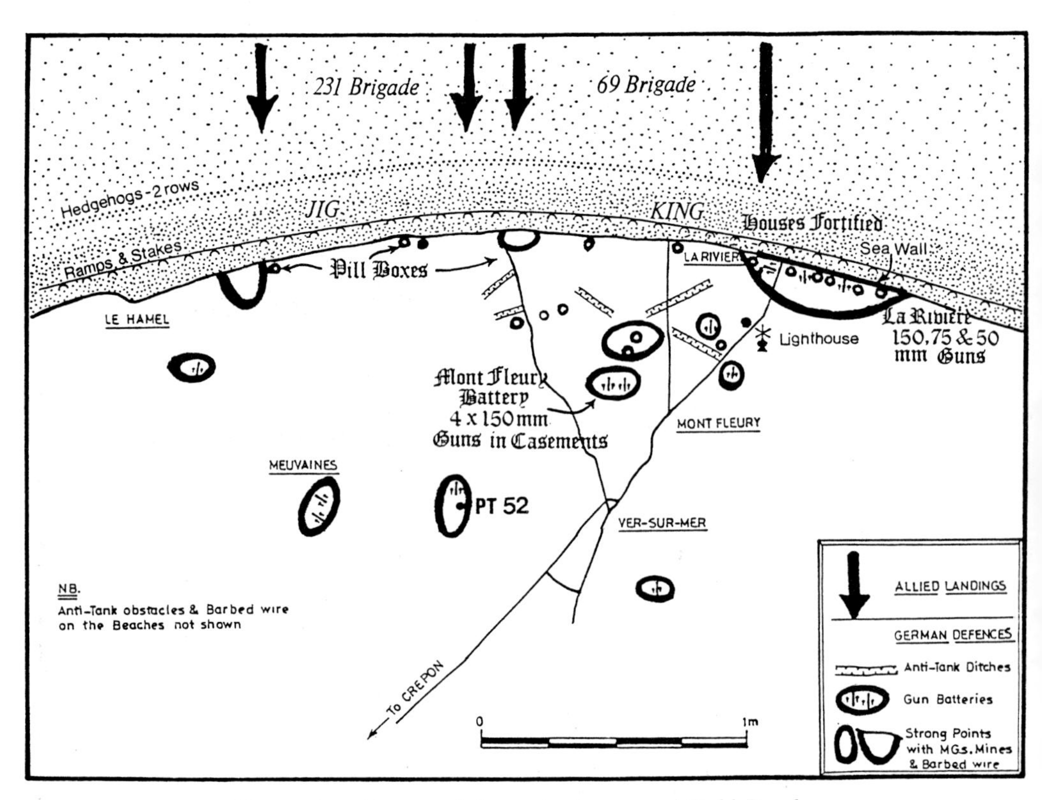

FIGURE 4. *German defences in the area of Gold Beach.*

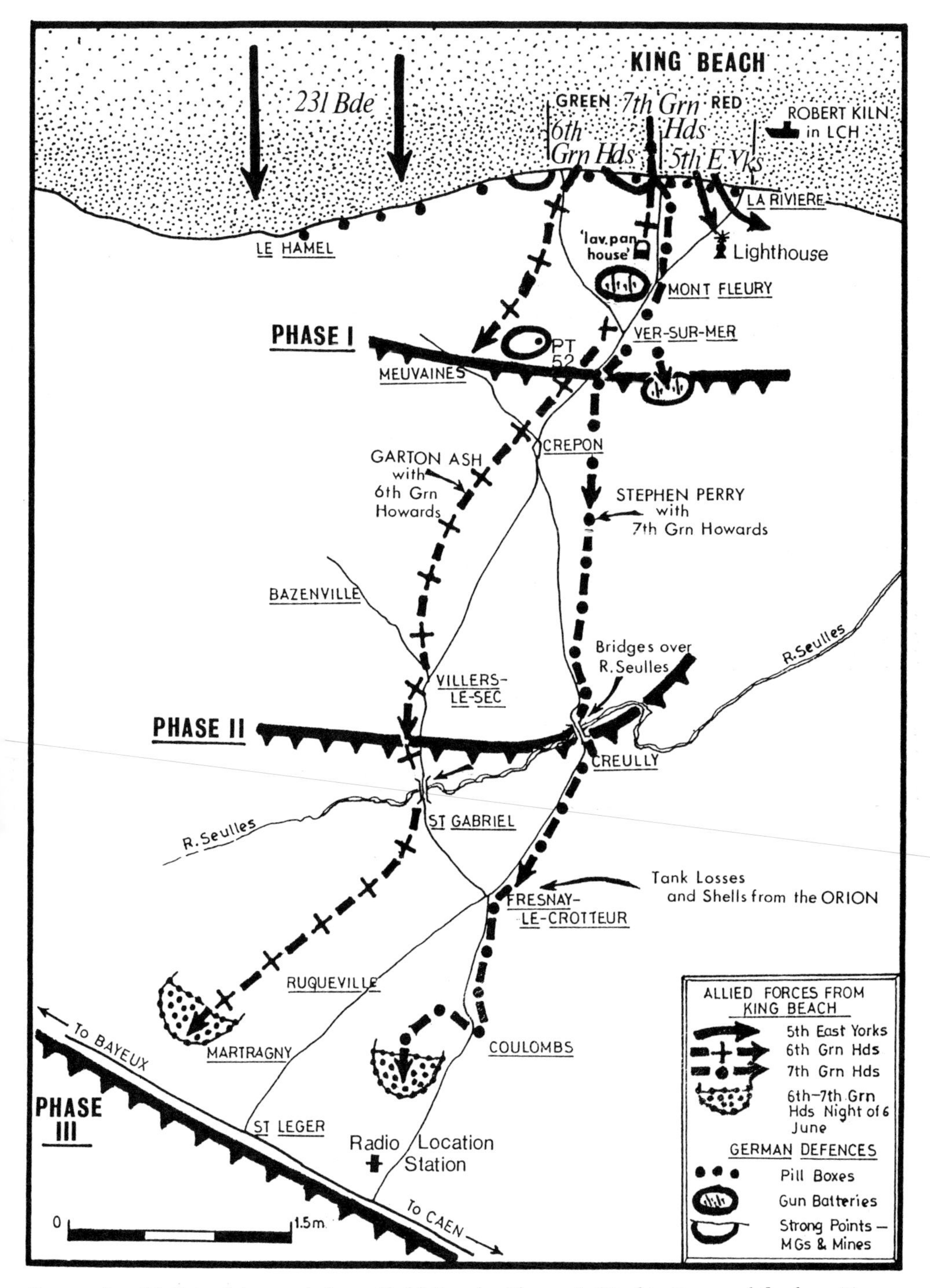

FIGURE 5. *69 Brigade's attack from Gold Beach: Phases I–III objectives and final positions, night of 6 June.*

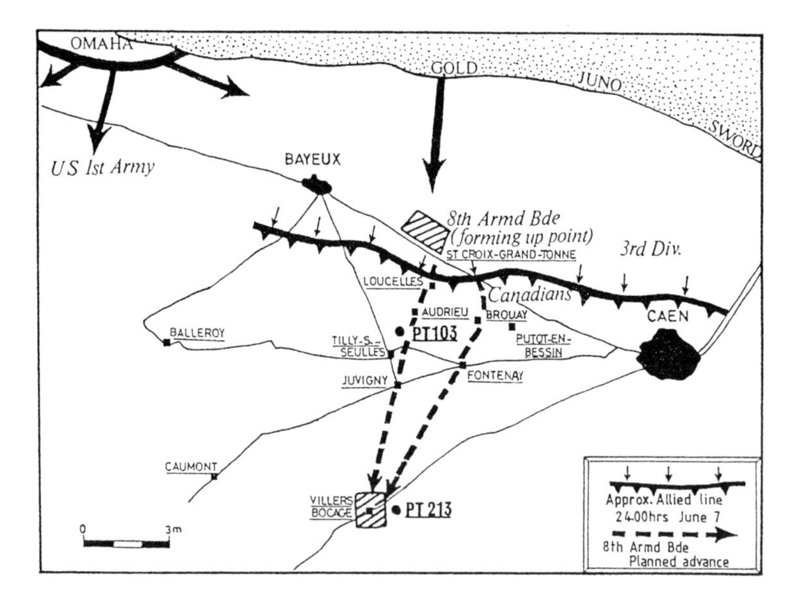

FIGURE 6. *8th Armoured Brigade's planned advance to Villers Bocage.*

FIGURE 7. *Gun positions and ranges from St Gabriel, Martragny and Jerusalem X-roads, 7–22 June.*

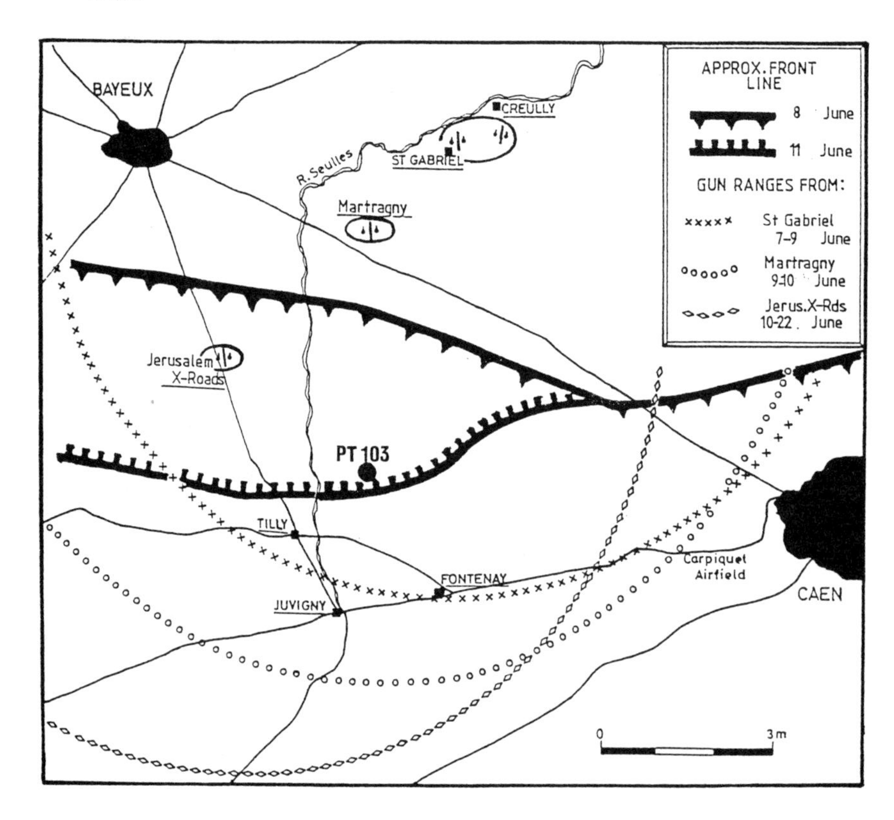

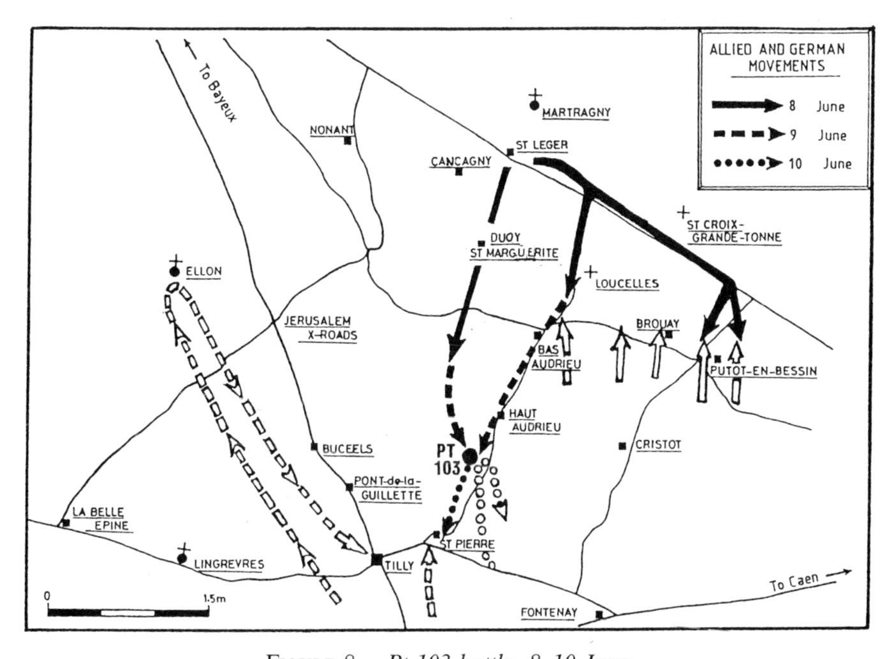

FIGURE 8. *Pt 103 battle, 8–10 June.*

FIGURE 9. *Pt 103: routes of Capt. Perry and Capt. Kiln, 8–9 June.*

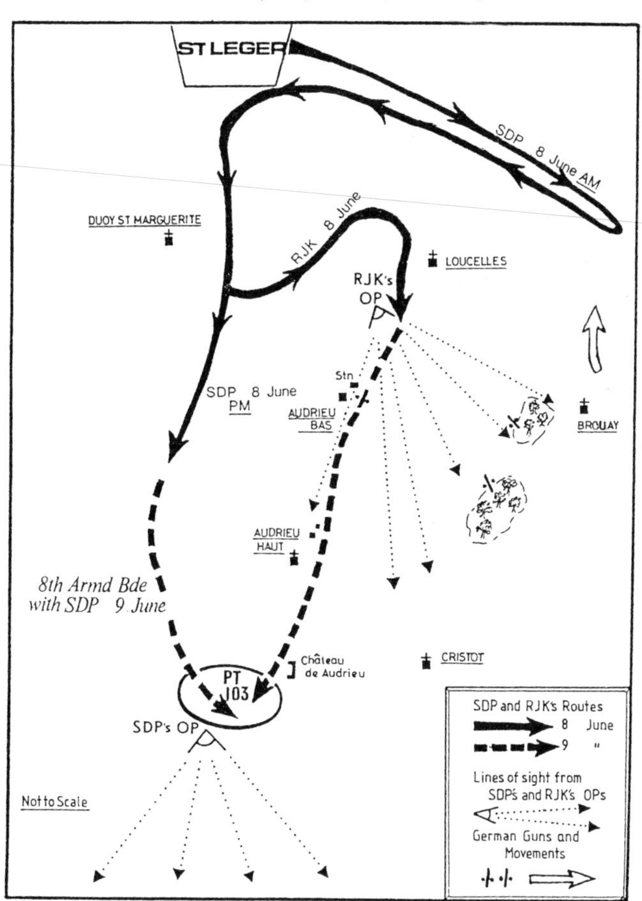

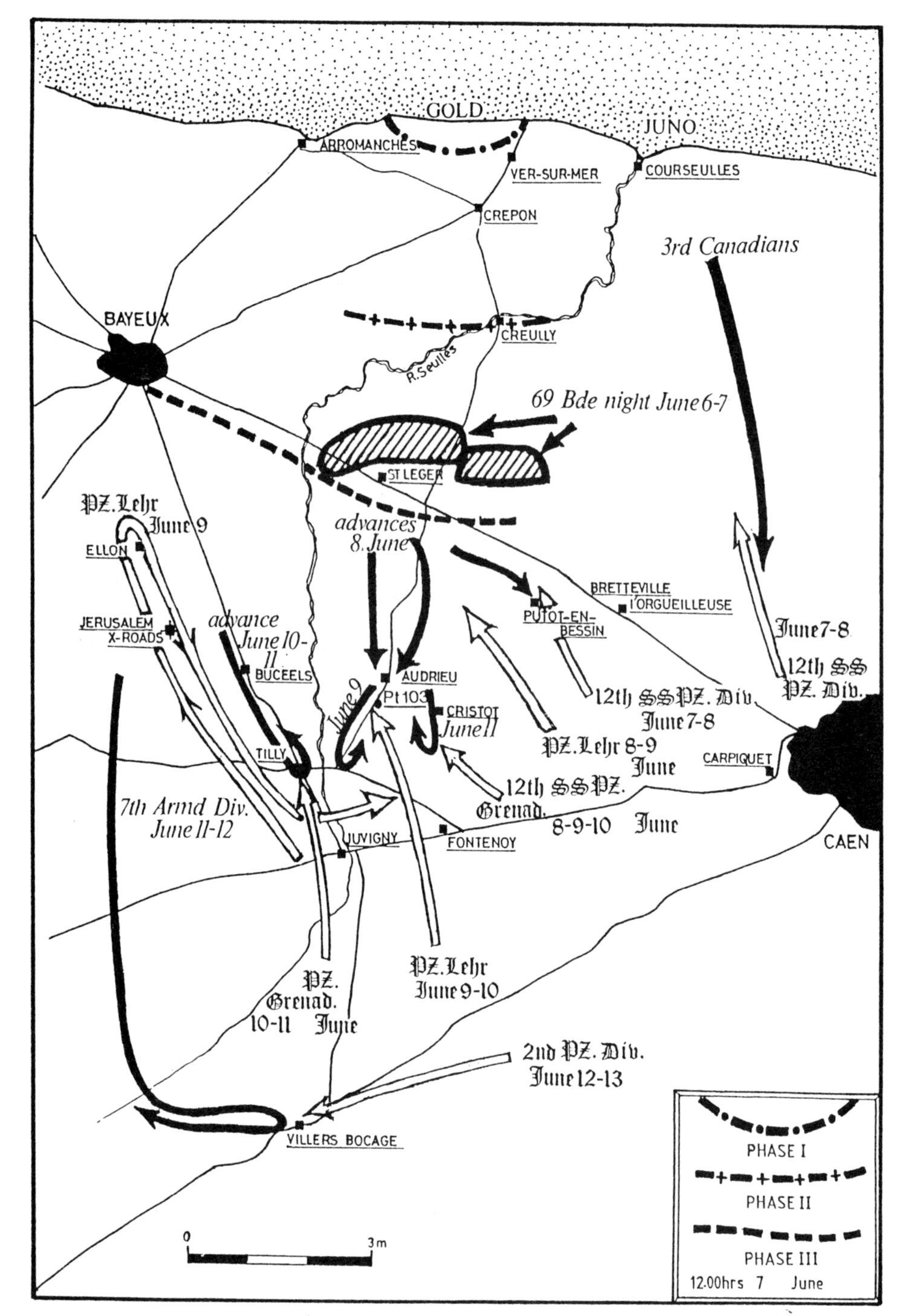

FIGURE 10. *50th Division's D-Day objectives and 30 Corps's battles 6–13 June.*

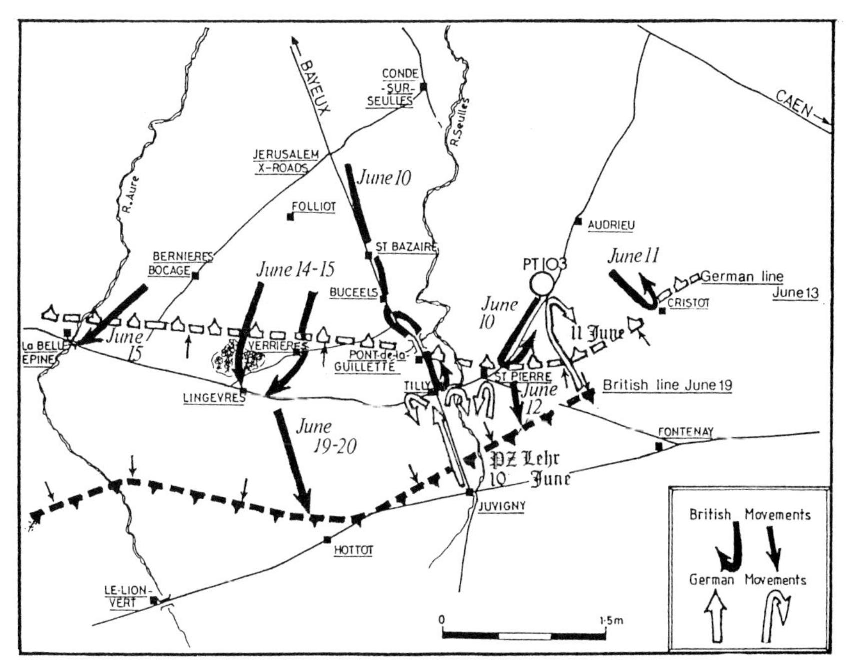

FIGURE 11. *Allied advance to Tilly-sur-Seulles, 10 June, and subsequent battles around Tilly.*
FIGURE 12. *Details of advance on Tilly and retreat, 10–11 June.*

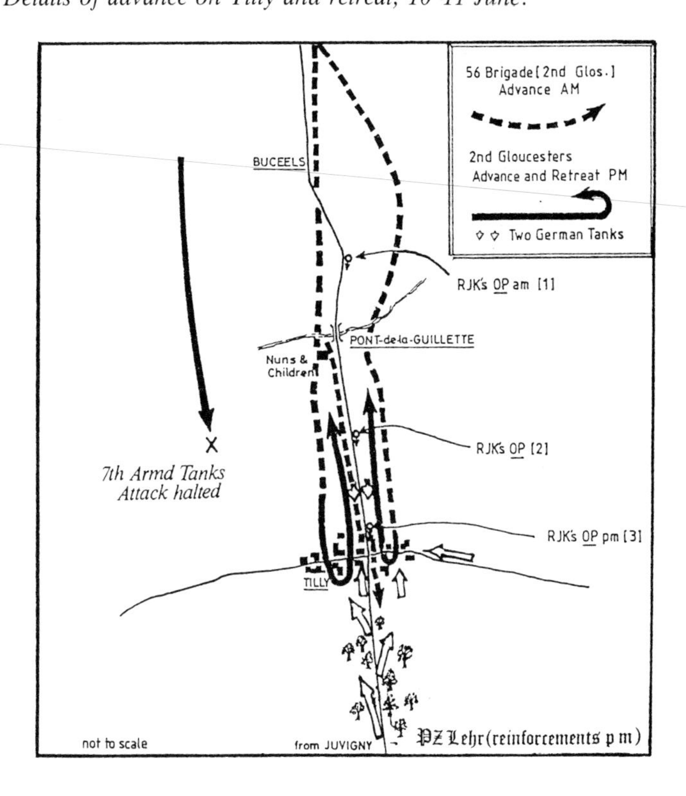

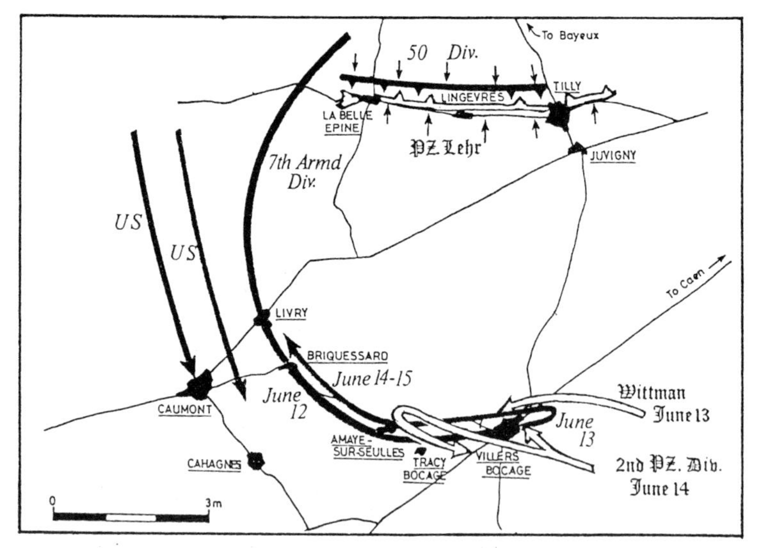

FIGURE 13. *7th Armoured Division's right hook, 12–15 June.*
FIGURE 14. *151 Brigade's attack on Lingevres, 14 June.*

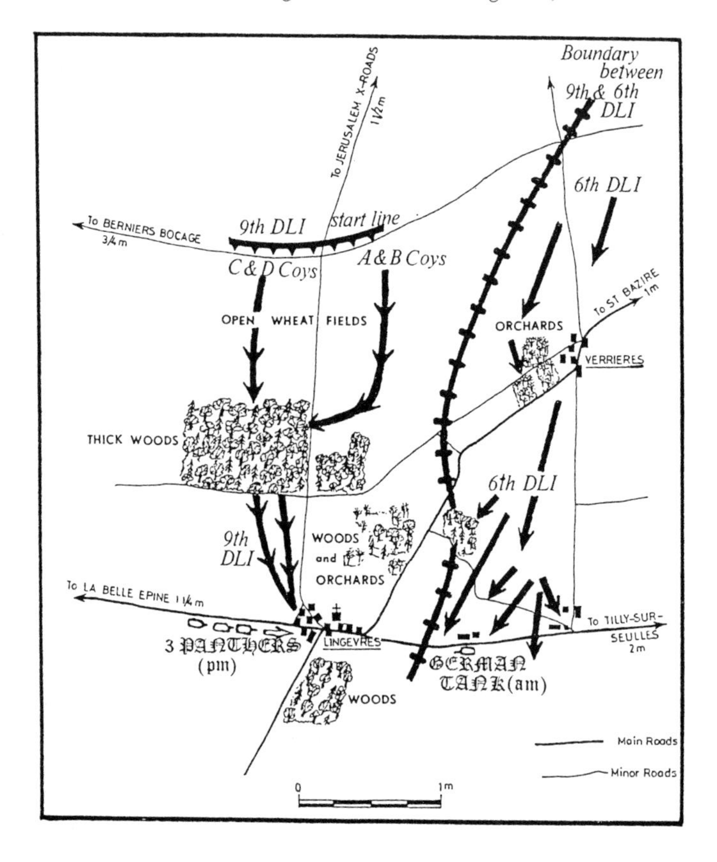

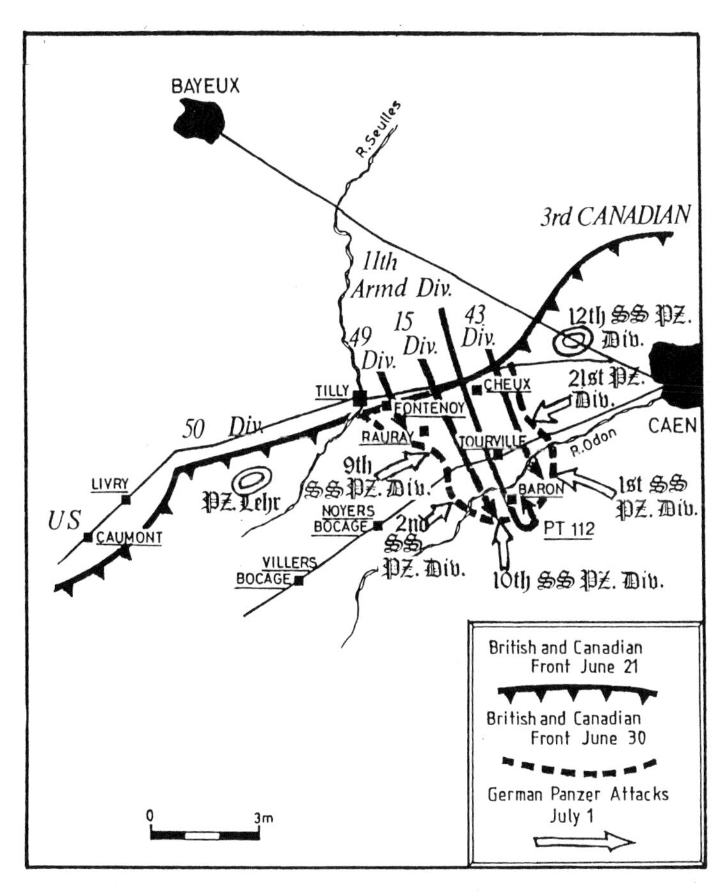

FIGURE 15. *'Epsom'.*

FIGURE 16. *German Panzer attacks 6–15 June: the whole assault was borne and repulsed by the British and Canadians.*

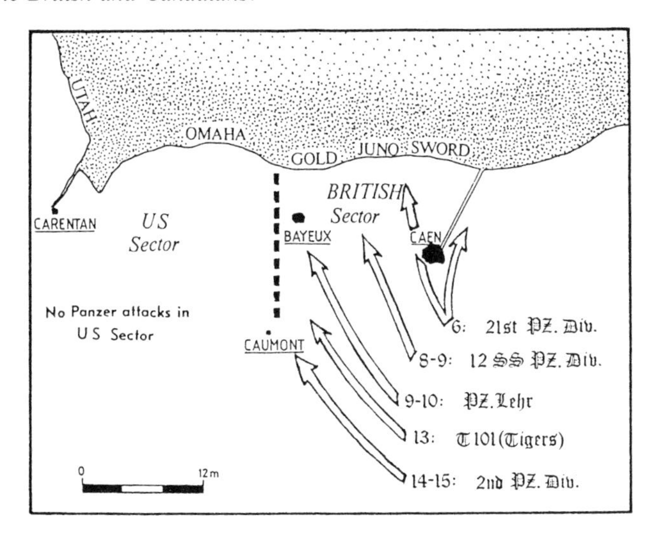

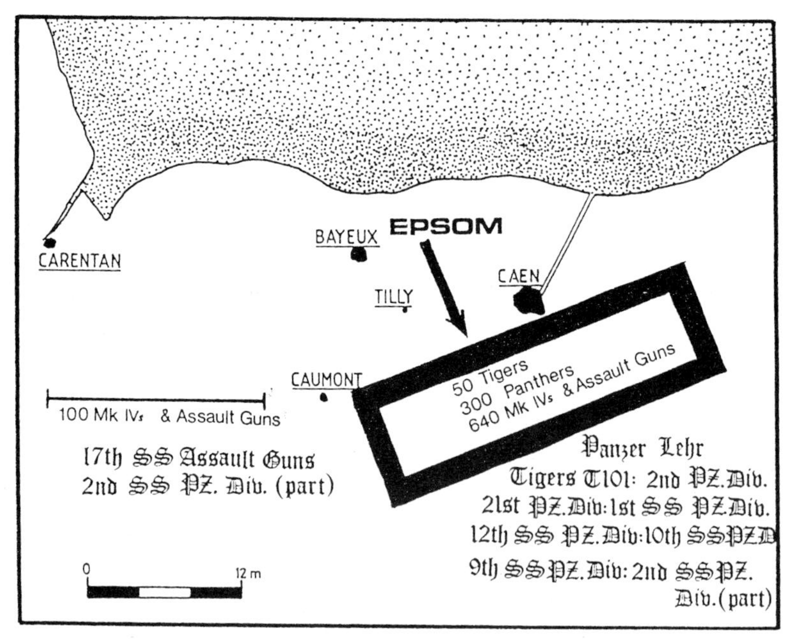

FIGURE 17. *Relative strength of German Panzer divisions facing US (left) and British and Canadian forces (right) after 'Epsom', end of June.*

FIGURE 18. *Relative strength of German Panzer divisions opposing 'Goodwood' and 'Cobra' in July, showing why 'Cobra' broke through while 'Goodwood' could not.*

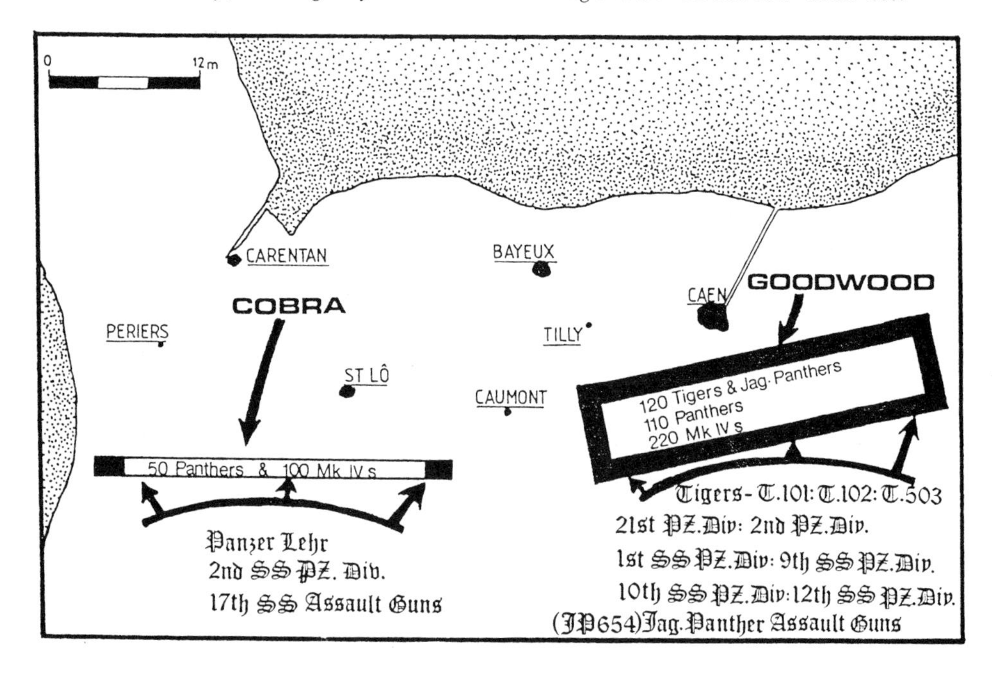

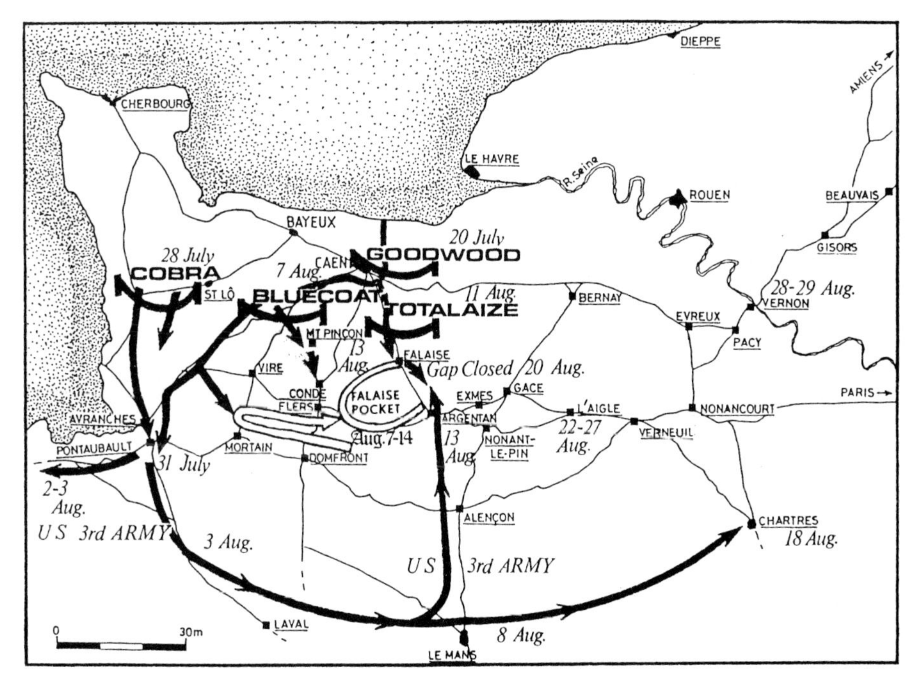

FIGURE 19. *The breakout from Normandy with operations 'Cobra', 'Bluecoat', 'Goodwood', and 'Totalaize'.*

FIGURE 20. *Operation 'Bluecoat' with 43rd Division.*

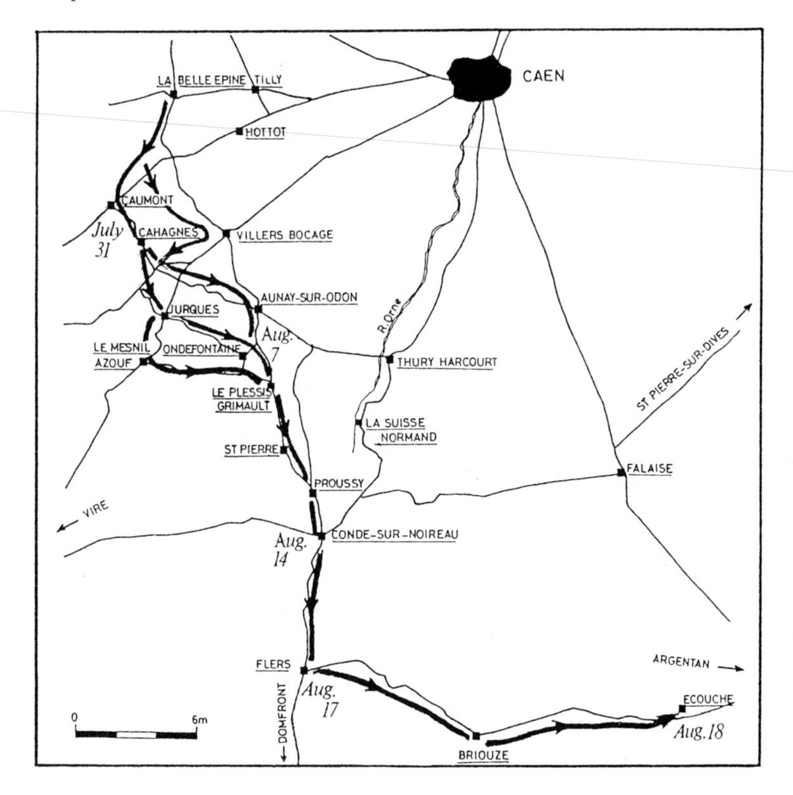

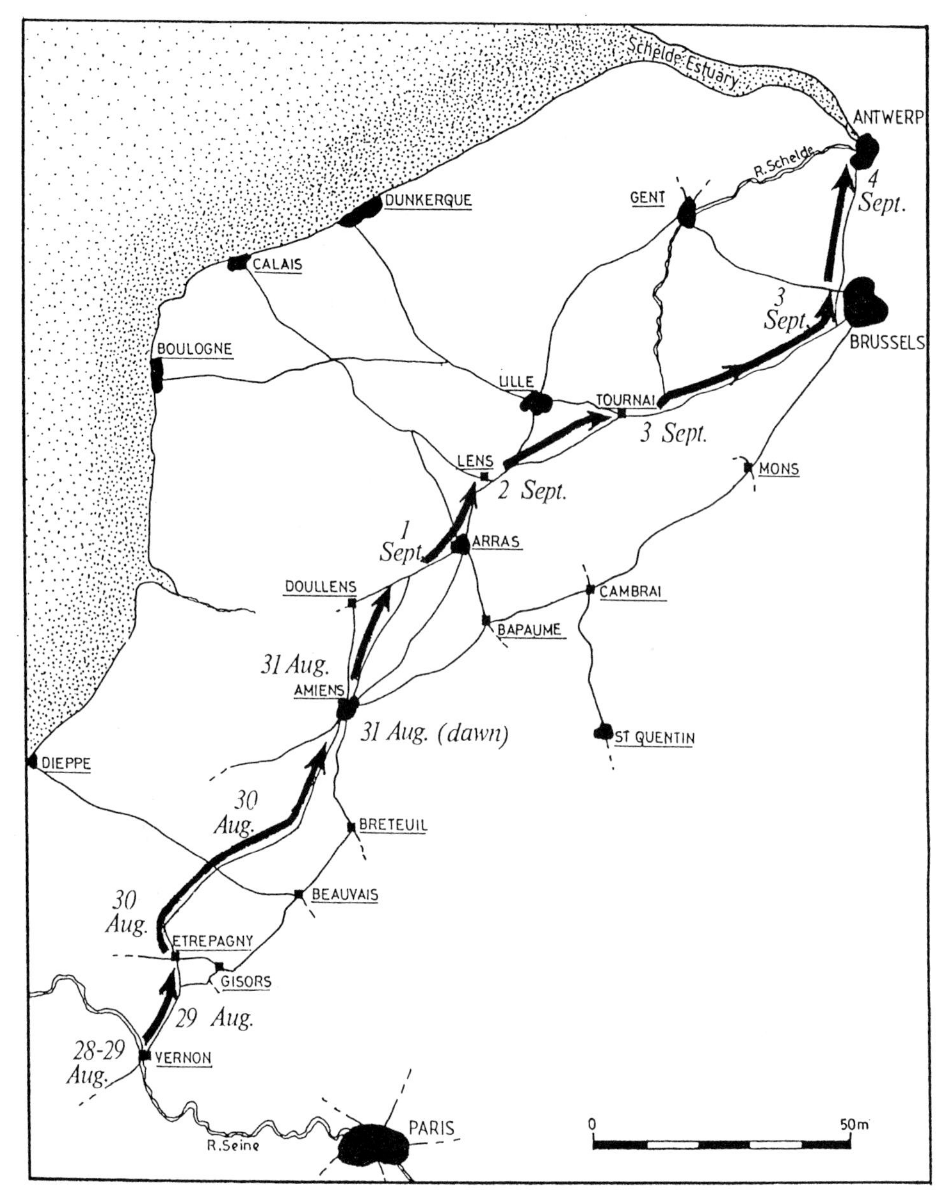

FIGURE 21. *Pursuit from the Seine to Antwerp, 28 August to 4 September.*

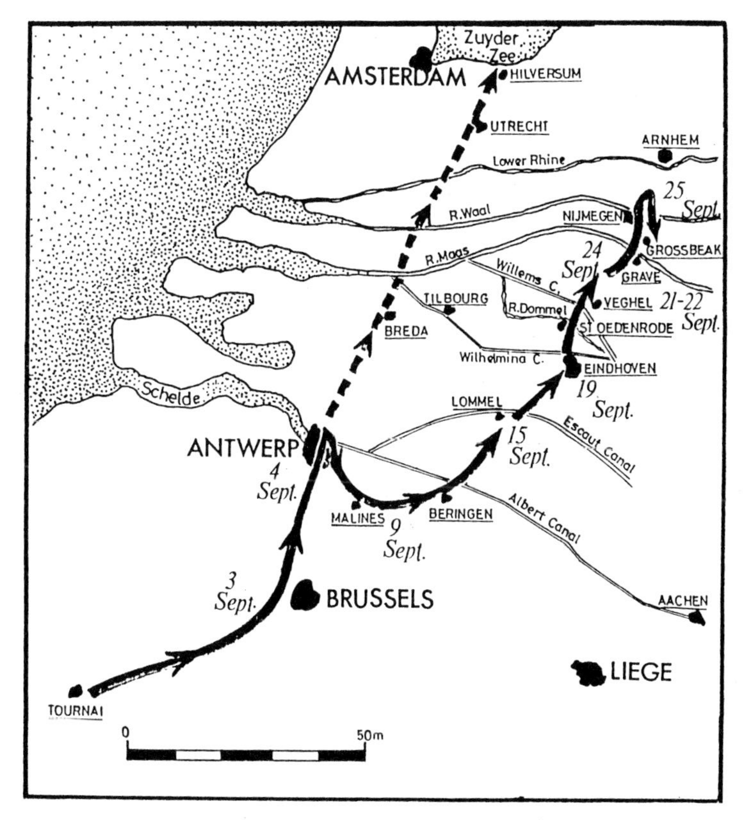

FIGURE 22. *Projected advance beyond Antwerp and actual advance to Nijmegen, 9–25 September.*

FIGURE 23. *Antwerp 4–8 September, details of attacks and movements (not to scale).*

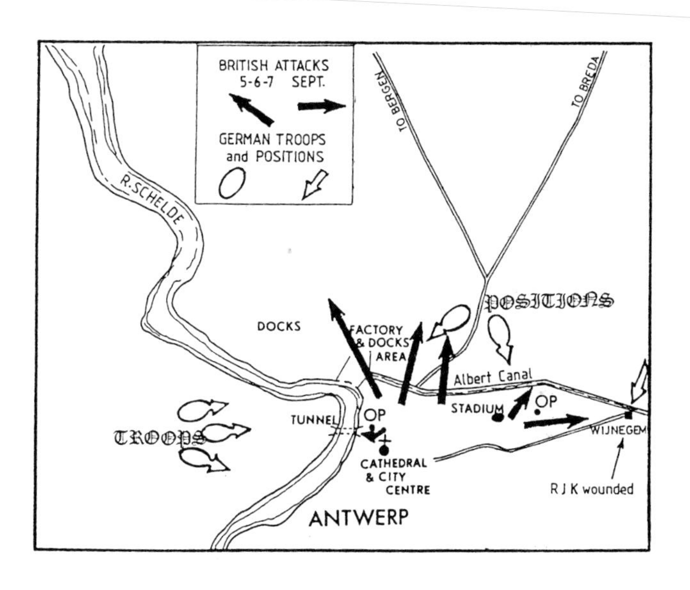

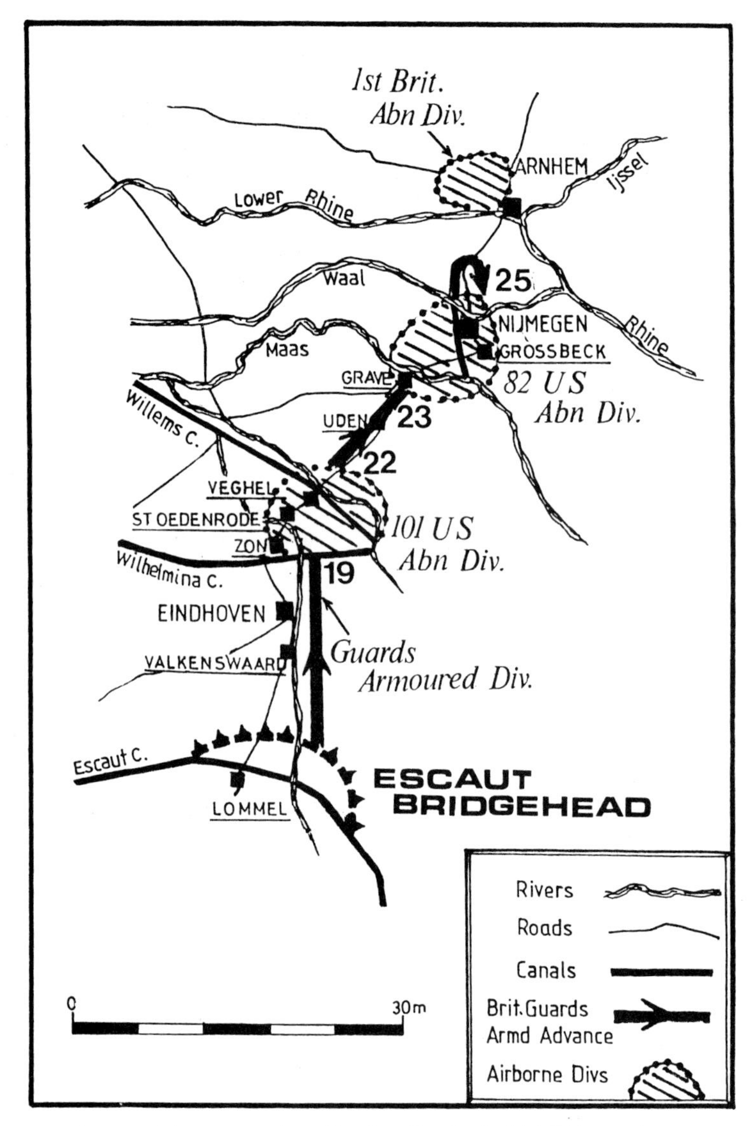

FIGURE 24. *Operation 'Market Garden', 18–25 September.*

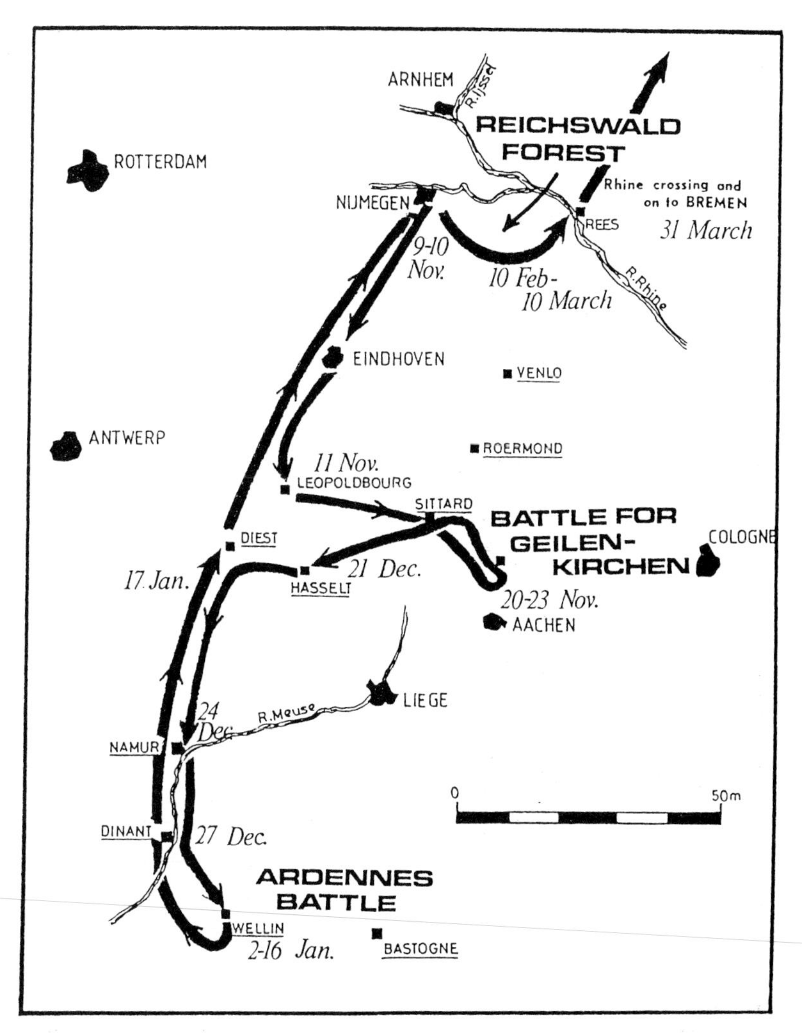

FIGURE 25. *The battles of Geilenkirchen (November 1944), Ardennes (December 1944/January 1945) and Reichswald Forest (February/March 1945).*

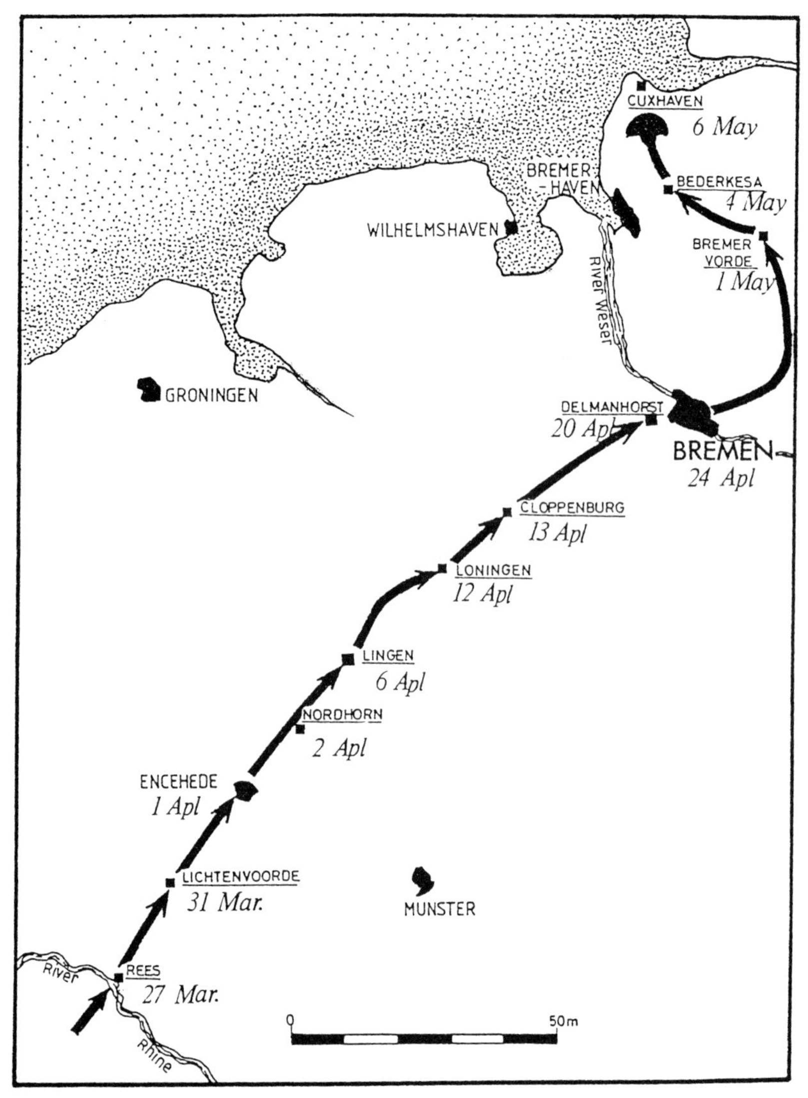

FIGURE 26. *Across the Rhine to Bremen and Cuxhaven: the regiment's advance 27 March to 6 May 1945.*